The Meaning of the Blues

The Meaning of the Blues

PAUL OLIVER

WITH A FOREWORD BY RICHARD WRIGHT

ORIGINALLY PUBLISHED AS *Blues Fell This Morning*

 COLLIER BOOKS

First Collier Books Edition 1963

Fourth Printing 1969

This Collier Books edition is published by arrangement with Horizon Press, Inc.

The Macmillan Company

Collier-Macmillan Canada Ltd., Toronto, Ontario

PRINTED IN THE UNITED STATES OF AMERICA

TO VALERIE

Foreword by Richard Wright

MILLIONS IN THIS our twentieth century have danced with abandonment and sensuous joy to jigs that had their birth in suffering: I'm alluding to those tunes and lyrics known under the rubric of the blues, those starkly brutal, haunting folk songs created by millions of nameless and illiterate American Negroes in their confused wanderings over the American Southland and in their intrusion into the Northern American industrial cities.

The blues are fantastically paradoxical and, by all logical and historical odds, they ought not to have come into being. I'm absolutely certain that no one predicted their advent. If I may indulge in an imaginative flight, I can hear a White Christian Virginia planter, say, in 1623, debating thus with his conscience while examining a batch of the first slaves brought from Africa:

"Now, these black animals have human form, but they are not really human, for God would not have made men to look like that. So, I'm free to buy them and work them on my tobacco plantation without incurring the wrath of God. Moreover, these odd black creatures will die early in our harsh climate and will leave no record behind of any possible sufferings that they might undergo. Yes, I'll buy five of these to be used as slaves. . . ."

But that mythical Virginia planter would have been tragically deluded. Not only did those blacks, torn from their tribal moorings in Africa, transported across the Atlantic, survive under hostile conditions of life, but they left a vivid record of their sufferings and longings in those astounding religious songs known as the spirituals, and their descendants, freed and cast upon their own in an alien culture, created the blues, a form of exuberantly melancholy folk song that has circled the globe. In Buenos Aires, Stockholm, Copenhagen, London, Berlin, Paris, Rome, in fact, in every large city of the earth where lonely, disinherited men congregate for pleasure or amusement, the orgiastic wail of the blues, and their strident offspring, jazz, can be heard.

How was that possible? I stated above that the possibility of those shackled, transplanted blacks ever leaving behind a record of their feelings about their experiences in the New World ran smack against historical odds. What were some of those odds?

First, those blacks were illiterate and it was not until some three centuries later that their illiteracy diminished to any appreciable degree.

Second, how could tribal men, whose values differed drastically from those of the Puritan Christian environment into which they were injected as slaves, ever arrive at an estimate or judgment of their experiences? How could they determine whether their lives were better or worse in America than in Africa?

Third, upon being sold into slavery, many tribes were deliberately separated one from another, so that the possibility of tribal inter-communication would be nullified, and, thus, the likelihood of revolt eliminated.

Fourth, not only were slaves bought and sold, employed as commodity-mediums of exchange, but they were intentionally bred as livestock, thereby augmenting the wealth of the planters.

Fifth, the spur to obtain the slaves' labour was brutality; the effort of the slave to learn merited punishment; self-assertion on the slaves' part met with rebuff; the penalty of escape, death.

How could such men, then, speak of what they underwent? Yet they did. In a vocabulary terser than Basic English, shorn of all hyperbole, purged of metaphysical implications, wedded to a frankly atheistic vision of life, and excluding almost all references to nature and her various moods, they sang:

Whistle keeps on blowin' an' I got my debts to pay,
I've got a mind to leave my baby an' I've got a mind to stay.

This volume contains three hundred and fifty fragments (a fraction of the material extant) of the blues, and I believe that this is the first time that so many blues, differing in mood, range, theme, and approach have been gathered together. We thus have here a chance to cast a bird's-eye view upon the meaning and implication of the blues. Certain salient characteristics of the blues present themselves at once.

The most striking feature of these songs is that a submerged theme of guilt, psychological in nature, seems to run through them. Could this guilt have stemmed from the burden of renounced rebellious impulses?

There is a certain degree of passivity, almost masochistic in quality and seemingly allied to sex in origin, that appears as part of the meaning of the blues. Could this emotional stance have been derived from a protracted inability to act, of a fear of acting?

The theme of spirituality, of other-worldliness is banned. Was this consciously done? Did it imply reflection upon the reigning American religious values?

Though constant reference is made to loved ones, little or no mention is made of the family as such. Was this because family life was impossible under slavery? (Family life among American Negroes has remained relatively weak until the present day!)

The locale of these songs shifts continuously and very seldom is a home site hymned or celebrated. Instead, the environmental items extolled are saw-mills, cotton-gins, lumber-camps, levee-banks, floods, swamps, jails, highways, trains, buses, tools, depressed states of mind, voyages, accidents, and various forms of violence.

Yet the most astonishing aspect of the blues is that, though replete with a sense of defeat and down-heartedness, they are not intrinsically pessimistic; their burden of woe and melancholy is dialectically redeemed through sheer force of sensuality, into an almost exultant affirmation of life, of love, of sex, of movement, of hope. No matter how repressive was the American environment, the Negro never lost faith in or doubted his deeply endemic capacity to live. All blues are a lusty, lyrical realism charged with taut sensibility. (Was this hope that sprang always Phoenix-like from the ashes of frustration something that the Negro absorbed from the oppressive yet optimistic American environment in which he lived and had his being?)

All American Negroes do not sing the blues. These songs are not the expression of the Negro people in America as a whole. I'd surmise that the spirituals, so dearly beloved of the Southern American Whites, came from those slaves who were closest to the Big Houses of the plantations where they caught vestiges of Christianity whiffed to them from the Southern Whites' cruder forms of Baptist or Methodist religions. If the plantations' house slaves were somewhat remote from Christianity, the field slaves were almost completely beyond the pale. And it was from them and their descendants that the devil songs called the blues came—that confounding triptych of the convict, the migrant, the rambler, the steel driver, the ditch digger, the roustabout, the pimp, the prostitute, the urban or rural illiterate outsider.

This volume is the first history of those devil songs; it tells how fortuitously they became to be preserved, how their influence spread magically among America's black population, and what their probable emotional and psychological meaning is. It would be very appropriate to recount that an American Negro was the first person to attempt a history of the blues and their meaning. But, like the blues themselves, this volume is paradoxical in its origin. It was written neither by a Negro nor an American nor by a man who had ever seen America and her teeming Black Belts.

Paul Oliver, the author of this interpretation of the blues, an interpretation that cuts across such categories as anthropology, economics, and sociology, first heard the Negro's devil songs on phonograph records when he was a child living in London. Those songs haunted that English boy. They spoke to him and he was resolved to understand them. For twenty years, as a student, a teacher, a lecturer, Paul Oliver studied the blues, collected records, pored over the literature relating to the Negro and created by the Negro, interviewed blues singers and jazz players, and has finally presented us with this interesting and challenging documentary volume.

As a Southern-born American Negro, I can testify that Paul

Oliver is drenched in his subject; his frame of reference is as accurate and concrete as though he himself had been born in the environment of the blues. Can an alien, who has never visited the *milieu* from which a family of songs has sprung, write about them? In the instance of such a highly charged realm as the blues, I answer a categoric and emphatic Yes. Indeed, I see certain psychological advantages in an outsider examining these songs and their meaning: his passionate interest in these songs is proof that the songs spoke to him across racial and cultural distances; he is geographically far enough from the broiling scene of America's racial strife to seize upon that which he, conditioned by British culture, feels to be abiding in them; and, in turn, whatever he finds enduring in those songs he can, and with easy conscience, relate to that in his culture which he feels to be humanly valid. In short, to the meaning of the blues, Paul Oliver brings, in the fullest human sense, what courts of law term "corroborative evidence."

I'm aware of certain possible difficulties. The Cold War climate in which this non-political book will appear might well militate in some quarters against its being received in the same warm, impartial, and generous spirit in which the author conceived and wrote it. Much of the material, factual and authenticated, and drawn from official sources, upon which Paul Oliver floats his interpretations of the blues, no longer "officially" exists: that is, American Negro middle-class writers as well as some American Whites with psychological vested interests might not only decry the material, but may seek to cast doubt upon its validity. If such were the case, it would be tragic indeed that material relating to æsthetics should come under the racial or political hammer.

Yet the contents of the 1954 Supreme Court decision regarding the integration of black and white children in American schools ought, at least, to open our minds a bit on this subject, and Paul Oliver's book, directly and indirectly, deals with that psychological area of tension and depression consequent upon social exclusion, documenting it, illustrating it.

Recently, when commenting upon the death of Big Bill Broonzy, a well-known Negro blues singer, a powerful and popular American Negro magazine announced the "death of the blues." But can anyone or anything hand down an edict stating when the blues will or should be dead? Ought not the contraction or enlargement of the environment in which the blues were cradled be the calendar by which the death of the blues can be predicted?

The American environment which produced the blues is still with us, though we all labour to render it progressively smaller. The total elimination of that area might take longer than we now suspect, hence it is well that we examine the meaning of the blues while they are still falling upon us.

RICHARD WRIGHT

Paris 1959

Contents

Author's Note and Acknowledgments

WHEN the present work was originally undertaken it had been my intention to write not only on the meaning of vocal blues but also on the historical development of the blues forms with summaries of the lives and work of principal singers. With this end in view I circulated a number of blues enthusiasts with a draft scheme requesting the assistance of those interested. Though many were fully occupied with their own researches the response from collectors was very generous, with the result that the information gathered from many sources far exceeded my expectations. To attempt to do some justice both to the subject and to the work of contributors I found that it was necessary drastically to reduce the original plan. Accordingly, I have devoted the present book solely to the meaning and content of blues, but a study of its form and history is now in preparation.

Though possibly no further removed from my subject in distance than the historian is removed from his in time, I am acutely aware of my remoteness from the environment that nurtured the blues. The help given me by visiting blues singers has therefore been invaluable and I would like to express to them my heartfelt thanks for their patient interest and kindly forbearance of my endless questions. In many hours of conversation Big Bill Broonzy drew from his inexhaustible fund of memories of half a century; Jimmy Rushing recalled at length the hey-day of the twenties; Brownie McGhee and Sonny Terry reminisced on blues and blues singers of the thirties and forties, demonstrating many points, and Brother John Sellers gave me the benefit of his wide knowledge of the blues in the post-war years.

The preliminary work for this book involved the written transcription of several thousand blues recordings from my own collection and from the record libraries of many collectors who generously put them at my disposal. A number of collectors also undertook the laborious task of transcribing records on my behalf and, though only a small proportion of these texts could be used in the final work, they all helped me to obtain a picture of the blues on record. For their help in transcribing records and for the information that they supplied my very sincere gratitude to Brian Davis; M. Jacques Demetre, blues columnist of *Jazz-Hot,* Paris; Jack Parsons, who also checked numerous items; Max Vreede of Holland, Race Research columnist to *Matrix,* and J. R. T. Davies who assisted him.

For the loan of records and the resources of their files my warmest thanks to Sam Benjamin, U.K. representative of the International Jazz Club; jazz and blues singer Beryl Bryden; Derek Coller, editor of the *Discophile* from 1948–1958, who also kindly solicited help through his magazine; Jim Davis who taped innumerable items; Brian Rust of the B.B.C. Gramophone Department; Derrick Stewart-Baxter, blues columnist of *Jazz Journal;* and Michael Wyler of *Jazz Publications* and Paramount specialist of *Jazz Monthly.*

Sincere thanks for many enjoyable record playing and transcribing sessions and for the loan of valuable items from their collections to Roy Crawford Ansell, who also joined me in research on Negro terminology; Graham Boatfield, *Jazz Journal* columnist; Peter Gammond of Decca Record Company; Gerry Grounsell and John Jack, Columbia Race catalogue specialists; Norman Jenkinson; John Langmead; Vic Schuler; and Eric Townley, *Jazz Journal* columnist.

Though the major proportion of the blues quoted in this book is of traditional and folk blues items, every attempt has been made to trace possible holders of copyright. In making this search I have been given every possible assistance by the Mechanical-Copyright Protection Society and in particular Miss M. D. Jarvis and members of her department who have been unstinting in their efforts and time. To them and to the publishing companies who have so kindly given permission for the quotation of items under their control, my warmest appreciation of their generosity. In this connexion I would like to express my thanks to the Directors of Cromwell Music, Ltd.; Empress Music, Inc.; Essex Music, Ltd.; Leeds Music, Ltd.; Milton "Mezz" Mezzrow; Pickwick Music, Ltd., and Southern Music Publishing Company, Ltd. Full details of the items held in copyright by these companies are given under the appropriate titles in the appendix, Acknowledgments in Discography. As far as is known, all holders of copyright have been traced, but the author requests the indulgence of any publishing companies whose copyright of a quoted blues and permission so to quote has been inadvertently overlooked.

I am greatly indebted to the distinguished authority on American folk song, Alan Lomax, and to the eminent Negro writer, Richard Wright, for their advice and encouragement. Likewise I am deeply appreciative of the interest and help of John Ball, Professor of English at Miami University, Oxford, Ohio, and Director of the Archive of Ohio Folklore, and of his wife, Mrs. Helen C. Ball, Special Services Librarian at Miami University; and of the valuable information on Negro affairs given me by Ralph H. Turner, Associate Professor of Sociology, University of California, and Philip H. Wikelund, Associate Professor of English, Indiana University.

To Richard C. Wootton, Cultural Affairs Officer of the United States Embassy, my grateful thanks for his help and advice, and to the Staff of the American Library for the loan of innumerable books and recordings from the Archives of the Library of Congress. Sincere thanks also to B. Bennett, Librarian of the Greenford Branch, Ealing Libraries, and his staff, for their trouble in obtaining many rare books for my use. Doug Dobell, Brian Harvey and Bill Colyer of Dobell's Record Shops have also loaned me books and recordings for which I am most grateful, and I have been greatly encouraged by the continued interest of Doug Dobell in the progress of this work.

Many other persons have helped me in divers ways. I would especially like to thank Sam Charters for information on singers; Tom Cundall, Editorial Director, and Jack Higgins, past editor of *Music Mirror,* in which magazine appeared the series of articles on which the idea of this book was based; Nat Hentoff, co-editor of *The Jazz Review* and late of *Down-*

beat, who kindly solicited help through his column; Max Jones of *Melody Maker* for much advice and aid; Donald Kincaid and Alexis Korner for technical information; Robert Koester, editor of the *St. Louis Jazz Report,* for his interest and generous notice in his magazine; Albert McCarthy, editor of *Jazz Monthly* and compiler of *Jazz Directory,* for his great help in enabling me to trace obscure discographical data; Anthony Rotante, columnist of *Record Research,* for discographical information; and Bert Whyatt, assistant editor of the *Discophile,* for the loan of Race Record publicity sheets. My warm thanks to all the other persons who have helped in different ways and who, by letter or in person, have expressed their interest in the project. In expressing my appreciation of the great help that I have received from all these persons, I would add that the selection of relevant material, the opinions stated and the conclusions drawn in the content of the book are entirely my own and do not necessarily represent those that might be made by any persons who have assisted me.

To no one do I owe a greater debt of gratitude, however, than to my wife Valerie, who has endured for many months the constant upheaval caused by sheaves of notes, stacks of books and piles of discs; who has nobly transcribed recordings, typed and filed transcriptions; who has checked discographies and typed the final manuscript; who has heard blues records incessantly and repeatedly; who has given me the right encouragement when enthusiasm has flagged, and who has somehow developed a passion for blues herself.

The Meaning of the Blues

Introduction

A FULL-FEATURED, curly-haired coloured woman from Cincinnati, Ohio, in her thirtieth year, stood before the horn of the recording machine in the New York Studios of the Okeh Record Company. With their instruments pointed down the bells of similar horns, a group of five musicians beside her at the signal of the recording engineer commenced to play an introduction, and then, in a clear voice, pitched a shade too high for comfort, she began to sing:

1. I'm worried in my mind, I'm worried all the time,
    My friend he told me to-day, that he was going away to stay,
    Now I love him deep down in my heart,
    But the best of friends must part. . . .

Perry Bradford, the composer of her song, stood near. It was he who had secured this recording date for 14 February 1920, when Sophie Tucker had been unable to record. Neither the occasion nor the recording seemed unduly auspicious, but the sale of the first disc to be made by a coloured singer, *That Thing Called Love,* backed by *You Can't Keep a Good Man Down,* sung by Mamie Smith, "contralto, with Rega Orchestra" on Okeh 4113 was sufficiently great to secure for the singer a second date on 10 August the same year. This time she cut Bradford's *Crazy Blues* with its choruses based on a twelve-bar structure, the first vocal recording to employ a blues form. For months the disc sold some 7,500 copies a week, revealing the existence of a market that the record companies were not slow to exploit. In Alberta Hunter's words, Mamie Smith had "made it possible for all of us."

If Mamie Smith had never entered a recording studio, if the blues had never been recorded in any form, it would have thrived as a folk music. Mamie's songs were on the very fringe of the blues, half-Vaudeville performances which marked a late stage in the development of the blues from a simple folk music to a form of sophisticated entertainment. When the first "Race Records"—those made specifically for Negro consumption—were issued, the blues had a history of some thirty or forty years and attempts to commit the music to musical notation had been made a decade before. But though the advent of recording was not necessary to the life of the blues, it did mark an important stage in its history for two reasons. In the first place Negroes throughout the United States were now able to hear the voices of blues singers who were not in their immediate field of acquaintance, and in the second place the blues as an improvised folk music, that depended on the inspiration of the moment, could now be preserved in permanent form.

Undoubtedly the issue of the records in itself moulded taste, stimulated attempts to sing in similar vein, and in turn increased the demand. But the remarkable sale of the first blues recordings indicated that the demand already existed and that the Negro populace was anxious to obtain its own music on wax. Examining the situation in the middle twenties when the recording of Negro artists was still young, the sociologists Odum and Johnson assessed the combined annual sale of records made by and for Negroes at a figure between five and six million copies. At this time examples of folk blues musicians had scarcely appeared, for contrary to the process of development of the blues it was the more sophisticated and more easily accessible forms that were first put on disc. As the record companies broadened their activities they found a similar demand in Southern country districts and commenced to record rural singers, first bringing them North to the studios, then taking mobile vans to record them nearer home.

By the end of the twenties Vaudeville and tent-show singers, circus artists and barnstormers, medicine-show entertainers and wandering troubadours, street beggars and field-hands, folk minstrels with guitars and gin-mill musicians at battered pianos, singers with boogie-woogie pianists, vocalists with washboard, jug and jazz bands were to be heard on record all singing and playing some form of the blues, and outside the phonograph supply shop queues would form of Negroes anxious to obtain the latest blues discs fresh from the presses. Saloon bars, barber shop parlours, drug stores, cigar stands and Negro business establishments of every description sold the records and the companies were ever advertising for more representatives. Discs could be bought from wandering vendors or through the mail-order catalogues of big shipping firms, and Negroes throughout the Northern and Southern States ground them to grey inaudibility on battered Victrolas, heavy-armed table machines and hand-cranked portables. This was their music, the blues of their own race, and families that could ill afford to do so bought their phonographs and surrendered their seventy-five cents a time for the records. Country "dog-trot" cabins and "shot-gun" houses, edge-of-town taverns and waterfront barrelhouses, red light honky-tonks and hole-in-the-wall cribs, music shops and street corner intersections, crowded tenements and apartment houses alike echoed to the rocking, moaning, hollering, singing of the blues throughout the Negro world of the United States.

Wider acceptance of the blues came much later and appreciation was, and for the most part still is, limited to the synthetic "blue" compositions of the Broadway show and the commercial confections of 52nd Street that purport to be blues by the inclusion of the word in the titles. But apart from the blues specialist and the occasional folklorist, interest in authentic blues has been confined to the enthusiasts of jazz. In the public mind the imprecise use of the term, not only in the field of popular music but also in dictionary definition, has sown seeds of perplexity as to the nature of the blues. But within the music itself there is room for confusion, for it does not conform to a simple definition. Were the blues a simple folk music local to one area, native to a small social group and tied to a firm tradition of standardized form and instrumentation, as is the case with many forms of folk music in various parts of the world, the identification and appreciation of its peculiar properties would present no undue difficulty.

But the blues is sung and played in districts that are literally thousands of miles apart where widely differing social, economic, physical and climatic conditions prevail: its distribution might be compared with a purely hypothetical folk music that flourishes at once in Copenhagen and in Rome, in London and in Cairo, though bonded by language and national unity. It is a music that is common to persons living under the most primitive rural circumstances and in the high pressure of modern city life. It is not the creation of a distinct troubadour group but is as common to the farmer as to the factory worker, to the hobo as to the union entertainer, to the lover as to the murderer. It has an ancestry that extends back into the nineteenth century and, some would contend, into the slavery period and it has continued to thrive during the migratory movements and social advancement of millions of people. In form the blues eventually determined its unique twelve-bar, three-line pattern but innumerable variants exist in stanzas of eight, ten, fourteen, sixteen bars amongst many others, whilst the fundamental element of instrumental and vocal improvisation which is a feature of the blues has proved an effective barrier against standardization. Blues vocals have been sung to the accompaniment of axes and hammers, home-made instruments, guitars and harmonicas, mandolins and banjos, pianos and organs, trumpets, clarinets and saxophones; to the small folk bands and improvising "traditional"-styled jazz bands, large jazz orchestras, rhythm and blues combinations —and to no accompaniment at all. Blues singers range in style and delivery from those whose voices are coarsely incomprehensible to those who sing in soft, burred, if not dulcet tones; unlike the flamenco singers with whom they are so often loosely compared, they vary from the taut to the supremely relaxed, the negligent to the precise. Some murmur, some moan, some holler, some declaim. Some there are who half-speak their words; others who shout and cry. There are blues singers with deep, rich voices, with gutteral, throaty voices; and there are others whose voices are high-pitched and shrill. And in the field of jazz there are the purely non-vocal forms of the blues where the means of vocal expression have been transmuted into instrumental terms; where the jazz musician plays the blues. If there is one simple common denominator in all these aspects of the music it is that the blues is a folk form of expression that is by superficial appearances the product of a racial group, the Negro in America; although the Negro stock has been so reduced through intermarriage and miscegenation during the centuries that it is doubtful if pure African blood can be found to any great extent in the United States, and the features of African cultural origin have been so modified and altered during that passage of time, ousted by compulsory and later voluntary absorption of a new culture, that their remains—if they exist—are vestigial. Yet the apparent fact remains that only the American Negro, whether purple-black or so light-skinned as to be indistinguishable from his sun-tanned White neighbour, can sing the blues. If there is a conclusion to be drawn from this it is that the blues has grown with the development of Negro society on American soil; that it has evolved from the peculiar dilemma in which a particular group, isolated by its skin pigmentation or that of its ancestors, finds itself when required to conform to a society which yet refuses its full integration within it. This enforced partial isolation has produced, in spite of the Negro's earnest desire to be accepted on wholly equal terms within the social pattern of American life, a certain cultural separation which has borne fruit in, amongst other things, the blues.

With some speculation on the origins of the blues, which are admittedly obscure, it has been possible to trace its process of evolution and change in a sequence which becomes progressively more clear after the turn of the century. Buried deep in the fertile ground of the Revival hymns, the spirituals, the minstrel songs, the banjo and guitar rags, the mountain "ballits," the folk ballads, the work songs and the field hollers, lie the roots of the blues which began to take form at some indeterminate time in the late nineteenth century. Above all the meandering, interminable "arwhoolies" and hollers, improvised by the field-hands of a thousand Southern plantations influenced the growth of this *ex tempore* song. They were sung by men at work but the blues evolved as a song primarily created by men at leisure, with the time and opportunity to play an instrumental accompaniment to their verses. With fiddle, banjo and, most of all, guitar they were able to add a second, answering voice which amplified the meaning of their own song. In accepting the certain restrictions that the instrument imposed they fell back on the simple three-chord harmony—tonic, subdominant and dominant of the hymnals and ballads, but the shadings, the bendings and the flattenings of notes which had so delighted the field Negro were preserved in the vocal delivery and found instrumental expression in the employment of flatted thirds, dominant seventh chords and whining notes achieved by sliding the strings, and the use of other unorthodox techniques.

From such beginnings evolved the folk blues, which originally had eight- and sixteen-bar forms related to the spirituals and ballads, but ever more frequently took shape in a pattern of twelve-bar stanzas of three lines each, wherein the first line was repeated giving the singer an opportunity to extemporize a third, and if he so wished, a rhyming line. With vocal lines of approximately two bars each the singer was able to play instrumental "breaks" between them that added greatly to the meaning and beauty of his creations. These folk blues of the rural South, strong, untutored but rich in textural variety, moving in expression and frequently accomplished, if unorthodox, in their instrumental accompaniments, are the "Country Blues," the "Southern Blues," though in the different styles recognizable in the work of singers from the Carolinas, from Mississippi, from Georgia or from Texas they merit more detailed identification. Sometimes the country singers were supported by other instrumentalists, playing stringed instruments in "juke bands" or the home-made instruments of the "jug band" and the "washboard band." These were popular in rural districts of the South but found ready support in the streets of Memphis or New Orleans in which latter city the similar "spasm bands" had more than a little influence on the development of jazz. In the cities and towns —Dallas, Birmingham, Atlanta—folk blues guitarists also worked, begging in the streets or playing in the saloons where "barrelhouse" pianists copied their rhythms and pounded out their versions of the blues. Some singers worked in the medicine shows and the touring carnivals, finding an audience for their blues in the "tank towns" and villages that they visited. In these shows the Vaudeville singers and tent-show burlesque entertainers met the blues singers and absorbed the elements of their folk music. Bringing to it the professional qualities of deliberate artistry they laid the foundations of the "Classic

Blues" which bridged the gap between the folk music and the world of entertainment. Whilst the classic blues singers, of whom the majority were women, brought the blues to the minstrel shows and the Negro theatres, the "City Blues" singers of the urban centres developed their harder, tougher forms which reflected the different character of their environment. Some were a shade slicker, yet a trifle less relaxed than the country singers and their somewhat more facile playing and singing was "dressed up" through their contact with a more sophisticated world.

From the honky-tonks of New Orleans came the "black butt" pianists who played powerful, aggressive blues in the tough dives of the "wide-open" city and the oil towns, the lumber-camps and levee-camps of Texas, Louisiana and Arkansas yielded the "Fast Western" pianists who sang as they played in imitation of the Southern guitarists, rolling eight-to-the-bar rhythms in the bass, and improvised endless blues variations in the treble. As "Boogie Woogie" their music found a home in the Chicago of the twenties. During the years of the great Negro migration they and the country singers, who risked the unknown life of the urban North, brought their blues styles to Chicago, Detroit, Cleveland and New York where the classic blues singers joined forces with those of the New Orleans and mid-Western jazz musicians who had also migrated. Whilst the clubs, theatres and dance halls rang to the blues of the classic singers, the tenements and speak-easies gave a home to the city blues and the rapidly urbanized country blues of the Southern-born Negroes.

The years of the Depression did not kill the blues, rather they gave good reason for singing them. In the South, where conditions could scarcely be worse, the blues did not change greatly in character; the guitarists still made the strings cry with knife blades and bottle-necks on their fingers as they moaned the blues. But in the North, blues guitarists and pianists combined during the thirties to produce, as conditions improved, the brash, exciting "Urban Blues" of Harlem and Chicago's South Side. Boogie piano, guitar, bass and drums in support of the singer made a frequent combination, often augmented by harmonica and on occasion by saxophone or clarinet. By now the classic blues had virtually died: linked with the traditions of Vaudeville and New Orleans-style jazz, it passed with them. Those elements that survived did so in the sophisticated forms of the blues which reached the night clubs and cabarets of Harlem or which were sung by the blues-jazz singers who worked in front of the large orchestras of the late thirties. But the strongly manned, blues-based bands that emanated from Kansas City with their riffing brass and "powerhouse" rhythm sections produced full-throated, deep-lunged "blues shouters" who declaimed their blues above the compelling music. Though World War II put a temporary stop to recording, it did not stop the blues, and when peace came the jumping, small group music of the urban blues groups and the driving, swinging jazz of the big combinations were wedded in the development of "Rhythm and Blues." In the "R. & B. bands," as they were soon to be known, the guitars, basses, even the harmonicas were electrified or amplified, and the post-war spirit was reflected in the optimistic and aggressive music which supported the strong-voiced blues shouters. Boogie pianos and guitars, honking tenors and heavily accented off-beat drumming characterized the post-war music of the city blues, and even in the Southern towns and the newly opened Negro West the same music could be heard. But with the popularity of R. & B. on the radio networks came a demand for the Southern country blues—now played on electric guitars.

Such might be a summary of the development of the blues with all the faults and inaccuracies that so brief a history must inevitably include. Blues, it must be stressed again, is a very individual form of music and the arbitrary classification of so personal an art must necessarily force singers into categories which do not adequately represent their particular merits, but rather tend to minimize them in the process of fitting them into a general pattern of conformity. But just as the folk singer is influenced by his environment, and his work is very largely a reflection of it, so too is he a part of his own tradition and in being so, bears certain elements of similarity with others working in the same idiom. Loose classifications can therefore be made which can justifiably distinguish the country blues singer from the urban blues singer or the Kansas City blues shouter. Through the work of them all run certain qualities of expression that characterize the blues as no other music, though the degree of blues quality tends to diminish as the music inclines to more sophisticated artistry on the one hand, or to the narrative ballad, rag or other form of Negro folk song on the other. For this reason the examples quoted in the present work are drawn primarily from the country and urban folk blues rather than from either the hollers or the classic blues. Likewise, as this is not intended to be an historical analysis, few examples have been taken from the work of big band blues singers and jazz blues vocalists, for an examination of their qualities as blues singers would be necessary. The omission of many great names is therefore in no way an indication of personal prejudice nor the inclusion of others an indication of preference. The examples that are quoted are taken from gramophone recordings, for these are the only means whereby the majority of persons can obtain any impression of the work of all but a few blues singers. Without the gramophone record the singing of scores of blues artists of the twenties and thirties would be unknown to us to-day and it is indeed fortunate that the recording of the blues, if it did commence somewhat late, at least came within the life-time of what may well have been the first generation of true blues singers.

To what extent the blues examples that are to be heard on record give a truly accurate picture of the whole field of the music is a matter of conjecture. In the almost total absence of any contemporary research in written or noted form let alone on record, the extent to which records illustrate the forms of the music that were prevalent in the first decades of the century cannot be ascertained. That there have been forms of the blues scarcely represented on record or entirely absent, and that some may still exist, seems likely enough and the dangers of dependence on gramophone recordings are readily apparent. It seems almost indisputable that the field hollers had a major formative influence on the blues, but no examples were to be heard on record during the nineteen-twenties, and until the late thirties none was committed to wax for public release. Certain forms of primitive unaccompanied blues have been recorded only in the post-war years for specialist collections and even these may have undergone a process of change, for the work of singers who have been consistently recorded over a period of perhaps thirty years has often shown many processes of change according to the altering circumstances of their environment. Similarly the considerations that determined if a singer ever appeared on disc are innumerable: whether he was in the vicinity when the recording engineers arrived; whether he was interested in being recorded, or like Freddy Keppard jealous of his material; whether his work appealed to the session supervisors; whether his name reached the talent scouts; whether he had sufficient personal drive to present himself; whether he kept the recording date, and so on. Again, the material that appears on wax, though in the case of the blues remarkably broad in scope and more uncompromising than in almost any other branch of song, still depended to a certain extent upon its possible appeal, on the danger that it may offend, and on its acceptability to the recording company.

It is evident that any examination of the blues on record must be made with the foregoing considerations borne in mind. Nevertheless, the gramophone record still remains the basis for any discussion upon the subject, for it is the only means whereby all interested can consider the merits of an identical example of the blues. Above all other forms of music, folk song is to be heard rather than read. It scarcely exists in a true sense in written musical notation though folk songs have been noted and adapted by musicians and collectors frequently enough. There are no fundamental standards in the manner of delivery, for this is essentially personal to the folk singer himself who is in no way striving after technical perfection and purity of tone. And of all folk song forms the blues may well be said to be the one which most requires to be heard. Fortunately its representation on gramophone recordings is truly remarkable and exceeds that of any other type of folk music. Though some singers are known by a single recording—some in fact by reputation only—the examples of blues by Big Bill Broonzy, Lonnie Johnson, Bumble Bee Slim and Leroy Carr, to take but four great and admittedly well featured singers, exceed a thousand titles. The factors that decide why a great singer should only appear for a single recording session may well be bound up in the circumstances of his private affairs and his personality, but there are literally thousands of blues by other singers which merit examination. In view of the abundance of recordings, the paucity of published works on the subject of the blues is truly surprising, and it is probably true to say that in proportion to the numbers of examples available to the public no folk music has been so neglected and so little documented. If it is true that the blues is to be heard and not written it is also equally true that the blues eminently deserves to be written about. Though it is fashionable at the moment to decry any suggestion that the blues has "significance" under the curious pretext that such a suggestion destroys the spirit of the music, the fact remains that the blues *is* socially significant. Failure to appreciate what the blues is about, failure to comprehend the implications of its content, is failure to appreciate the blues as a whole.

Not that the blues has been entirely neglected: it is customary to include in any anthology of American folk song a selection of blues verses. But the blues has not the traditional sequences of stanzas of the narrative ballad, and seldom chronicles an historical event exterior to the experience of the singer. Consequently, blues verses plucked out of context and entered unexplained in such an anthology have a certain appeal as emotive fragments, but as a whole seem strangely bleak. Only in the histories of jazz does the blues receive closer examination. It is an undeniable fact that, complex though the beginnings of jazz undoubtedly were, in the assimilation of the influences of the marching parade music, of ragtime, the spasm bands and the popular music of the turn of the century, in its final emergence as a coherent art form the blues played a major formative part. Because of the dependence of jazz upon blues—the acceptance of the fact that the blues has proved to be a basic element in every aspect of the music, traditional, mainstream and modern—to use the current nomenclature—as no other single feature has proved to be, the blues has been studied in some detail. Through the blues have been traced the links of jazz music with earlier Negro musical traditions of the spirituals, the work songs and the hollers, and the history of the music itself has received diverse and at times contradictory attention. Nevertheless these examinations of the blues are clearly made from the standpoint of the jazz enthusiast, historian and critic. The influence of the blues on jazz was a musical one, eventually to be developed in a purely musical non-vocal form of expression. Though the jazz band accompanied the blues singer it could just as well play the blues without the singer's presence and in the course of time the importance of the singer became less as the jazz musicians used the blues form instrumentally. Perhaps naturally, if not wholly justifiably, such analyses, though making some incursions into the content of the blues, are primarily concerned with its musical elements and the relationship of the vocal blues to instrumental jazz.

For the majority of collectors, it may be fairly suggested, the appeal of listening to blues records lies mainly in the appeal of their musical qualities and often quite apart from the meaning of the blues verses themselves. But the music is the vehicle of expression; the true blues singer does not sing needlessly and his song is the medium by which he expresses what he intends to say. To appreciate the music without appreciating the content is to do an injustice to the blues singers and to fail to comprehend the full value of their work. In view of his peculiar social status and the complexities of the racial relations in the United States the world of the blues singer is circumscribed. His blues have meaning for him and he has ideas to express; it is impossible either to enjoy or to understand the blues to the full through the musical qualities alone.

One may wonder why there was such a market for the blues when the records of Mamie Smith first appeared on the stands. Why did the blues recordings sell in such numbers for so many years, and why do they still do so? What was it that attracted the purchasers of the blues discs and caused them to spend hard-earned money on the blues as they would on no other art form? It was not for the music alone. It was because the music had meaning not only for the singer but for every Negro who listened. In the blues were reflected the effects of the economic stress on the depleted plantations and the unexpected prosperity of the urban centres where conditions of living still could not improve. In the blues were to be found the major catastrophes both personal and national, the triumphs and miseries that were shared by all, yet private to one. In the blues were reflected the family disputes, the upheavals caused by poverty and migration, the violence and bitterness, the tears and the happiness of all. In the blues an unsettled, unwanted people during these periods of social unrest found the security, the unity and the strength that it so desperately desired.

The blues does not reflect the whole of Negro life in the United States, and a social study of the Negro problem does not explain the blues. But in order to understand the blues singer it is necessary to explore the background of his themes, and to try to enter his world through them, distant and unapproachable though it may seem, cruel and hard though it may be.

Chapter 1

Got to Work or Leave

FOR ONE REASON alone is the Negro to be found on the American Continent: the enslavement of his ancestors. Their labour in bondage accounts for his presence there, no matter what his place in society may be to-day. Over a period of three centuries coloured men and women in their millions were torn from their African homeland, chained, shipped, sold, branded and forced into a life of toil that only ceased when death froze their limbs. Their children worked in the fields from the day when they could lift a hoe to the day when they dropped between the shafts of the plough. Brutal planters there were, and humane ones too. Some Negroes were given their freedom, some managed to buy theirs and even that of their womenfolk; some gained positions in the households as personal servants, some became skilled artisans and craftsmen. But it was the great multitude of common labourers, uneducated, unskilled, deliberately kept in ignorance and held in perpetual, unrelating bondage on whom the South relied. On the results of their sweat and toil depended its economy.

With the end of the Civil War came the "Day of Jubilo," the Liberation, but many slaves failed to grasp its meaning. There were tears on both sides, from the eyes of both slave and owner on many a plantation when the promised freedom came. Uncertain groups of Negroes stood in the gateways not knowing what to do. Some begged to be taken back, some stumbled off along the highways until hunger and helplessness forced them to return, whilst others walked on till they starved by the wayside. In the terrible years of the "carpet-bagger" administration when ignorant Negroes were given sudden power under the unscrupulous direction of Northern adventurer politicians, the South, both Black and White, suffered, and the good that the many able and educated Negro legislators did for the country did not afford a sufficient salve for the wounds that were borne. With the Reconstruction, Negroes, who were tilling the farms that they had been given when the plantations were abandoned, found themselves driven away as these were restored to former Confederates or claimed by the railroads. Ruthlessly and systematically the embittered Southerners deprived the Negro population of their Civil Rights, in open defiance of the Fourteenth Amendment, and embarking upon a succession of legal measures that enforced "Jim Crow" laws of segregation in every aspect of life, effectively disenfranchised the coloured population. On the plantations that were being re-established Negro workers found that they were again working under conditions of virtual slavery and that the share-cropping system which had seemed a just method of dividing the labour amongst families employed by one owner had become an iniquitous method of holding men in a bondage

Reconstruction brought new work in different spheres for those Negroes who had kept on walking when they stepped from the plantation gates to Freedom, though it was work of the most strenuous kind. Railroads that had been destroyed were rebuilt and new ones constructed; the river levees were repaired and graded and the expansion of trade on river and railroad gave work to roustabouts and stevedores. Mines were opened, saw-mills built, and they attracted the Negro labourers who were being squeezed out of other occupations by the continual flow of immigrants from Europe and the closing ranks of segregated Unions.

The last quarter of the nineteenth century saw an ever-increasing movement of Negro workers from state to state. By 1910 nearly one and three-quarter million Negroes had left their home states for others and of these some had moved West and half a million had gone to the North. As the pressure of hostile opinion and legislation became ever greater, Negro workers sought new employment and travelled long distances in order to find it. In the ensuing years they were to be followed by thousands more.

REFRAIN
2. Poor boy, poor boy, poor boy, long ways from home.

I was down in Louisiana doin' as I please,
Now I'm in Texas I got to work or leave.
Poor boy, *etc.*

"If your home is in Louisiana, what you doin' over
    here?"
Says, "My home ain't in Texas and I sure don't care."
Poor boy, *etc.*

I don't care if the boat don't never land,
I'd like to stay on water long as any man.
Poor boy, *etc.*

When my boat comes a-rockin' feels like a drunken man,
Says, "My home's on the water and I sure don't like
    land."
Poor boy, *etc.*

Tied in permanent debt to the planters on whose lands they were share-croppers or tenants, a vast number of Negroes were still forced to remain, for the share-cropping system was flourishing in the twenties and is by no means over to-day. In this the Negro farmer or the "poor White" lets his labour and that of his wife and family in return for "furnishings" of food and equipment, plough and mules and a percentage of the proceeds of the crop that he produces. These are hired to him on credit at the beginning of the year and are paid off when the crop has been gathered and "ginned," or compressed and cleaned of oil and foreign matter. The "cropper's" share seldom represents more than a fraction of the sum that his crop can realize, and when he has paid for the rent of his farm buildings and for the food that he has received, he generally finds himself in debt to the landowner. To pay this he must pay in labour and as the years pass he finds himself more and more firmly enslaved to the "Boss man." He secretly calls the

White man Mister Tom, Mister Charlie or Mister Eddie and tries to convince himself that he "gets along" and will one day earn enough to free himself and seek work elsewhere. In his broken, incoherent but profoundly moving voice, Sleepy John Estes claims that "Mister Tom's all right with me" whilst he outlines the compromises that he has made with the injustices of his situation:

3. Tom is good, some say mean,
   Hauling cotton, if y'ain't got no team,

   REFRAIN
   Now tell me how's about it? Yes, tell me how's about it?
   Tell me how's about it, Mister Tom's all right with me.

   Tom ain't so tall, no showin' in th' row,
   Everybody in Brown' say he got him plenty of dough.

   You out in the fiel' givin' ain't enough a' rule,
   Ask him for a li'l money he say, "Boy, share yo' mule."

   Tom lives in the country, Mis' Robert's in town,
   Soon this morn' Mis' Robert gonna hit that black man
      lyin' down,

   Now tell me how's about it? Yes, tell me how's about it?
   Tell me how's about it, Mister Tom's all right with me.

In his "dog-trot" cabin with its crumbling foundations, leaking walls and wind-swept corridor dividing the four rooms, the share-cropper raises as large a family as he is able, sometimes marrying a widow and taking her children into his home. For children mean labour: labour to dig, to plough, to hoe; labour to chop cotton, to "buck-jump" or weed cotton, to pick cotton. The plough-hand dreams that one day he may break free, and swears that he will no longer plough and hoe. But the winter threatens and he finds himself once more in a harness as real as that which holds his mules.

4. I was a plough-hand for forty years, I swore I would
   never plough no more, (twice)

Now I'm a married man now, oh Lord, there ain't no
 more so and so.

I'm going back to my plough, now a woman is the
 cause of it all, (*twice*)
Now she says, "Bill, if you ain't raising cotton, oh Lord,
 we'll have no money in the fall."

"Farming is all right, little girl, if you knows just what
 to do, (*twice*)
'Cause it killed my old grandpap, oh Lord, I declare I'm
 going to make it kill me too."

Every night, I'm calling John, Jake an' Pat. (Sing it
 boy, sing it.) (*twice*)
Now I had a dream last night, oh Lord, there was a
 mule in my hat.

The money he realizes from his crop will barely keep him
and his family alive through the year. In theory the cropper
receives half of what he produces from the sales prices, but
as the Negro has so often sung:

Ought's a ought, figger's a figger,
All for the white man, none for the nigger.

For the Negro who "cain't read, cain't write" there is little
protection against ruthless exploitation, and his rights are less
than were those of a peasant working under the conditions of
medieval feudalism. He is powerless to dispute the reckoning
when the scales weigh against him and has no means of legislation against the system that keeps him in serfdom. His farming methods are not of the best for he has to try to get the
largest crop he can, and rotation farming means a year or two
of starvation. Thus even the most fertile lands can have farms
of exceptionally low standard; the rain corrugates the land
and washes away the top soil on the slopes, and the under-
nourished land is starved for fertilizer that the cropper cannot afford. In the principal states producing cotton in 1930
there were a million and a half share-croppers working under
the system and of some 225,000 tenant families in Mississippi

at that time—of whom more than seventy per cent were Negro—over 135,000 were in the lowest economic category.

It was a little insect barely a quarter of an inch long that set the seal on the destruction of the South's cotton economy. In 1862 the boll-weevil was observed in the cotton fields of Mexico, and thirty years later it was ravishing the plantations of Texas. Within a few years it was to be found throughout the entire South where the warm, humid conditions were perfect for its propagation. Attacking the cotton bolls where the weevil laid its eggs, the grubs reduced them to empty shells and the dismayed planters and field-hands alike were powerless to prevent the pest. Thousands of Negro share-croppers were thrown out of work but not out of debt as the weevil destroyed their crops. They composed a ballad about the indestructible insect, even paradoxically found some sympathy for it as they saw their own unbreakable spirit symbolized in its invincibility. Years later, in the particularly bad years of the mid-twenties, the ballad became a blues and the cotton worker would sing as did Kokomo Arnold:

5. Boll-Weevil, Boll-Weevil, come out of my parlour there, (*twice*)
   Says, "We got the boll-weevil mama, Jesus, boll-weevil everywhere."

   Well I went to my captain, and I asked him for a peck of meal, (*twice*)
   He said, "Leave here Kokomo, you got boll-weevils in yo' fiel'."

   Mister Weevil, Mister Weevil, you left us in an awful fix, (*twice*)
   Done et up all our home, left us nothin' but the sticks.

   Says the merchant to the doctor, "You won't sell no mo' C.C. Pills (*twice*)
   'Cause the boll-weevil down here in Georgia done stop all these cotton mills."

   Now Mister Boll-Weevil if you can talk, why don't you tell (*twice*)

'Bout poor Kokomo down here in Georgia catchin' a lot
of hell?

A number of the larger plantations managed to survive the
ravages of the boll-weevil and continued to produce cotton on
the old system of share-cropping. Amongst the largest of these
was that owned by the Delta and Pine Land Company—a
British Syndicate of mill-owners, the Fine Spinners' Association of Manchester whose 3,300 croppers in a thousand families were earning in the late thirties an average of $525 a
season, two-thirds of which being expended on credit furnishings. Centred on Scott, Mississippi, it is to-day the largest
plantation and though attempts have been made at social reforms it still maintains its share-cropping system.

When the recording of blues commenced the cotton-boll
economy of the South had already virtually collapsed. Many
of the small plantations were forced to change their crop as
the weevil in the space of thirty years brought waste and destruction to every part of the cotton belt. Now, other districts
further to the South-West have demonstrated that they can
effectively produce the crop, and mechanization has largely
replaced the manual labour of the Negro cotton-worker.
Though it is still grown in considerable quantities in the South
many planters have had to turn to "goober peas"—ground
nuts—and to the eye crops—black-eyed peas and potatoes—
for their source of income. For many Negroes this meant a
change of work but no change of status for they were still in
virtual bondage, whilst others working on tenant farms had to
face penury and the competition of the dispossessed.

Lack of incentives, lack of opportunity, lack of hope will
dispirit a man until he no longer wishes to live or to work
and so he may resort to protest that manifests itself in deliberate idleness. Knowing that he cannot benefit from his
labours he is determined that no one else should do so either.
Sings a Florida Negro, Gabriel Brown:

6. Now I started at the bottom, and I stays right there,
   Don't seem like I'm gonna get nowhere.

   REFRAIN
   I'm gonna take it easy, I'm gonna take it easy,
   I'm gonna take it easy, babe, that's what I'm gonna do.

> You can have a job, maybe as hard as salt,
> You try to say something and they lay you off.
>
> What your bosses are doing you can never tell,
> They're always trying to cut the personnel.
>
> I've got myself together, made my mind up now,
> I won't have a doggone thing nohow.

Powerless to act in open hostility he may resort to more cunning methods, such as that mentioned by Big Bill Broonzy in his *Plough Hand Blues* when he declares that he is "always setting my backband back, oh Lord, to prevent my little plough from going too deep." Such methods only spite the perpetrator, who does no one as much harm as he does to himself. So the Negro field-hand finally resigns himself to being "a steady-rolling man," and by working himself unstintingly throughout the year, and finding other occupations during the lay-off periods, eventually saves sufficient money to purchase his own mule and equipment and rise fractionally up the scale to the status of tenant-farmer. As Robert Johnson says:

7. I'm a hard-workin' man, have been for many long years
    I know. (*twice*)
   I'm the man that rolls when icicles hanging on the tree,
   And—mmmmm—you hear me hollerin', baby, mmmmm
    down on my bended knee.

Tenant-farmers have a small degree of independence in that they own their equipment and livestock and have therefore less to hire from the plantation, or the company. Some may eventually gain complete freedom and, if they are fortunate, buy their own land, but the odds are heavily against a tenant-farmer becoming prosperous. He must still sell his crop in the open market and is subject to discrimination that may force him to sell at a ridiculously low price. At the mercy of the weather, his livestock and the efficiency of his tools, when the crops "give out" he, his family and his livestock suffer.

8. Well, I'm a poor farmer, what am I gonna do? (*twice*)
   When my corn done give out, whoo, whoo, I take a load
    on my mule.

Well, my mule was named Jim, he was too lazy to wag
his tail, (*twice*)
Police told me if I hit that mule again, well, they would
put me in jail.

Well, that mule's back was sharp as a razor, 'cos he sure
couldn't get no corn, (*twice*)
When the middle of my face gets hairy, takes the shave
off his back bone.

Well, that old mule sat down, when he heard what the
police said, (*twice*)
That mule looked back at me and smiled, bucked his
head and crossed his legs.

I don't blame that old mule and neither could nobody
else, (*twice*)
Before that darn old mule would wiggle, woo Lord, I
set to hauling myself,
I set to hauling myself.

Both share-cropper and tenant-farmer had to "stay in
good" with their White overlords and in that period of strain
during the twenties no Negro dared raise his voice aloud in
protest or assert his rights when he was the victim of racial
discrimination. So he maintained an air of happy indolence,
played up to the stereotypes that traditional jokes had
moulded for him, hid his sufferings and struggled to survive.

9. Well, I drink to keep from worrying and I laugh to keep
from crying, (*twice*)
I keep a smile on my face so the public won't know my
mind.

Some people thinks I am happy but they sho' don't
know my mind, (*twice*)
They see this smile on my face, but my heart is bleeding
all the time.

Frustrated and disillusioned by the conditions of work and
the poor rewards for his labours, discouraged by discrimina-

tory practices that lowered his receipts or threatened to put him out of work altogther, the Negro farm-hand sought work elsewhere, hoping to find employment in a different district that would enable him to save sufficient to bring his family.

10. If I mistreat you, babe, I don't mean you no harm, (*twice*)
    I'm just a little country boy, right out of the cotton farm.

    I'm just from the country, never been in your town before, (*twice*)
    Lord, I'm broke and hungry, ain't got no place to go.

    I was raised in the country, I been there all my life, (*twice*)
    Lord, I had to run off and leave my children and my wife.

Eventually he would find work on the "jobs." However fierce the competition may be from White workers, from immigrants and "poor buckra"—White persons of the lowest economic class—there are certain occupations that are—in the superbly ironic euphemism currently employed—"protected" for the Negro. These are known simply as "the jobs" and their nature is such that none but the poorest White men will be employed in them. The conditions of work are usually so appalling, so injurious to health, to life and limb that only the most underprivileged classes will be found undertaking the tasks. Amongst these are the turpentine workers who "gutter" the slash pines with their knives, collect the resin and press and distill the turpentine. Working often in unbearable heat and using material which is dangerous to health, they live in camps under the crudest of conditions, fenced in by barbed wire and suffering miserable privations. Pigmeat Pete and Catjuice Charlie, two Negro entertainers, brought many wry smiles when they sang in mock-contented tones:

11. The hoss we had done seen his best,
    Walk four blocks and he sit down to rest,
    Sit down one day in some turpentine.
    Now the poor hoss done lost his mind,

On our turpentine farm, umm-hmmm
On our turpentine farm,
Where the work ain't hard, and the weather is warm.

From the turpentine-camps the migrant workers would move on to the logging-camps, where however, their lot was very little better. Whereas three-quarters of the entire personnel employed by the turpentine industry were Negroes, coloured men represented in 1930 only some thirteen per cent of the labour force in forestry throughout the country. In the South alone, however, they formed the majority of the workers employed. The logging companies had paid the lowest wages possible, restricting the workers to a forty-hour week and paying them from twenty-three to forty cents per hour. "Dummy lines" which could be easily lifted and relaid connected some of the remotely placed logging-camps with the main railroad lines, but the men were confined to their shack and tent townships and bought all their requisites from the company stores. And from the exploitation of loggers and public alike the Weyerhauser syndicate massed its hundreds of millions of dollars in profits. Though logging tops the list in industrial fatalities relative to the man-hours worked, the Negro lumberman sings of the "rainbow round ma shoulder" as his diamond-blade axe flashes in the sunlight. In the extreme South the loggers face each other in their "pirogues"— their dug-out canoes—and without rocking their clumsy boats expertly felled the cypresses with their singing cross-cut saws.

Meanwhile in thigh-boots and rubber coat the mule-skinner strives to endure the suffocating heat and the sweet stench of rotting wood whilst he fights off the attacks of the mosquitoes and gallynippers that plague him in his "shanty" home and wherever he goes. "Mosquitoes worry me so," says Blind Lemon Jefferson, "I cain't hardly stay on my feet."

12. I bought a spray last night 'n I sprayed all over the house, (*twice*)
Mosquitoes all around my door won't let nobody come out.

Mosquitoes all around me, mosquitoes everywhere I go, (*twice*)
No matter where I go, they sticks their bills in me.

    I would say gallynipper, these gallynippers bites too
       hard, (*twice*)
    I stepped back in my kitchen and they springing up in
       my back yard.

Through the slime of the swamps in the river bottoms the
mule-skinner urges his mule, drawing the "skiff" on which the
logs are carried to the river. When the water is deep he floats
his skiff, when it is shallow he drags it behind him. Other
mule-skinners are pulling the logs that the "chokerman" has
hitched with a wire noose behind the mule; it is a cruel life
with the considerable danger of being crushed by rolling
timber, of sinking to a gruesome death in the swamps, of
mutilation or even of murder at the hands of one of the loggers being ever present. But as he drives his mule to the levee
he will sing a blues:

13. This man is a long way from home, an' he's got a
      brownskin woman,
   An' he knows pay-day's comin' pretty soon,
   An' the ole woman's shoutin' for some mo' pay-day.
   An' the ole mule is hon'n' and the sun is going down,
   An' the man wishes that pay-day would move off a little
      further
   So he wouldn't have to pay the woman nothin'.
   I'm goin' t' tell ma woman like the—Dago tell the Jew,
   You don' wan' me, and honey, I don' wan' you.

On the levee the overseers worked the women as they worked
the men—tough women who could handle the mule teams
and who fought with single-trees and knives. Life was cheap,
or at least the lives of men; the lives of the mules were more
greatly prized. Murder could be committed with little fear of
legal retribution—if the victim was a Negro and if he was not
a "rolling man," an exceptionally strong worker. Yet the
levee-graders took pride in the hard lives that they led. As in
the past the roustabouts boasted of the weals that seared their
backs and the punishments meted by the "mean mates" who
handled the river men, so the levee-workers relished the
stories of their more vicious captains. As the loading crews-
men boasted of the weights they could carry up the swaying
gang-planks of the stern-wheelers—it was reckoned that one

man could carry what two of the rising crew could lift on to his back—so too, the mule-skinners would vie each other in their skill with skiffs and bull-whips.

13. . . . The women on the levee, honey, holler, "Whoa. Haw. Gee."
   The man on the levee holler, "Don't cha murder me,
   Please baby, please baby, please baby, please baby."
   "Honey, I'm a long way from home.
   Honey, I'm down in the bottoms, skinnin' for Johnny Ryan,
   Puttin' my initials, honey, on the mule's behind
   With my line babe, with my line babe, with my line babe. . . ."

From way up the Ohio, on the Mississippi and many a tributary to the Brazos Bottoms the work of laying the giant mattresses and building the artificial banks that hold back the flood waters is continuous. The work commenced in the eighteenth century, and by 1828 the levees extended from the Delta to the Red River. During the Civil War they were damaged or neglected and the disastrous flood of 1874 proved their ineffectiveness. The Government made a grant of $5,000,000 towards the repair of levees improving navigation, though not for the protection of the land, and the Negroes whose homes were threatened cut the willow canes, wove the hurdles and constructed the mud walls, establishing a traditional source of work for the migrant labourers. The loaders fill the skiffs with clay and rubble; the skinners bring the carts to the levee where the dumper unloads them for the graders' use.

14. Which way, which way, does that Blood Red River run?
   Honey, from my back door to the risin' sun.

   Go down to the camp, an' tell ma Brother Bill,
   That women he love is sho' gonna get him killed.

   I just stopped here, baby, to catch ma livin' wind,
   Soon as the weather break, honey, I'm up and gone again.
   I'm gonna tell you somethin' bout that Blood Red River now. . . .

Well, the dumper tol' the loader, "Boy, send me six feet
o' clay,
Well, the Blood River rises six feet ev'ry day."

A system operated in such labour camps not greatly dissim-
ilar to that which binds the share-cropper, for the "fixin's"
or "furnishings" were deducted by the companies from the
total pay and the balance, if there was any, was paid to the
worker at the end of the week. If he found himself in "debt"
he would leave. No one would follow him, for there were men
waiting in the "queue" to be taken on, as there were at the
railroad-camps, the road-camps and the rock- and gravel-
camps. Similar in character, erected from temporary shacks,
railroad wagons or tents, the camps housed the men who dug
gravel, quarried and pounded the hard rock, and built up the
highways and gradients from the rubble. Conditions of labour
seldom varied; the men were worked "from sun to sun"—from
daybreak to sunset—expecting, and receiving, harsh treatment if they failed in their tasks, and little commendation
when they worked well. In a voice so rough, strong and wild
that his pronunciation is scarcely comprehensible, one such
worker recorded in Atlanta—Lewis Black—told of catching
a fast train by the tail wagon and going in search of such work
so that he could send for his wife:

15. Goin' out on the queue, goin' out on the queue, (*twice*)

Ef Ah find anythin', comin' back after you.

Soon one mornin' hour pas' four, (*twice*)
Say mama, come'n look-a-you ketch the *Cannonball*.

Ah got on behin'—say now mama, com'n looka—Ah got
on behin', (*twice*)
Say, you can't leave me, say you can't help cryin'.

When Ah leave fum hyah, gwine out on the Ohio,
(*twice*)
Ef Ah doan fin' no log-camp, Ah'll fin' a gravel-camp
sho'.

Mmmmmmmm what's the matter, what's the matter
heah? (*twice*)
Ain't nothin' goin' on wrong, but mama, Ah doan keer.

The belief that the Negro is a brute animal more capable of
standing such gruelling work provided that it does not require
mental effort is a legacy of the slavery period that has been
handed down from generation to generation so that it is
seldom disputed in the present. Curiously it finds support also
from the Negro, who has accepted the belief and has found
in it a source of racial pride, drawing satisfaction from the
conviction that he can undertake work from which the White
"cracker," his economic equivalent, is debarred by physical
weakness. Sometimes he realizes that the perpetuation of the
fallacy keeps him in perpetual servitude; that the work may
break him but that he will never break the work. Taking a
lesson from the ballad of the self-destruction of John Henry
which had been an incentive to work for inumerable steel-
drivers and spike-drivers on the Southern railroads, Mississippi John Hurt sings the blues of a spike-driver who has
worked himself to breaking point:

16. Take this hammer and carr' it to the captain, tell him
I'm gone,
Tell him I'm gone, you can tell him I'm gone.
Take this hammer an' carr' it to the captain, an' tell him
I'm gone,
Jes' tell him I'm gone, I'm sure is goin'.

This is the hammer that killed John Henry, but it won't
kill me,
But it won't kill me, but it won't kill me.
This is the hammer that killed John Henry, but it won't
kill me,
But it won't kill me, ain't gonna kill me.

It's a long way from East Colorado, honey, to ma home,
Honey, to ma home, honey, to ma home.
It's a long way from East Colorado, honey, to ma home,
Honey, to ma home, that's why I'm goin'.

John Henry's a steel-drivin' boy, but he went down,
But he went down, but he went down;
John Henry's a steel-drivin' boy, but he went down,
But he went down, that's why I'm gone.

There are other jobs to which a Southern Negro worker can go with a reasonable chance of securing work: the tobacco and fertilizer plants, the cement factories and the saw-mills. In all of these the dust hangs thick and heavy, and in the majority extractors are not a part of the fixtures. The owners are in the business for the purpose of making money and dust extractors are a needless expenditure when workers can be obtained who are prepared to suffer the inhalation of the injurious particles, and, in the instances of the tobacco and fertilizer plants especially, the sickening odours that make the senses reel. But the simple and uneducated Negro accepts readily enough the conditions along with the regular pay-check.

17. I didn't build this works, but I sure don't care a damn,
    (*twice*)
    An' when I'm on my job, mama, I don't want no man
    hangin' around.

    Yes, I'm workin' on the saw-mill, sleepin' in a shack six
    feet wide, (*twice*)
    I see my gal every pay-day and I'm perfectly satisfied.

Whilst the loggers worked and the "short dog" trains on the "dummy lines" took them deeper into the woods, the process of felling and shipping timber to the saw-mills continued, but the avarice of the landowners often caused them to destroy timber at a rate far in excess of any attempts at reforestation. By 1933 there were eighty-three million acres of timberlands laid waste, leaving hills gullied and dry, infertile and scarred by the ugly wounds where trees had been uprooted or felled without thought of restocking. A further two hundred million acres were dangerously deteriorating, and in the ensuing years vast areas were irrevocably lost to future cultivation. When the logging company or the railroad had reduced the country to the "stump lands" the temporary lines were shifted, the landings in the bottoms fell into decay, and the saw-mills closed down leaving its workers with no employment.

18. I was lyin' in bed this mawnin', an' heard the mill whistle
     blow like it was cryin'. (*twice*)
     Ole saw-mill has cut all that timber, ain't no mo' work
     for that man of mine.

Industrialization came slowly to the South—too slowly for the Negro. The insecurity of Southern rural economy which was so markedly to his disadvantage caused many a coloured worker to move from the country areas and gravitate to the towns and industrial centres where wages were better and more stable. From the North came reports of good prospects for Negroes and better opportunities of obtaining employment, and from 1910 there was a steady stream of migrating coloured men moving from state to state with the Northern cities as their ultimate goal. In the steel factories many of the jobs were restricted, but the "open-hearth" sections offered ready employment for Negroes; few others would work under the almost insufferable heat from the furnaces. Field-hands weighed their chances against the disadvantages of severing themselves from their homes; the mills of Bessemer and Gary called, and they were gone.

19. To-day, mama, to-day—to-morrow—I might be 'way,
     (*twice*)
     Going back to Gary, that's where I intend to stay.

     Not o'clock in the mornin', mama, not o'clock in the
     afternoon, (*twice*)
     When I leave for Gary, some good man can have my
     room.

     Shine on harvest moon, harvest moon shine on, (*twice*)
     For you will be shinin' after the days I'm gone.

Work in the steel-mills was tough, demanding precision timing, great physical strength and considerable powers of endurance. Southern Negroes were used to strenuous work but employment in a semi-skilled capacity precluded many who had been used only to heavy, menial, unskilled labour. The mills wanted men, and those who applied were eager enough to learn. Soon there were more Negroes employed in semi-skilled work than there had ever been before. They bragged of their physical prowess and the less fortunately endowed men jeolously watched the women who were attracted by them.

20. If you get a big-leg woman now in this old town,
    These steel-mill mens now will run her down.
    Get a woman even out in this old town,
    These steel-mill mens now will run her down.

The prestige attached to working in the mills was an effective if minor adjunct to the recruiting drive, and the representatives of the mill-owners exploited this as much as the more obvious inducement of financial gain, in order to draw conservative spirits from the South.

21. I used to have a woman that lived up on a hill, (twice)
    She was crazy 'bout me, ooh well, well, 'cause I worked at the Chicago Mill.

    You can hear the women hollerin' when the Chicago Mill whistle blows, (twice)
    Cryin', "Turn loose my man, ooh well, well, please and let him go."

    If you want to have plenty women why not work at the Chicago Mill? (twice)
    You don't have to give them nothin', ooh well, jest tell them that you will.

In 1914 the continual flow of immigrants from Europe to the United States ceased and the Northern industrialists, whose work was expanding with the demands of impending war, required cheap labour in quantity. Restricted immigration still operates to-day but it now has no major influence on the national economy; during the years of World War I when the stream of European unskilled labourers was halted there was an acute labour shortage in the industrial North. Recruitment officers were sent South to draw Negro workers from the plantations, and special freight cars were chartered to bring them to the North. Many of the labour officers were literally tarred and feathered or expelled from Southern towns and villages at the point of a gun, and Negroes who left the plantations were forced back by county sheriffs who implemented hastily drawn laws designed to stem the tide of migrant coloured workers. The extreme was reached in Macon, Georgia, where a labour agent was required to pay a licence fee of $25,000 to operate, and only then if he had the recommendations of twenty-five businessmen, ten ministers and ten manufacturers of goods. Elsewhere, heavy fees were demanded and operating agents were put into jail. Though they were often technically in debt through the perniciousness of sharecropping, countless numbers of Negroes left the country farms that had been their whole world for their entire lives and, having little or no conception of Northern urban life, prepared to face the risks involved in the hopes of a better future. The cessation of the influx of European immigrants coincided with Henry Ford's pronouncement, in 1914, that none of his workers would earn less than five dollars per day, and it was in that year also that he commenced to employ Negroes on his assembly lines. As his huge plants in Detroit continued to expand and more coloured workers were taken on, the news reached the remotest corners of the South and attracted men who had been living in penury.

22. I'm goin' to Detroit, get myself a good job, (*twice*)
Tried to stay around here with the starvation mob.

I'm goin' to get me a job, up there in Mr. Ford's place, (*twice*)
Stop these eatless days from starin' me in the face.

When I start to makin' money, she don't need to come around, (*twice*)
'Cause I don't want her now, Lord, I'm Detroit bound.

Because wild women lives in Detroit, that's all I want to see, (*twice*)
Wil' women and bad whisky would make a fool out of me.

The pictures that the recruiting men painted were bright and colourful, and to the simple Southern Negro with his limited experience and his folk ways the prospect of work in the North was infinitely attractive. If he questioned the employers' motives or stopped to consider what his ultimate destiny might be, he was too familiar with poverty and exploitation to let the thoughts deter him long. Ford, it is alleged, with a long distasteful history of anti-Semitism in his industrial dealings had his reasons for employing Negro workers. He put considerable sums of money in the Negro "Urban League," paid good wages to his coloured employees, and used them to block the organization of labour unions within his firm. As the Unions gained strength he employed more Negroes, but few were aware of these motives.

23. Say, I'm goin' to Detroit, I'm gonna get myself a job.
    (*twice*)
    I'm tired of layin' around here workin' on this starvation farm.

    Say, I'm goin' to get me a job now, working in Mr. Ford's place, (*twice*)
    Say, that woman tol' me last night, "Say, you cannot even stand Mr. Ford's ways."

But when the eruptions between Ford and the Unions came to a head in the mid-thirties, it was to the Unions that the Negroes gave their votes. In the ensuing years there were many Negroes in all parts of the country who had good reason to be glad of the dependability of Henry Ford's products, and in particular the celebrated "Model T," when they could afford to purchase one of the ancient and out-of-date models.

24. Well, well, when you feeling the winter, please throw your wild oats in the bin, (*twice*)
    Well, well, papa, next spring, eeh-yeah, I want t'take up my T-Model again.

    Well, T-Model Ford, I say, is a poor man's friend, (*twice*)
    Well, well, it will help you out, yeah when your money is spent.

Well, one thing about a T-Model, you don't have to
shift no gear, (*twice*)
Well, well, just lay down your brake and feed the gas,
eeh yeah, and the stuff is here. . . .

Throughout the war and the immediate post-war years Negroes in the North were able to have a share in the general
prosperity; there were jobs in plenty in Pittsburgh and Cleveland, New York and Chicago, and if one source of employment failed, it was still possible to secure alternative work.

25. I don't care, streets they is covered with snow, (*twice*)
I got to work at the warehouse and bring my baby the
roll.

Burnt half-way down, got to wait till they build again,
(*twice*)
I'm cuttin' grass now but I'm still bringing the money in.

They build and build till they finally done got through,
(*twice*)
You know in the mornin' just what I got to do.

I've got to get up every morin' till I wear my poor self
out, (*twice*)
Going down town working at the new warehouse.

Negroes were getting a share in the national prosperity of
the era, even if it was only the small surplus that dribbled
down the sides of the gigantic and ill-founded structure of
the commerical pyramid, rather than an integral part of it.
The orgy of speculation which the stockholders enjoyed during the late nineteen-twenties was to bring a sudden and devastating collapse of that unhappy erection: the index of common stock prices averaged a hundred in the year 1926; by
September 1929 it had more than doubled to 216. The big
profits that accrued from this speculation went into the pockets of only a small percentage of the nation, though it seemed
that everyone who had a few dollars to spare attempted to
invest them to his profit, and in doing so contributed to the
nation's eventual loss. The crash came in October 1929 when
the shareholders desperately tried to sell out. Sixteen million

shares were sold on the 29th of that month and the total loss exceeded the National Debt. Factories closed; the whistles sounded for the last time and the workers were laid off as the Depression settled on the land.

26. The rollin' mill it was done broke down,
    They ain't shippin' no iron to town.

    The longest train I ever seen,
    Run round Joe Brown's coal-mine.

    Her engine was there at the coal-mine's hill,
    And the captain never left town.

A shocked nation stared at its shattered industry, beheld in stupefied horror the closure of the banks, the collapse of capital investment. Inevitably those who had been signed on last were the first to lose their jobs. The Negroes who had streamed forth in happy anticipation a decade before, now found themselves workless, laid off with considerable fear and no regrets, no thanks. Men huddled together in mind-shattered despair on the street corners, stood with tin cups in the soup kitchens, and queued for long hours in the bread lines.

27. I was down and I cried that those jinx won't come at
        night, (*twice*)
    And it's tough to see a man go to the wreck and almost
        fall and die.

    I stood on the corner and almost bust ma head, (*twice*)
    I couldn't earn enough to buy me a loaf of bread.

    Baby, times is so hard, I almost call it tough, (*twice*)
    I can't earn no money to buy no bread an' I can't buy
        my snuff.

    My gal's a housemaid and she earns a dollar a week,
        (*twice*)
    I'm so hungry on pay-day, I can't hardly speak.

Now gather round me people, let me tell you true facts,
(*twice*)
That tough luck has struck me and the rats is sleepin'
in my hat.

On the outskirts of the large cities crude shack towns—
"Hoovervilles"—with dwellings made from tar-paper, packing
cases and metal advertisements housed the penniless. In conditions of mutual suffering White and coloured lived side by side
but there remained the perpetual fear that the Negro might
take any work that was available, and the sight of a dark-
skinned face was an unwelcome one.

28. I know just how, baby, a broke man feels, (*twice*)
    There's no one, baby, that will do him a real good deal.

    I've been broke all day, baby, did not have a lousy dime,
    (*twice*)
    I'll be all right, baby, I swear some other time.

    Lord, I don't feel welcome, mama, in St. Louis any
    more, (*twice*)
    'Cause I have no friends, baby, and no place to go.

Workless Negroes begged in the streets, rummaged through
the garbage-cans for scraps of food that they could salvage.
Coats wore thin, trousers were patched with rags, and feet
and knees were bound in gunny sacks as clothes fell apart and
shoes broke at the seams. With the coming of winter many
homeless and despairing men wished themselves back once
more in the hostile South.

29. Winter-time is coming, can you hear that howlin' wind?
    (*twice*)
    You better get ready cause the summer's done gone in.

    Cold wave make me shiver, cold wave gets my goat,
    (*twice*)
    I feel so disgusted, ain't got no overcoat.

Shoes ain't got no bottom, feets standin' on the ground,
(*twice*)
When it starts to snowin' be Alabama bound.

Winter-time is comin', ain't got a single sou, (*twice*)
With my pocket empty, tell me what I'm goin' to do?

This was a period when every man was for himself. There were twelve million unemployed in 1932. Consuming poverty ate into the hearts of men, and human feelings were wrung dry. With the election to the presidency of Franklin D. Roosevelt and his optimistic introduction of the policy of the New Deal, there was a slow but perceptible return to economic stability. Negroes found that at first they were still George Schyler's "mudsill of America" and in the struggle for employment they had lost ground even in the hated "jobs." Accustomed to the fight for survival, they accepted the situation philosophically.

30. I woke this morning laughing, laid down last night a-crying, (*twice*)
    Lost all my money, broke and didn't have a dime.

    When I had money, I had friends for miles around,
    Hmmmmm—mmm I had friends for miles around,
    Ain't got no money, my friends don't seem to know me now.

For all too many of them conditions were not markedly different from those that they had endured when the nation as a whole was enjoying a period of relative prosperity, and it was only half in humour that Lonnie Johnson declared that "Hard Times ain't gone nowhere."

31. People is raisin' 'bout hard times, tell me what it's all about,
    People is hollerin' 'bout hard times, tell me what's it all about,
    Hard times don't worry me, I was broke when it first started out.

Friends, it could be worser, you don't seem to understand, *(twice)*
Some is cryin' with a sack of gold under each arm and
a loaf of bread in each hand.

People ravin' 'bout hard times, I don't know why they
should, *(twice)*
If some people was like me, they didn't have no money
when times was good.

The New Deal brought employment to hundreds of thousands of workless men and with the institution of the schemes
of national relief by Roosevelt with Harry Hopkins at his
side, Negro families were given a chance to resuscitate themselves. In the mid-thirties some fifty per cent of the Negro
families in the North were receiving national assistance, but
in Atlanta sixty-five per cent were on relief and eighty per
cent in Norfolk, Virginia. The optimism of earlier years had
gone, to be replaced by more cautious hopes, but the North
still afforded better chances for a man to obtain some form
of employment and perhaps to save sufficient to bring his
family to him. The migration North continued.

32. I left my babe in Mississippi, picking cotton down in
New Orleans, *(twice)*
She says, "If you get to Chicago, please write me a letter
if you please."

(All right. . . .)
I said, "Baby, that's all right, baby that's all right for
you, *(twice)*
You'll be picking cotton down there. . . . Oh, baby
shall I get through?

"Baby, when I get to Chicago, I swear I'm gonna take
a chance, *(twice)*
I know when I get back to Mississippi, I'm sure gonna
change your name."

National relief gave him sufficient to live above starvation
level, but it did nothing to give the unemployed man the self-

respect that working for his living promoted. This the Public Works Administration, the Works Projects Administration and other schemes provided, and the ambitious programme of river dams, public highways, bridges and other municipal and federal construction undertakings gave direly needed employment though the fear of losing it remained a very real one.

33. Lord, Mister President, listen to what I'm going to say, (*twice*)
    You can take away all of the alphabet but please leave the P.W.A.

    Now you're in Mister President, an' I hope you're there to stay (*twice*)
    But whatever changes you make, please keep the P.W.A.

    P.W.A. is the best ol' friend I ever seen, (*twice*)
    Since the job ain't hard, and the boss ain't mean.

    I went to the poll and voted, an' I know I voted the right way, (*twice*)
    Now I'm praying to you Mister President, please keep the P.W.A.

Though the men were not driven as many of them had been on the Southern plantations and the work was not by these standards hard, yet the road grading, the drilling and manual labour involved in many of the construction schemes was heavy enough, and the work paid only moderately well. Faced with the high rents that are charged in Negro sectors, and the debts incurred by having goods on credit in lean times, a labourer still had good reason for anxiety.

34. Working on the project with holes all in my clothes, (*twice*)
    Trying to make me a dime, to keep the rent man from putting me out doors.

    I am working on the project, trying to make both ends meet, (*twice*)
    But the pay-day is so long, oh well, well, until the grocery man won't let me eat.

Working on the project with pay-day three or four
weeks away, (*twice*)
Now how can you make ends meet, ooh well, well,
when you can't get no pay?

If he was married or had a woman living with him, he had
little time for her unless she could help bring the money in,
though opportunities for work for her were few, as W.P.A.
employment for women was confined to indoor occupations
and these were limited.

35. I don't want no woman to sit around on her D.B.A.
Hell, I don't want no woman to sit around on her
D.B.A.
She got to bring me some kind of a job—if it's working
on the W.P.A.

A percentage of the work to be undertaken for any particular project was reserved for Negroes but the proportion
was often grossly unrelated to the number of Negro unemployed, especially in the South where discriminatory practices
operated against them. A man was fortunate to be on the
W.P.A. for generally the wages, though low, were still higher
than the sums that he might earn on the farms, or obtain on
relief—one reason for the discrimination against him: the
Southern farmers did not wish to see him obtain more on
Relief projects than he would in their employ. The majority
of Negro project workers were unskilled with the result that
their pay was in the lowest of categories. But the Negro
worker looked at his fellows who were unable to obtain any
form of employment and was thankful enough. By 1940 there
were some 237,000 Negro workers on W.P. A. projects repre-
senting a slightly higher proportion of the total than their
representation in unemployment figures. But outside the
P.W.A., W.P.A. and the United States Housing Authority,
there was little thought for the unemployed Negro and few
attempts made by official forces to give him work.

In the meantime the Unions had grown in power, and
fierce disputes raged between them and the employers. The
sheets were by no means clean on either side—gunmen and
spies were hired by both Union men and employers, and bitter
battles were fought at the picket lines and the factory gates

throughout the States. Atrocities of an appalling nature were committed by both factions, for in fighting for their livelihood the men were literally fighting for their lives in this period of devastating national distress. Negro workers were often taken on as strike breakers; labelled as "scabs" they were brutally man-handled by the striking workmen, though frequently they were unable to see that they were being exploited as tools for the employers. At this time many Unions made emphatic legislative measures to ensure that Negroes were excluded from their number; other rejected them by tradition even though no clauses in their constitutions specifically demanded Negro exclusion. To their everlasting credit there were some Unions that prohibited discrimination, though they were in the minority. Consequently when a strike occurred at the factory or mine the Negro provided willing non-Union labour. His woman rejoiced when pay-day came and neither stopped to count the cost.

36. My man is done the mine, he's got a Cadillac Eight,
And I have got the job to keep his business straight.

REFRAIN
I've got a ma–a–an in the 'Bama Mine,
I can spend his dollars, like I can his dimes.

You let these women fool you and give me the air,
I tried to be in reason, now I don't even care.

(*Spoken*) Yes, I got a man in the mine. You women ought to get a man like me. He mighta look dirty when he comes out—but he knows. . . .

Pressure was relieved for the White worker with the entry of the United States into World War II. Whilst hundreds of thousands of men were being drafted into the armed services it was estimated by the Bureau of Labour Statistics that close on one and a half million extra workers would be required between April 1941 and April 1942 to meet the demands of the defense industries. But in spite of this need for a vast army of civil workers, it was to be a White man's war. Grimly deliberate, the plants sought to exclude Negro workers from the factories even though there was an ever-increasing number of coloured men on relief and insufficient workers to meet the demands of industry. Four hundred thousand Negroes lived in New York, but of over twenty-nine thousand employees in ten defense plants in the area, a meagre one hundred and forty were coloured. Westinghouse, with Government contracts worth over $8,000,000, employed three Negroes out of its eight hundred workers in its Baltimore factory; there were only a dozen Negroes amongst the twelve thousand workers in the aircraft industries of Southern California and the deplorable story could be illustrated indefinitely. So, in this time of national emergency the Negro would sing:

37. Please give me a match to light this short I've found,
      (*twice*)
    I know it looks bad for me, picking tobacco up off the ground.

    Lord, it's zero weather an' I ain't got a lousy dime,
      (*twice*)
    I'm walking from door to door an' I can't find a friend of mine.

    I'm going back to the lowlands, and roll up my jumper sleeves, (*twice*)
    Then I'll be sitting pretty, baby—long as I kill grass and weeds.

Negroes who had gone North to find better employment became disillusioned; the South that they had left in bitterness now seemed less cruel. Cotton prices had risen to nine cents in 1940, to fourteen cents in 1941 and were to rise to twenty cents in the following year. Many Negroes were attracted Southwards.

38. I'm going back South,
    Where men are men, and women are glad of it.

    Oooh—I've got those Southern blues, (*twice*)
    Cotton prices going higher, an' I ain't got no time to lose.

Chicago and Detroit. Folks have you heard the news?
(*twice*)
Old Dixieland is jumping—I've got the Southern
blues. . . .

Exasperated with the situation in the war and factories,
Negro leader A. Philip Randolph called for a march on Washington to be made by some fifty thousand Negroes on 1 July
1941. Four days before it was to take place President Roosevelt wrote his Executive Order 8802 which, in urging a policy
of non-discrimination in industry, caused the cancellation of
the march and the establishment of the Committee on Fair
Employment Practice. Negroes were taken on in defence
factories though they had good reason to fear the effects of
the lay-off with the cessation of hostilities.

39. I had a little woman working on that National Defence,
(*twice*)
That woman got to the place, I'm glad she did not have
no chance.

Just because she was workin', makin' so much dough,
(*twice*)
That woman got to the place she did not love me no
mo'.

That Defence has gone, just listen to my song, (*twice*)
Since that Defence has gone, that woman done lost her
home.

Much of the good that was done during the latter part of
the war in obtaining good and equal employment for Negroes was spoiled when the companies retrenched with the
end of the strife. Returning White servicemen claimed their
previous posts, or better ones, whilst the Negroes who had
been brought into the factories at a later stage were the first
to be laid off. But there was no Depression parallel to that
of the post-World War I years and by comparison the Negro
was economically somewhat better placed. In the West Coast
cities there had been a phenomenal growth in the Negro populations owing to the opening of defence factories to Negroes,

which presented many problems of post-war adjustment. The Fair Employment Practices Commission lost much of its effectiveness, and some of its branches actually acted as screens for discrimination. California voted against its continuance but consultants were appointed to take its place.

Though an analysis made in 1948 revealed that the average Negro family was still earning little more than half that of the medium White family, there has been over all a slow but undeniable improvement in the labour situation of the American Negro. He still finds his principal sources of employment in the non-skilled and semi-skilled categories, but he has made small yet significant inroads into the professional and technical fields. Integration is gradually taking place, perhaps most successfully when it is not the result of Supreme Court Decisions backed by armed intervention. The coloured man who has profited by the great advances in Negro education, by the experiences of the war and by those improvements in industrial and social relations that have taken place looks more astutely and with greater understanding at the problem than hitherto. His philosophy is summed up by Charles (Crown Prince) Waterford when he sings of living in Los Angeles, a city where he finds Southern attitudes of mind still persisting; where overcrowding makes a Negro's automobile his front parlour; but where, if he meets conditions half-way and is prepared to give and to take, he is confident of ultimate concord.

40. Well, some call it the Land of Sunshine, some calls it
    Central Avenue, (*twice*)
    I call it a big ole country town where the folks don't
    care what they do.

    Well, if a man can make it Los Angeles, he can make
    it anywhere (*twice*)
    But you got to have one of those Cadillac cars, yes, and
    you can't stay where.

    Well, some like fried chicken, well, I'll take a pie,
    (*twice*)
    But don't eat it too fast boys—you'll get the gravy in
    your eye.

> Yes, every wink don't mean I'm 'sleep, and every good-
> bye don't mean I'm gone, (*twice*)
> I'm gonna settle down on the West Side and make L.A.
> my home.

Slow though its acceptance of the inevitability of industrialization may have been, the South had to develop for its
own survival. Employment of Negroes in industry ultimately
came to the South in spite of the persistence of the beliefs in
the Negro's incapacity to undertake such work, and though
the majority of Negro workers are still employed in unskilled
jobs the proportion of farm labourers dropped from thirty-
six per cent in 1900 to a mere six per cent a half-century
later, whilst the total of Negro industrial employees rose from
a miserable one per cent to thirty per cent within the same
period. And in the Mississippi Delta regions, where progress
is slower and old traditions and modes of thought die hard,
there are signs of change and the glimmerings of hope for
the coloured people there.

41. I worked all the summer, yes, and all the fall,
    Going to spend Christmas in my overalls,

    But I'll get a break yes, somewhere before long,
    —Yes, before long.

Chapter 2

Railroad for My Pillow

IN 1890 eight out of every ten Negroes lived in rural districts and during the course of the next thirty years a further fifteen per cent of the coloured population moved towards the towns. Significant of a change in the pattern of Negro life though this was, the ensuing decade witnessed a still more marked increase in the urban population: in 1930 nearly half of the Negro population was living in the towns. Between 1910 and the entry of the United States into World War II close on two million Negroes had migrated from the South to the Northern urban centres. The war brought a further million, whilst large numbers moved to the West where Negroes hitherto had been few in number. The process has continued and though to-day more than three-quarters of America's Negroes still live in the South, the shift from the agricultural to the urban communities has been remarkable, for by 1950 less than a fifth lived in Southern rural districts. Thus there has been a considerable movement of coloured people within the South itself, and though the Great Migration to the North was an extraordinary phenomenon the effects of which were made outstandingly apparent by reason of the startling growth of the coloured sectors in the cities, this internal circulation within the South has been no less spectacular.

The redistribution of the Negro population witnessed during the past fifty years has been largely dependent upon the changing conditions of employment and the new requirements of industry in the twentieth century, but this movement of coloured workers has given support to the deliberately stimulated notions of Negro shiftlessness. Accusing fingers have been pointed at the wandering workers and families and bitter tongues have spoken of the work-shy, the unreliable, the undependable Negro who has in fact only moved on through dissatisfaction and the desire to better his economic status. Even though the Negro worker can earn to-day approximately four times his wage of 1940, whilst he continues to earn little more than half the salary of the average White wage earner, the circulation of labour is likely to continue. It will only abate when he can attain parity of esteem with his White competitors.

During these years of Negro migration the blues has developed and it is no doubt largely as a result of this circulation of coloured people that it has spread in so remarkable a manner. A folk music reflects the environment of the people who create it, and when their background is a constantly varying one it is scarcely surprising that the images that are mirrored in the blues have much to do with the movement of the Negro. Not only does the blues illustrate his search for work compatible with his talents and appropriate to his needs; it also reveals the personal quarrels, the human foibles, the weaknesses, the qualities and defects of spirit and character that have caused men to leave their homes in the hope of finding new and happier surroundings; it gives a glimpse of what it must mean to be one among the many rejected, homeless migrants—to be one single unit in the impersonal statistics that represent the millions of rootless men and women.

If the search for employment constitutes the principal reason why large numbers of Negroes leave their homes, there are nevertheless many other motivating factors which for the individual may be no less impelling. Amongst the most significant of these must be the reaction against segregational practices, when the frayed material of human endurance has been worn through. For years a man may suffer the petty indignities that are as much the manifestations of racial discrimination as the lynchings. He may take his seat in the back of the bus; may stand, herded with his fellows in the inadequate Jim Crow cars of the trains. He makes his exit from the station by the door marked *Coloured*—he drinks from the water fountain marked *Coloured*. He is accustomed to the policy of "separate but equal" educational facilities that can mean that he has been taught by an unqualified teacher in an unheated, ill-equipped shack. He enters by the back door, never by the front; he takes his hat off when he speaks to a White man and notices that no hand is lifted to the hat when a White man speaks to his wife; he answers to "Uncle" or "Boy" but never hears himself addressed as "Mister"; he steps off the pavement when a White person approaches and is careful not to look too hard at a White woman. He sees the White boys trying to "make" the young Negro girls and knows that he dare not protest. If he is a "good Nigger" and "knows his place," if he is not "uppity" and makes no attempt to assert his rights as an American citizen, he lives in an uneasy peace. And his personal pride hurt, his individuality suppressed, he wonders to himself why he has merited such discrimination, and what the future may bring. He listens to the teachings of the preacher that all men are children in the eyes of God and tries to equate the words with the facts of his own experience and the revelations of his own eyes.

42. They say we are the Lawd's children, I don't say that ain't true, (*twice*)
But if we are the same like each other, ooh, well, well, why do they treat me like they do?

I want to live on, children, children, I would like to see, (*twice*)
What will become of us, ooh, well, by nineteen and fifty-three.

Some of the Good Lawd's children, some of them ain't no good, (*twice*)
Some of them are the devil, ooh, well, well, and won't help you if they could.

Some of the Good Lawd's children kneel upon their knees and pray, (*twice*)
You serve the devil in the night, ooh, well, and serve the Lawd in the day.

But the singer, Peetie Wheatstraw, was never destined to wit-

ness the improvements in race relations that were gradually
taking place in 1953, for he was killed in a car accident on
a level crossing at Clarksdale, Mississippi, in 1941.

Comes the day when the pattern of racial discrimination
becomes in its total effect upon him almost unbearable and
the Southern Negro considers making the break. It is not
simple for him; share-cropping, work on the levee or on the
turpentine farm may keep him with a heavy debt to pay before he can be free to leave.

43. Say, if I ever get a dollar to pay this debt I owe, (*twice*)
    Says I never will in this world get in debt no more.

A man who has seldom travelled further from home than he
can walk in a day, a man who lives a few score miles from
the nearest city, some five miles from the nearest village, a
man whose whole horizon has been bounded by cotton-wood
trees, who has never seen a Northern newspaper, who has
never possessed a radio, finds it hard to break himself away
from the little world he knows; to leave his friends and his
kinfolk in order to try his fortune in a country of which he
knows nothing—such a man may never summon the courage
to make so bold a move. Instead he may content himself with
the resolution that he will leave if "he still feels the same way,
to-morrow," and in doing so canalizes the burning anger and
frustration that might have prompted him.

44. Bye-bye Arkansas. Tell Missouri I'm on my way up
       North now, baby,
     I declare I ain't fooin' gal, if I can just—
     Feel in the mornin' like I feel to-day.
     I declare I'm gonna pack up, pack up now, baby,
     And make my getaway.

But the threads that tie him to his home begin to snap, the
strain becomes greater, the tautening of racial tensions becomes too much. To him "Black is Evil," for his colour he
knows is the basis of his trouble. He begins to resent the
colour of his people, the colour of his own skin which he
feels is burned to the depths of his very being, to his black
soul. He hears of better conditions in the distant North where
discrimination is supposed not to exist and where employ-

ment is to be gained for the asking. Though he treats the stories with a certain amount of scepticism, he resolves to move to the North, bearing in mind the thought that, if his hopes are not realized, he can return to the Jim Crow South again.

45. I'm tired of this Jim Crow, gonna leave this Jim Crow town,
    Doggone my black soul, I'm sweet Chicago bound,
    Yes, I'm leavin' here, from this ole Jim Crow town.

    I'm going up North, where they say—money grows on trees,
    I don't give a doggone, if ma black soul leaves,
    I'm goin' where I don't need no B.V.D.s.

    I'm goin' up North, baby, I can't carry you,
    Ain't nothin' in that cold country, a sweet gal can do,
    I'm goin' get me another gal, baby, I'm through with you.

    Lord well, if I get up there—where they don't suit—
    I don't start no crying. Go tell that ole ma'am of mine,
    Lord I'm ready to come back to my Jim Crow town.

Euphemistically, a Negro may call racial discrimination "bad luck" and sing of its effects, but sometimes it is a chain of misfortune rather than the effect of direct discrimination that leads a man to take such a step; trouble with his crops, with his domestic affairs, with the police and with his friends, may drive him to the point where he would rather leave the district than remain. It is not always a case of failing to face his responsibilities, for the future may hold nothing for him, and in spite of the fear that a simple man may have of the unknown outside world, to remain where his family have lived and died in the cotton rows, to stay where his own failure has made his wife hostile to him may be unbearable.

46. Trouble, trouble, I been havin' it all my days, (twice)
    Now it seems like trouble gonna put me in ma lonesome grave.

I'm scared to stay here, scared to leave this ole Bad
    Luck town, (*twice*)
But when I get back early mornin', my head goes round
    and round. (*twice*)

Now listen here, people, I don't want no one's advice,
    (*twice*)
I done change ma way of living, gonna find someone
    to treat me right.

I'm gonna tell everybody what bad luck I've had in
    ma life, (*twice*)
I killed my sisters and my brothers; now that woman
    done wrecked ma life.

Returning home when the sun has gone down, his pockets
empty of all save his calloused hands, the share-cropper pauses
before his clap-board shack, with its patched walls and crumbling piles. Bellies swollen with pellagra, his children watch
him solemn-eyed, whilst his woman now cooking the grits in
the skillet "loudmouths" him for his laziness, for his uselessness. She does not understand why his work never seems to
get them out of debt, but she knows that she has to bear
children, raise, clothe and feed children and try to keep a
home together. She curses him in her own helplessness for
bringing them to such misery and turns him from the door.

47. The time has come for us to part,
      I ain't goin' to cry, it won't break my heart,
      'Cause I'm through with you and I hope you don't feel
        hurt.

      You're like an old horseshoe that's had its day,
      You're like an old shoe I must throw away,
      I'm through with you and I hope you don't feel hurt.

      You ain't got no money, you're down and broke,
      You're just an old has-been like a worn-out joke,
      So I'm through with you and I hope you don't feel hurt.

The house does not belong to him, the land is not his own;

the peck of meal in the bin and the rusting plough beside the outhouse belong to the company store; his woman has no further use for him; the bolt is slammed across the door. So he turns away and the dust slowly settles where he has dragged his aimless feet.

48. Yes I'm leavin', mama, but I don't know which way to go, (*twice*)
'Cause that woman I been living with for twenty years, mama, says she don't want me no mo'.

An' I feel like walkin', mama, an' I feel like lying down, (*twice*)
'Cause the woman I been livin' with for twenty years, mama, she done sold me down.

I got holes in my pockets, baby, I got patches in my pants, (*twice*)
I'm behind with the house-rent, mama, Lord, Lord, he want it all in advance.

For the woman no less than for the man, the conditions of living and working under the share-cropping system can be so frustrating as to leave her with no will to work or to share his life. Rather than remain with a woman who has no desire to look after his needs, her husband may quietly "quit" her, failing to return one day from his work, seeking solace and comfort in the home of another woman. Small deficiencies of character may be magnified in eyes whose vision is distorted by misery, minor disputes become inflated by fear and despair into family-shattering rows. The catalogue of real and imagined injuries and injustices is paraded, accusing fingers pointed, vicious words uttered and blows struck. "A workin' man," sings Blind Boy Fuller, "ain't nothin' but a woman's slave." And Lee Warren looks back bitterly on the years during which he has been exploited:

49. Cooked my breakfast this morning, pretty mama, had my dinner on time,
Split my last dollar like you split my last dime.

REFRAIN
Well I'm gettin' tired of fattening frogs for snakes,
Take me so many years to learn my mistakes.

When I had plenty money you pulled me in your door,
Soon as I got bad luck you 'suaded me from your doggone room.

When I first met you, pretty mama, didn't have so many
clo's,
No house-rent, almost sleepin' out-doors.

Declaring that "I'm going away to wear you off my mind,"
another man has stepped into the dirt road, "another man
done gone." It is better that he should go than he should turn
his woman from her home, for he stands slightly more of a
chance of obtaining employment elsewhere whilst she may not
have to look far before another man takes his place. Children
are capital in a community where freedom from virtual slavery can only be obtained by maximum output of work. A
Negro would therefore often be prepared to accept as his
own the children of his wife by a former husband or lover
and raise them along with his, provided that they work in the
fields and help to clear the cropper's debt. Only with the
gradual rejection of the crop-lien system and better marital
relations, resulting largely from improved educational facilities, has this loose form of family tended to disappear, to be
replaced by a firmer and socially more secure structure based
on mutual responsibility. The substitute parent was not necessarily resented by the man who left, who was frequently prepared to accept the situation philosophically. Departing without rancour towards the man who had displaced him he
would "make his getaway" to a new district, sometimes to
better his fortunes in the process.

50. She had a man, onl' a man; had a kid, man, onl' a kid,
Had a man on' a man; had a kid man—on' a kid.
She had so many men, until she could not keep it hid.

I left that woman, one mornin', jus' about the break
of day, (twice)
You know I packed my suitcase, made my getaway.

Here I am, in Chicago, and I'm going very well, (*twice*)
I don't find that woman, I live just alone by myself.

Figures that illustrate the extent of the Migration are necessarily few, for the full import was not fully appreciated at the time nor were there reliable methods of measurement available. Nevertheless certain statistics do indicate the degree to which Negro men left their homes, and the numbers of desertions of their wives and families that had taken place. Of some two hundred thousand homeless men in Chicago in 1930 some ten per cent were Negro transients and a sample taken of these indicated that more than half had been married. Of these who had been married nearly three-quarters had deserted their wives and families. A similar pattern was evident in New York, where of some seven thousand, five hundred and sixty Negro arrivals, the same proportion of married men was to be found and of these thirty-five per cent had deserted their families. These alarming figures were to be echoed in the scores of cities to which the Negro men migrated during the twenties and thirties and caused serious social problems in the South, where many families were left with the mother alone to care for them. Not unexpectedly the Negro mother tended to be more admired—and more missed—by her offspring than was the father, and she was remembered with respect and without false sentiment by them in later years.

51. What a sad old Sunday, people, this year in May,
(*twice*)
I think of my mother and I kneel down to pray.

Mother was a woman sure to me, I really do know,
(*twice*)
I'll never have a friend like my dear old mother no more.

Since we didn't have people to make a home like it should be, (*twice*)
But although poor mother doin' the best she could for me.

In the ante-bellum years the Negro family was a true matriarchate. The importance of the father was deliberately reduced under the slavery system and Negro children seldom had great respect for their male parents if indeed they knew who they were. At this time strong and well-developed Negroes were literally kept at stud on many plantations with the sole purpose of procreating children likely to be effective as workers or as saleable material. The women were informed whom their mates were to be and love played no part in their relations in all save the most humanitarian plantations —and slavery was not a humanitarian system. Furthermore the young Negro girls were reserved for the sexual excesses of the young White planters and the coloured concubine was normal in the South. Some were well provided for, but the majority were cast back into the slave-quarters to bear their children and to continue to labour as soon as they had fulfilled their purpose. Consequently the mother was frequently the only parent that the Negro child knew, and his affections were naturally centered upon her. With the conclusion of the war there was a period of extreme promiscuity amongst Negroes which was a manifestation of the new-found Freedom, but there was also considerable evidence in an increasing sense of self-respect on the part of the coloured man and as the years passed an assumption of responsibility that showed that he wished to assert himself as the head of his own family. Nevertheless the rule of the mother and of the grandmother persisted in a very large number of instances and Negro families have continued to show a proportionately much higher rate of female "heads" than have the White families.

Greater opportunities for escape and for evacuation, the promiscuous living attendant with overcrowding in slum areas, and many other factors combine to make the proportion of families with female heads greater in the urban than in the rural areas and greater in the rural non-farm areas than in the farming districts. Thus the rural areas often show a figure of some fifteen per cent, whereas in the cities the numbers of such families may often be in excess of a third of the total. For example the Negro sociologist, Franklin Frazier, states that in 1930 nearly forty per cent of the sixteen hundred Negro and mulatto families in Nashville, Tennessee, had female heads—a term which covers mothers, married and single, foster-mothers and elder sisters.

With the problems of maintaining a family, and of securing an income, many women readily accepted another man in the home but, though such relations could be harmonious, they also stimulated much jealousy and disunion. The problems besetting a mother who has to cope with the combined passions and desire for freedom of the many children in a large family, as the boys approached their maturity, were often too great, and the young men did not heed the warnings and entreaties of their parents.

52. I've treated my dear old mother, I've been treatin' her
     so unkind, (*twice*)
    Without a mighty change I believe I'm gonna lose my
    mind.

    So many men are in trouble and their mothers have
    been their slave, (*twice*)
    So much grievin' and worryin' I've carried her to her
    grave.

    If I had to go back home, I'm gonna fall down on my
    knees, (*twice*)
    I will never leave my happy home no more because
    my poor old heart would bleed.

Some would find the remonstraces of their parents boring or unintelligible; they would ignore the advice given them, delight in their reputations as irresponsible children, and take advantage of any indulgence towards them. Young and with voice still unbroken, Isaiah Nettles rebels against the half-hearted restraint of his parents.

53. Aaaah cryin', mama, papa said, "Doodadoodado—do
    Cryin'—eeeh don't let him—doodadoodado—"
    She's a high-steppin' mama, I don't care what you do.

    I was a li'l boy, on ma way to school,
    Was a little boy—ooh—on ma way to school,
    An a high-brown woman, an' she broke my mammy's
    rule.

> Mama said I'm reckless, daddy says I'm young and
>   wild,
> Mama said oooh; daddy said I'm young and wild—
> Said, "He's so reckless, he's my baby's chile."

Seriously accepting their responsibilities, many parents
would try to restrain their children and try to set an example
to them that might help to negate that which they often saw
about them. But the family structure was too loose, the problem too great and not always was it possible to cope. Sons
and daughters were lured away from home by false and attractive promises against the advice of their parents. At times
of national or racial stress the number of children on the
move greatly increased. Such catastrophes as the East St.
Louis riots of 1917 and other cruel disturbances made little
sense to the children who failed to realize their seriousness.

54. Lay down at night, trying to play my hand,
    Through the window, out stepped a man,
    I didn't know no better, oh boy, in ma girlish days.

    My mama cried, papa did too,
    My daughter, look what a shame on you,
    I didn't know no better in ma girlish days.

    I flagged a train, didn't have a dime,
    Tryin' to run away from that home of mine,
    I didn't know no better, oh boy, in ma girlish days.

    I hit the highway, caught me a truck,
    1917, when the world was tough,
    I didn't know no better, oh boy, in my girlish days.

Children wandering aimlessly on the roads presented a
major problem in the twenties and thirties and the researches
of the Children's Bureau conducted in 1932 by Dr. McMullen
of Chicago University suggested that there were then some
two hundred thousand child hoboes on the roads and railroads. Later examination revealed that the number was
probably in excess of half a million. These vagrant children
of all national and racial groups, but of whom a considerable
proportion was Negro, were tough and embittered, homeless

and independent; they scorned the camps of the Civilian Conservation Corps—the C.C.C., subject of more than one blues—though the corps drew more from children who were in unhappy homes than from those who had left them. The victims of families broken by economic stress, the defections of parents and the vice of racial prejudice, many suffered abominably and were ruthlessly exploited; others, becoming bitter and mean, begged and thieved, drifting readily into crime.

55. I don't know my real name, I don't know where I was
      born, (*twice*)
   The trouble I've been having, seems like I was raised
      in an orphan's home.

   My mother died and left me when I was only two years
      old, (*twice*)
   And the trouble I've been having only the Good Lord
      knows.

   I've been treated like an orphan and been workin' like
      a slave, (*twice*)
   And if I never get my revenge, evilness will carry me
      to my grave.

A visible sign of the acuteness of the Depression, the droves of coloured men, women and children who were to be seen scuffling along the dirt roads were unwelcome to both White and coloured communities. As the years wore on and money became scarce, when the poverty of those who wandered in the streets was almost equalled by that of the residents of homes for which they could not afford the rent, the begging cup of the hobo "bumming his chuck" and seeking a "handout" became more resented.

56. I have walked a lonesome road till ma feet is too sore
      to walk, (*twice*)
   I beg scraps from the people, oh well, till my tongue is
      too stiff to talk.

   Anybody can tell you people, ooh well, that I ain't no
      lazy man, (*twice*)

But I'll guess I'll have to go to the poorhouse, mmmm
   well, well, and do the best I can.

I am what I am, and what I was born to be, (*twice*)
Mmm, hard luck is in ma family and it's rollin' down
   on me.

When I get off ma troubles I'm gonna bring my money
   down, (*twice*)
And change my way of living, oh well, so I won't have
   to tramp aroun'.

In the blues songs of the homeless and workless there is
little evidence of the self-pity that Odum and Johnson declared was a characteristic of Negro song. Pride, philosophical acceptance of the present situation and often a strong
vein of hope are constantly recurrent features which mark
the blues. The poverty and the unhappy conditions described
were a clear statement of fact and in no wise born of self-pity.

57. Seem like I was born in Bedlam, just a bad luck chile
   and everything goes all wrong, (*twice*)
I came home this morning, my baby has packed up
   and gone.

I will always remember what my mother told me and
   every word she said was true, (*twice*)
I've had so much trouble, I didn't know what in the
   world to do.

I'm gonna quit worryin' and will stop grievin' 'cause
   the bad luck will change some day, (*twice*)
It's hard to walk in that straight and narrow way.

The blues acted as a catalyst for the blinding anger, humiliation and frustration that sought to demolish the moral
codes and spirit of a man, and the act of artistic creation
brought satisfaction and comfort both to him and to his
companions. Essentially the blues singer is a realist and his
statements are accurate portrayals of his state of mind, uninhibited in their self-expression. Singing of his condition

brings relief to his heart and order to his disturbed thoughts, though many a blues indicates that the singer has come close to moral and mental disintegration.

58. Well, I'm broke and hungry, Dulcie, you got the feast
       for me, (*twice*)
     My stomach's filled with nothin', nothin' else but grief.

     My friends don't see me, no, they just pass me by,
       (*twice*)
     I wouldn't mind it so much, but they hold their heads
       so high.

     Now I'm roamin' the highways and pickin' up cigarette
       butts and everything I can find, (*twice*)
     I mean I'm broken-down and disgusted, I sure got evil
       on my mind.

     Now I'm eatin' wild berries and I'm sleepin' on the
       ground, (*twice*)
     I'm broken down and disgusted and I'm tired of
       trampin' around.

Much of the Southern rural scene is a broad and under-developed landscape in which small, condensed communities exist in isolation connected only by unmetalled tracks. Making their various ways towards the cities, the Negro transients had little more than the sun to guide them and a vague conception of the direction in which they had to go. For those who had hitherto been confined to limited areas, penetration into the unknown regions beyond held unsuspected terrors and the tedium of pacing the winding, endless roads was shattering on the nerves.

59. Look down that long old lonesome road, (*twice*)
     My poor feet is tired but still I've got to go.

     There's no trail to my home town, there ain't but one
       way to go, (*twice*)
     There's mile after mile, stepping down that long old
       muddy road.

> There ain't but one thing that worries me both night
> and day, (*twice*)
> That's the place they call Death Valley, and it's just
> half-way.
>
> I've been tramping this lonely road, night after night
> and day after day, (*twice*)
> If your prayers don't help me, you know I'll die trying
> to make my way.

A lift on the tail-board of a wagon going to town, of a cotton
cart going to the gin might help to bring him a little nearer
to his destination, and so, in Bobby Grant's words he goes
"down that dirt road, that long, long dirt road, that lonesome
old dirt road; I'm goin' down that ole dirt road till somebody
lets me ride. . . ." His best hope is to reach one of the main
highways or turnpikes that seam the face of the United States,
for once on these his direction is clear and there may be the
chance of P.W.A. work on the highway itself. To the homeless man the highway itself is as good an address as any
other.

> 60. Yes I'm goin', yes I'm goin' away, (*twice*)
> I'm gonna leave here walkin' down on Jeff Davis High-
> way.
>
> When you get lonesome, try and write me some day,
> (*twice*)
> An' if I don't pay for no account, baby, I'll be down
> on Jeff Davis Highway.
>
> The woman I was lovin', she's so far away, (*twice*)
> That's the reason I'm gonna leave here, walking down
> on Jeff Davis Highway.

For the migrant Negro with his eyes focused on the far
horizon the long ribbons of the "odd" numbered highways
have a magnetic fascination. Harsh edges unsoftened by wayside vegetation, their stark concrete whiteness causing them
to glare cruelly in the unrelenting sun, they guide his steps
to the North. He sings of Highway 49 which leads him from
Gulfport through Jackson to Clarksdale, or more recently,

of Highway 99 which takes him up the Pacific Coastal route from Los Angeles. Often he sings of Highway 61 which begins in New Orleans and by way of Natchez, Vicksburg, Memphis and St. Louis, continues northward to St. Paul and Port Arthur; or of its fellow, Highway 51, on whose hard causeway countless thousands of flapping soles and bare black feet have made no indentation. Highway 51 runs also from New Orleans and by way of Jackson, Mississippi, and Memphis, Cairo and Decatur, Illinois, swings eastward of Chicago through Madison. These are the best-known routes to the Southern Negroes: to Tommy McClennan who lived on the highway way out of Jackson, where he could watch the cheapest form of road transport available to the fare-paying migrant—the Greyhound bus.

61. Now if I should die, before my time should come,
    I said if I should die jus' before my time should come,
    I want you to please bury my body out on Highway 51.

    Now hyah come that Greyhound, with his tongue stickin' out on the side, (yes, yes)
    Now heah come that Greyhound with his tongue stickin' out on the side,
    If you buy your ticket, swear 'fore God and they'll let you ride.

    Now my baby had won five dollars and now, now she spend it—
    My baby won five dollars, she spend it out on a V-8 Ford, (yes, yes)
    So's I could meet that Greyhound bus on that Highway 51 road.

With money a man could make a speedy departure by way of the Greyhound bus, for, in the words of Lee Brown, "Baby, ain't you ever been to the Greyhound bus depot? Babe, that's the fastest bus running on Highway 51. . . ." But for those who had not got the fare there were certain hazards in walking the highways. Few truck drivers would pick up a Negro; there was always the chance of arrest for vagrancy or one of the other charges designed to keep Negroes from migrating. The railroad tracks offered a less conspicuous, but at the same time, an equally certain indication of the route. Talking to himself to keep from falling between the lines through the hypnotic effect of walking the ties, the hobo would follow the hard iron road.

62. Keep on walkin' and walkin', talkin' to myself, (*twice*)
Gal I love's with somebody else.

I got the hard road blues, walkin' on down the line, (*twice*)
Maybe some day my gal will change her mind.

It's a hard, hard road when your baby done throwed you down, (*twice*)
Goin' keep on walkin' from town to town.

I'm goin' find my baby, don't think she cain't be found, (*twice*)
Goin' walk this hard road till my moustache touch the ground.

For Southern Negroes the appeal of the railroads has always been both a real and symbolic one. In the Slavery periods when Negroes were unable to travel between districts without written "bonds" from their owners, the snorting engines, with brilliant furnaces tracing their progress and clouds of black smoke that hung in the still air above the tracks long after the screaming whistles had died away, inspired in them an awe which their descendants still retain. For them the train that appeared from the horizon and roared towards the plantations to roll on into the unknown regions beyond was a symbol of power, of freedom and of escape. When organized escape routes were planned for Negroes to make for the free North they were known collectively as the "Underground Railroad," lending further significance to the railway system. But this time the hay-lofts and barns owned by friendly Whites were the "stations," and the "conductors" were the anti-slavery sympathizers, who risked imprisonment, even their lives, to guide the slaves to freedom. This symbolic importance of the railroad was imprinted on Negro religion and the spirituals told of the "Glorious Gospel Train"; to-day the trains that take the Damned to Hell and the Righteous to Glory are still favoured themes of sermons. As the blues developed in the post-bellum years the railroad figured prominently in the songs; the symbolic had become reality and now the trains bore northwards innumerable Negroes who were leaving the South, for,

63. When a woman gets the blues, she hangs her head and
    cries.
    But when a man gets the blues, he flags a freight train
    and rides.

Perhaps the morality is questionable; there are grounds for criticizing the Negro who escapes from his problem rather than remaining to face it, considering "bumming" a free ride on a passing train to be deserving of contempt. But to a wretched, friendless, workless and hopeless man these are arguments that are unlikely to make sense or reason, and the temptation to make a rapid escape to another and remote district where prospects may be better is irresistible.

64. I'm standing here by this lamp-post with my mind in a
    different land,
    I ain't got no home, woman's got some other man.

    And some people singin' the blues just because they
    know the song,
    But when you hear me singin', I ain't gonna be here
    long.

    I dreamed last night that the whole round world was
    mine,
    I woke up this mornin', didn't have one lousy dime.

    I gambled, 'clare gambled, but I can't win no more,
    Every once in a while rent-man knocks on my door.

    So I'm leavin' here to-night if I have to ride the blinds,
    Catch a freight train special—Engineer, lose no time.

    I'm stone bare-footed and my last pair of pants is tore,
    'Clare I've never been in this hard luck before.

As the long freight train takes a curve, a figure breaks from cover and dashes towards the track, taking advantage of the slowing of the train to make boarding possible, and of the bend to hide his movements. Crooked fingers clutch the couplings and he swings perilously on the swaying truck before getting a firmer grip. He may make for the "blinds" if he can. These are the baggage cars next to the tender, which are "blind" or, in other words, have no side door. Sitting on the step he is safe and out of reach of the brakeman's club, but to reach the blinds he must come close to the tender and may be observed in doing so. More dangerous, but out of sight and unapproachable, are the brake rods that run beneath the freight cars. Risking his life he may try to worm his way across these, or if he is unusually adept he may carry a small board to throw across the rods and then precipitate himself upon it in the narrow gap between them and the underneath of the truck. Holding on to axle beams, brake rods or coupling links throughout the day and night, in icy winds, in the choking poisonous fumes of the railroad tunnels, he may freeze to numbness or succumb to exposure and drop to certain death to the track below. To hobo a ride takes the determination of the utterly desperate, and cold, reckless nerve. It is not the escape for the faint-hearted.

65. Well, I'm blue and evil, so many things to learn, (*twice*)
   So many things to worry, so many ways to turn.

   I had so much trouble, swear my nerves is weakenin'
      down, (*twice*)
   I would swing on a freight train, but I'm afraid to leave
      the ground.

   Whistle keeps on blowin' an' I got my debts to pay,
      (*twice*)
   I've got a mind to leave my baby an' I've got a mind
      to stay.

There is no room for mistakes; no second chance: the loss of a limb is the least penalty for failing to "nail a rattler" successfully the first time. But the children learn from the older, more experienced hoboes who generally like to have a child with them to make their fires, to cook and to solicit for alms when they reach the cities. Living promiscuously and dangerously they continue to hop the flat-cars, swing on to the gondolas until disablement of mind or body forces them to beg their rides from the "mean old fireman" and the "cruel old engineer." "I decided I'd go down South the last time and take it as it comes. I reckoned that mean old fireman and engineer would too," commented King Solomon Hill:

66. Now some of these people have gone down to-day,
    And this fast train Northern and Southern, travelling light and clean.

    Mmm mm—I wanna ride your train,
    I said, "Looka hyah engineer, can I ride your train?"
    He said, "Looka hyah you oughta know this train ain't mine an' you askin' me in vain."

    Said, "You got to go to the Western Union, you might get a chance."
    (*Spoken*) I didn't know the Western Union run no trains.
    Said, "You go to the Western Union and you might get a chance. . . .

    You write to your wife and some of your people, your papa be standin' right here."
    (*Spoken*) Hadn't thought of it that way before.

    I wanna go home, and that train is done gone dead,
    I wanna goooo and that train is done gone dead,
    I done lost my wife and my three little children and my mother's sick in bed.

    Mmmm—please, let me win my fare,
    'Cause I'm a travellin' man, boys, an' I can't stay here.

Appealing to the railroad men seldom had any effect, although the engineers on some lines were Negroes. But they were anxious to retain their jobs in days when jobs were scarce enough and when hoboes and "bums" constituted a major problem to the railroad companies. The hoboes hated the "snakes"—the switchmen, whose lapel buttons with an "S" motif earned them their names, and most of all the brakemen, the "stingers"—so named from the "B" that they wore on their buttons. Firemen would turn their hoses on the hoboes who clung to the tops of the box-cars so that their wet clothes would freeze to them and they would fall from their perches; brakemen swung the clubs with which they tightened down the brakes in defence against the tough and desperate hoboes. They are the traditional enemies of the railroad bum and their ranks are supported by the railroad "bulls"—the company police who with "billy" and "nightstick" fight off the tramps and wield their clubs through the hobo encampments. To protect themselves against assaults of the railroad officials and police, the hoboes frequently band together and ride in groups upon the cars, especially the Negroes, who have also to contend with racial prejudice. Out of a racial clash between two such groups and a White gang with a couple of White prostitutes arose the terrible Scottsboro affair. Having reached a district in which they may hope to find work, or where they intend to settle for a while, the bums gain strength and protection from the railroad police by living in the hobo "jungles."

67. Now when I came in on that *Mae West,* I put it down all at Chicago Heights, (*twice*)
Now you know the hobo jungle and that's where I stayed all night.

Now if you, hobo, if you brown you better not be sleepin' out, (*twice*)
Now Mister Wynn will get you and Mister Callahan will wear you out.

Now I was East road-bound, bound for my home town, (*twice*)
Now if you ain't got the fare, that's where they will let you down.

Hidden deep in the wayside brush but known to the experienced tramps, the jungles are primitive shack towns made from scrap metal, wood and cardboard, and the packing cases that hoboes have tipped off the trains. On the bare earth the denizens of the jungles, some of whom have made the disease-ridden tips their permanent homes, cook their coffee and beans. In a Negro dialect so marked and in tones so rough and deep that his indistinct words can only be detected with difficulty, but accompanying himself with delicacy and subtle originality on his one personal possession, the guitar with which he earns a few nickels and dimes, Son Bonds sings with only a trace of bitterness of the ultimate frustrations and misery that a migrant life between the jungles brings.

68. I'm a broken-hearted bachelor, travellin' through this wide world alone, (*twice*)
     It's the railroad for my pillow, this jungle for my happy home.

     This ole jungle, this old jungle, has me sleepin' by myself, (*twice*)
     Well, I'll believe I'll go, honey, find somebody else.

     Well jungle, this ole jungle, cinders blowin' back in ma face, (*twice*)
     I'm gonna get me a little woman, gonna fin' me another place.

Of the vast army of "transients" who were "on the bum" during the thirties—estimates ranged from two to four millions—a large proportion relative to their national percentage were Negroes and of these only a small number were true "boomers" or migrant workers. Far too many had no prospects whatsoever and toured aimlessly, with the police ready to arrest them for vagrancy or for failing to pay their fares. Living from day to day, skipping aboard the freight trains as they rattled slowly across high trestle bridges, clambering on to the passenger trains as they gathered speed on leaving the stations behind, they let the great locomotives carry them to distant cities where, their dreams assured them, opportunities awaited their coming.

69. *Green Diamonds* blowin' her whistle, train's comin' round the trail, (*twice*)
     I can't ride Pullman, guess I'll have to ride the rail.

> Chicago, Chicago, that is the town for me, (*twice*)
> Drop me off on the Lake Front, that's where I'll be
>   contented to be.
>
> Oooooey, hoooey. . . . I'm just dreamin' dreams,
>   (*twice*)
> The whole round world is mine, things are not like
>   they seem.

There were some who were scared to pay though they might have the money: they were the Negroes who had been recruited to the Northern labour forces in war periods and those with some form of criminal record or debt to pay who knew that their presence at the ticket box would be noticed and reported. For the man in trouble the railroad affords the swiftest method of avoiding apprehension, and the long distances that the trans-continental trains cover may ensure that he can get outside the state where he may gain immunity from the local arms of the law. So in St. Louis the singer, Walter Davis, knows that the M. & O. Line—strictly speaking, the G.M. & O., or Gulf, Mobile and Ohio, will take him South from the city more than five hundred miles to Mobile Bay, Alabama.

> 70. My baby got unruly, and she called the Chief of Police,
>   My baby got unruly, called the police up to my door,
>   I believe to my soul gonna have to ride that M. & O.
>
>   I'm a railroad man and I love that M. & O. (*twice*)
>   An' when I leave this town I ain't comin' back no mo'.
>
>   I'm in a world of trouble an' I believe I got to go,
>   (*twice*)
>   I'm gonna leave here people, gonna catch that M. & O.

The train means protection and with its fast-moving coaches he feels a close bond. To Negroes living in particular areas served by one railroad company or another, the trains become familiar friends and the field-hands welcome their passing as they mark the progress of the day. They recognize the peculiarities of the whistles of certain trains and the "signature"

of the firemen who operate them. On those lines where Negroes were employed the firemen arranged the steam whistles
or "quills" so that a simple tune could be played, and on the
Illinois Central, the famous I.C. which runs from Chicago
to New Orleans, the firemen would send a rudimentary blues
wailing across the Delta by "quilling" on the whistles.

71. Nobody knows that I.C. like I do, (*twice*)
 Now the reason I know it I ride it through and through.

 That I.C. Special is the only train I choose, (*twice*)
 That's the train I ride when I get these I.C. blues.

 Mister I.C. Engineer, make that whistle moan, (*twice*)
 Got the I.C. Blues and I can't help but groan.

 I got the I.C. Blues and box-cars on my mind, (*twice*)
 I'm gonna pack my grip and beat it on down the line.

Countless blues are sung about individual trains which appear to have their own peculiar personalities, especially the
Cannonball, the *Redball* and other famous express engines.
Impressive in their speed and immense proportions, chilling
the spine with their shrieking whistles in the night, thrilling
the blood with the roar of their engines as they pass, even
the more obscure trains have their importance for Negroes in
the remoter districts. So the blues singer may tell of the *Flying Crow* which runs Northward from the Texas Coast:

72. *Flying Crow* leaves Port Arthur, calls at Shreveport to
 change her crew, (*twice*)
 She will take water at Texakarna, yes, boys, and keep
 on through.

 That *Flying Crow* whistle sounds so lonesome and sad,
 (*twice*)
 Lord, it broke my heart, and took the last woman I had.

At times the trains themselves take on the stature of the folk
hero that the railroad worker—John Henry, Joe Mica, Casey
Jones—once provided in the Negro ballad, and the singer

finds in the character that he has made of the locomotive the qualities that he himself would like to possess, though such fancy is usually tempered with the flame of a burning reality.

73. If I could holler like the *Bob Lee Junior* blows, (*twice*)
Then I would call my baby, ooh, well, on the killing floor.

If I had a head-light on some passenger train, (*twice*)
Then I would shine my lights and call the red a sham.

Well, the *Bob Lee Junior* passed me with my baby all on the inside, (*twice*)
And the conductor said, "I'm sorry, buddy, but your baby she got to ride."

So marked is the imprint of its character on his mind that the singer often personifies the train, addressing his complaints and his comments to it and thinking of its crew and the engine itself as one, a transference characteristic amongst men who work and live in close contact with ships and vehicles the world over, though not always found in their song. The machine becomes the scapegoat for faults that might be laid at the door of the singer himself or the substitute for the blameworthy when events cannot be explained.

74. *Big Four, Big Four*, why are you so mean? (*twice*)
Why, you the meanest ole train that I ever seen.

You taken my baby away and left me standin' here, (*twice*)
Well I ain't got no one to love, I swear I cain't go nowhere.

Engineer, I heard you when you blowed your whistle, fireman, I heard you when you rang your bell (*twice*)
Well, I hate to see my baby—my baby, fare you well.

In the train the folk Negro invests a character that he admires or hates according to the circumstances of its relationship to him and to his life. The *Big 80* or the *Dixie Flyer* may be a friend as it thunders on to the Southland:

75. *Dixie Flyer* come on and let your drivers roll, (*twice*)
Wouldn't stay up North to please nobody's doggone soul.

Blow your whistle, tell 'em mama's coming too, (*twice*)
Wake it up a little bit cause I'm feelin' mighty blue.*

—but the *Sunshine Special* or the *Panama Limited* that takes away a loved one becomes the object of bitter resentment:

76. I've got the choo-choo blues, had 'em all night and day, (*twice*)
'Cause the *Panama Limited* carried my man away.

There goes that mean ole train, leavin' for New Orleans, (*twice*)
Lord, I got the blues, I could almost scream.

More sinister and more deeply hated are the trains that bring the convicts to the prison camps, the modern counterparts of Joe Turner the "long-chain man," whilst the feelings are mixed when the *Midnight Special*—recalled in a famous penitentiary ballad—and the *Shorty George* bring the women for one night in the month to the prisoners on the State Farms, and then take them away again.

77. The *Shorty George,* ain't no friend of mine, (*twice*)
Takin' all the women and leavin' the men behind.

Shorty George, done been here and gone, (*twice*)
Lord, he's left many a poor man a long ways from home.

In Negro folksay there is a rich vein of railroad lore and this is strongly represented in the blues. Known by their initials or words derived from them, the Chesapeake and Ohio (C. & O.), the Texas and Pacific (T. & P.), the Louisville and Nashville (L. & N.), the Missouri, Kansas, Texas line known more familiarly as the Katy, the lines known simply as the Southern, the Seaboard, the Wabash and a few score of others all figure prominently in the blues of the migrant Negro. He tells stories and sings of the Kaycee—the Kansas City Southern Line, or of the Yellow Dog, one of the most famous themes of the railroad blues. The Yazoo and Mississippi Valley Road, which is crossed by the Southern Line at Moorhead, Mississippi, is known widely as the Yellow Dog, some persons contending that it was named in humour or ignorance from the initials of the shorter term for the line Yazoo-Delta. But in Rome, Mississippi, they declare that it was named after a mongrel hound that noisily greeted every train as it passed through, whilst employees of the line say that it was the derisive term used by workers on a rival line—for railroaders call a small dummy-line train a "short dog." But it scarcely matters: another fragment is added to the great body of Negro folk-lore; a little more material for the blues is created, and every coloured hobo understands when the blues singer cries:

78. I was standin', lookin' an' listenin', watchin' the Southern cross the Dawg, (*twice*)
    If ma baby didn't catch the Southern she must've caught the Yaller Dawg.

    I'm goin' to Moorhead, get me a job on the Southern Line' (*twice*)
    So that I cin make some money jus' to send for that brown of mine.

    The Southern cross the Dawg at Moorhead, mama, Lawd an, she keeps on through, (*twice*)
    I swear ma baby's gone to Georgia, I believe I go to Georgia too.

To "come from across the tracks" is to have been born in the lower-class section of a town, but the phrase has even more significance for the Negro, for the poorest sectors are those that back on to the railroad tracks, where the great locomotives as they gather speed on leaving the immense railroad termini of Chicago, Kansas City or St. Louis cause the poor frame houses to shudder to their inadequate foundations, blacken their walls with grime and smoke, crack the ceilings, and kill the vegetation; it is in the poorest parts that the Negro quarters are to be found—along the tracks. When Sippie Wallace sings of seeing her lover pass the window in the train she speaks literally rather than metaphorically.

79. I looked through the window, as the train was passing by,
Ran to the window as the train was passing by,
Lord, he gives me the blues so bad I tho't I would die.

The railroad holds few illusions for the Negro. Living beside the tracks in South-side slum or hobo jungle, walking the ties, riding the blinds, nailing the rattlers, firing the engines, greasing the bearings in the "round-houses"—he is too close to the ties, the tar and the tallow for romantic notions. As transient, as tramp, as wanderer or worker he sings from experience rather than sentiment.

Chapter 3

Sweet Honey for Me

THERE ARE ten, twelve, fourteen million Negroes in the United States, according to the conflicting figures given by various writers. This confusion is understandable for the identity of the individual Negro is not easy to define. Half a century ago the State of West Virginia officially declared a Negro to be a person with one sixteenth or more of his ancestral blood coloured, but in 1930 they broadened this to include all persons with any "ascertainable Negro blood," which means that to-day there must be many hundreds, and in the U.S.A. many hundreds of thousands of persons technically Negro, though they may well be unaware of the fact. Every year a few thousand Negroes "pass for White" and submerge themselves in the White world leaving their Negro background behind them. They are the Negroes of whom the sole justification for so designating them is that they are perhaps seven-eighths White. Quite half of the Negroes in America are mulatto, as much White as they are coloured, but stigmatized by a fundamentally illogical system that measures only the degree of Negro blood in their veins. A man may live next door to a swarthy, dark-skinned American of Italian or Balkan extraction, and though his own eyes may be blue and his hair blonde he must sit in the rear of the street-car marked *For Coloured* whilst his neighbour sits in the section for Caucasians. For many years the Negro has been officially termed "Non-

Caucasian," a euphemism designed to show that he does not stem from the cradle of Indo-European stock. At the opposite extreme the pure-blood African Negro is as difficult to identify, for although George Cable was still able to distinguish nearly a score of African tribal groups in the 1880's it is doubtful whether there are in the States to-day more than ten per cent pure African Negroes, and some authorities would dispute even this figure.

Between the extremes of colour—from the black-skinned Negro with tightly curled hair and marked prognathism to the light complexioned Negro with straight hair and aquiline nose —lies a multitude of types of skin pigmentation, skull structure and greater or lesser degrees of African and European characteristics. These have arisen from a multitude of causes in cross-racial intermixture but above all from the extensive miscegenation that was practised during and after the slavery period. It was the custom for Southern planters to keep one or even several concubines amongst the Negro women and to maintain a coloured "second wife." The second wives, or coloured mistresses, were often well treated, well housed, even well provided for in the wills of their masters, though others fared less happily. Their progeny became slaves on the plantations as did the children who resulted from the casual and often brutal unions enforced by the younger Southern White men, who marked their adolescence with the rape of a Negro girl. The extreme brutality of these sexual excesses is staggering in a region that prided itself on the courtly manners and aristocratic bearing of the Southern Gentleman. Negro slaves were powerless to intervene when their wives, sisters and daughters were demanded, for any attempt at prevention would result in disfigurement, the severing of a limb— even death. In many states legislation was introduced forbidding mixed marriages and sometimes punishing adulterous unions between White and coloured, but the exercise of the legal powers was used with extreme caution, and the measures in almost every case were more rigorously applied against the Negro than the White offender. In the rural South such practices have persisted to the present day, and in many areas Negro girls live in fear of young White students and planters who follow the herd instinct and seek to prove their virility and "courage" before their fellows.

Curiously, in the "Big Houses"—the homes of the Southern plantation owners—the house slaves and servants were privileged, even pampered and many were often looked after with affection. The Negro "mammies" who wet-nursed the children, who showered kisses and sympathy upon them and shared their secrets and love intrigues, were the objects of devotion amongst the younger White children, whilst the stable-boys and Negro valets were often similarly respected. From this confusing pattern there developed in many White persons a pathological mixture of guilt, sex and affection that found later expression in beatings, brandings and burnings, and which eventually amounted to a regional sexual complex that has manifested itself over the years in hideous lynchings, castrations and mutilations of Negroes who have often been unquestionably guiltless.

For the Negro, whether he is purple-skinned and blue-gummed or pink-skinned and red-haired, his colour is his problem, both within the Negro community and in the community as a whole. It is this which determines that his whole social life shall be different from that of his fellow Americans, for his colour and his cast of feature are the outward indications of his ancestry. Only the Filipinos, the Mexicans and the Puerto Ricans suffer more than the Negroes from the effects of their racial and national origins and their recognizable characteristics in hue or physique. Sometimes the element of colour creeps scarcely perceptibly into the blues, like a trace of high seasoning that lingers on in the skillet when the next dish is prepared.

80. I been half-way worried, for 'bout a year or two, (*twice*)
   I have had my ups and downs, I hope my plans come
      through.

   I have one woman in mind, I wonder will she take that
      chance with me, (*twice*)
   Cool, calm and collected, describes her to a T.

   But women are so tricky, they'll try to tell you white is
      black, (*twice*)
   To get a woman nowadays, is just like buying a pig in
      a sack.

But at other times the characteristics of the Negro race in features and colour have a more ominous significance in the content of the blues and hint that they are indirectly the cause of social troubles:

81. Now my hair is nappy and I don't wear no clothes of silk' (*twice*)
   But the cow that's black and ugly, has often got the sweetest milk.

   Now when a man starts jivin' I'm tighter than a pair of shoes, (*twice*)
   I'm a mean tight mama, with my mean tight mama blues.

For the Negro the result of the inter-racial admixture, in which he knew better than to have any willing or active part as initiator, has been the creation of a complex caste system based not on economy but on colour. Notwithstanding the poor example frequently before him he has generally aspired to the condition of being White, as he sees the better jobs, the higher standard of living that they enjoy. He attempts to emulate the Whites and to copy their features and characteristics, spending large sums of money on hair-straightening greases and combs that are supposed to remove the kinks in the Negro's hair. The Negro women will dye their hair to a brick-red colour, powder their faces and apply artificial colour in order to make their skins lighter and their complexions more "White."

82. Wasn't for powder and the straightening comb,
   Wasn't for the powder and the straightening comb,
   The De Kalb women would not have no home.

Often the lighter-coloured Negroes obtain employment more readily than those with a darker skin hue, for persons who can accept the presence of a light-skinned man often feel a sense of unreasonable revulsion when in the company of a very dark Negro. This primitive distinction by colour has been passed on to the Negroes themselves and the coloured population is many times divided by grades of skin pigmentation.

In the caste system that has evolved from this arbitrary means of discrimination, the lighter-skinned Negroes tend to be on a higher plane, whilst the extremely black-skinned man is looked down upon, the lowest grade being the "blue-gummed nigger" in the Negro's own offensive term, which identifies the darkest and most African of their number. It is instructive that the term is also applied to mean and recalcitrant Negroes: the generations of children that have lived in fear that "a black man will eat you up" have grown into adults who have retained that fear and the belief that the black Negro is criminally-minded, and they have passed the belief across the colour line. The dark-skinned Negro feels the distinction and resents it bitterly.

83. Now I hear my black name ringin' all up and down the line, (*twice*)
Now I don't believe you love me, mama, I believe I'm just throwin' away my time.

Well now, I had the blues before sunrise, oh, with the tears standing in my eyes, (*twice*)
Now gotta make me out such a funny feelin' man, a feelin' I do despise.

When conditions cannot become worse they are, in Negro parlance, "too black bad," and the term "black is evil" becomes comprehensible when it is realized that the stigma of a dark skin precludes hundreds of thousands from any of the privileges that they legally and constitutionally deserve. Contemptuous terms that have long been used to identify dark-skinned persons—"shine," "snowball," "shade," "eight-ball"— are exceedingly offensive to Negroes, to whom the terms "coon," "darkie" and "nigger" are equally objectionable when used by Whites though they may use them in an endearing way amongst themselves. To differentiate between their many shades of colour they have evolved many words which are applicable to certain shades: "ashy black," "chocolate-brown," "coffee," "sealskin-brown," "brightskin," "high yaller," "lemon," and others, though some become offensive as the years pass, whilst others remain acceptable and even flattering. Negroes of one particular skin hue often keep together and may certainly have a preference for that colour, looking with contempt on those that are darker than they, but also with disapproval on those who have a high proportion of White blood.

84. So glad I'm a brownskin, so glad I'm a brownskin, chocolate to the bone,
So glad I'm brownskin, chocolate to the bone,
An' I got what it takes to make a monkey man leave his home.

Black man is evil, yaller man is so low-down, (*twice*)
I walk into these houses just to see these black men frown.

I'm just like Miss Lillian, I'm just like Miss Lillian, I mean Miss Glinn you see, (*twice*)
She say, "A brownskin man is just all right with me."

And indeed the brown-skinned Lillian Glinn whom he admired had expressed just this opinion though she had been more careful or more generous where others were concerned:

85. Now all high yellers you ought to listen to me,
A yellow man's sweet, a black man's neat,
A brownskin man will take you way off of your feet.

And if you don't believe what I say,
Just get him to shake the shivaree,
That's why I say a brownskin man's all right with me.

To Barbecue Bob the black man was evil, and the yellow man low-down, but to the light-skinned Texas Alexander the relative merits of these coloured people were very different:

86. Brownskin women are evil, black women are evil too,
Brownskin women are evil, black women are evil too,
I'm gonna get myself a yeller gal, see what she will do.

In some sections of Negro society the lighter-skinned Negroes are mistrusted for it is assumed that they have less racial pride than those who cannot hide their origins. Some grounds exist for this assumption for a light Negro may cross the colour line and "pass for White," if he can make the necessary cultural and social adjustment. Whereas the practice of "day-time passing" in which Negroes obtain jobs normally reserved for White persons but return to their race at night is considered to be something of a joke at the expense of the White Americans, permanent passing is considered to be "deserting the race." Amongst racially conscious groups the darker-skinned members are often considered more reliable and their more evident African ancestry meets with approval.

87. My mama told me before I left home,
     My mama told me before I left home,
     You better let them Jacksonville women alone.

     The women want yeller and some women want brown,
     Some women wan' a yeller man and some want brown,
     I know a black man will beat you but he sure won't fall
        you down.

To those attributes that may seem to have some justification are added others, which, true or imagined, help to determine the Negro's place in his own society and affect his choice of partner. The virtues of one group—distinguished as always by colour—may be extolled to the detriment of others. Popular superstitions arise, such as the belief that even in the lighter-skinned Negroes their colour will eventually reveal its true self in a "stripe" of deeper pigment, a notion that is almost as widespread as the "black baby bugaboo," the fear that a light couple may produce a black child. In pointed metaphor the blues singer advises that his listener accepts the situation:

88. High yeller, she'll kick you, that ain't all,
     When you step out at night 'nother mule in your stall.

     REFRAIN
     A brownskin woman, best brownie after all,
     They'll stick by you, winter, summer, spring and fall,
     A brownskin woman, best brownie after all.

     Anybody tell you a yaller girl's all right—
     When they get twenty-five, they drive a black stripe.

Ashes to ashes, and dust to dust,
If you can't ride the train catch the ginger bus. . . .

So the problem of colour obtains not merely between the races but within the Negro race itself and there is not only one colour bar, but, in a sense, many. That this is also a bar to the progress of the Negro cannot be denied and the integration of the race is clearly retarded because of it. Love, of course, transcends these artificial barriers in many instances, but there is a tendency for darker-hued Negroes to marry the darker-skinned Negro women, adhering to the belief—anathema to many of lighter skin—that "the blacker the berry, the sweeter the juice." Lighter-coloured Negroes prefer to marry lighter still, and over all there is probably a tendency to a preference where possible for a lighter partner, when a preference is, in fact, expressed. In the course of love, colour may not play a very great part, but in the initial selection of the group with which he associates, and from which his partner may eventually be drawn, the Negro is undoubtedly influenced by skin hue, about which he is almost pathologically self-conscious by the very fact that he is perpetually reminded of its existence as a social barrier. Here, deep-skinned beauty is more than skin-deep in its influence.

Physical attractiveness amongst Negroes does extend beyond skin colour and "White" attributes are often much admired—"good" hair for example, which is long and straight and has no kinks. To improve their appearance some Negro women buy "rats," "rats' tails," or artificial hair.

89. Yes, you know I carried my wife to the hairdresser and
      this is what the hairdresser said: (twice)
    She say, "I can't treat your woman's hair, God knows,
      but I can treat her head."

    I told her, "No," if her hair ain't no longer than mine,
    Yes, you know she ain't good for nothin' but trouble,
    Yes, she's buyin' rats all the time.

    Yes, you know I woke up this morning, people, folks
      there even wake up 'bout the break of day, (twice)
    I even found a rat on her pillow where she usta lay,

I don't want no woman if her hair ain't no longer than
    mine,
Yes, you know she ain't no good for nothin' but trouble,
Yes, she be buyin' rats all the time.

There are some features which appeal to Negroes that do
not come into the categories of beauty normally or expressly
admired in White groups. Contrast with dark skin accentuates
the beauty of the teeth, and this is a feature to which attention is frequently given. Many are the blues that extol the
virtues of a woman whose "teeth shine like pearls." To draw
attention to the teeth it was fashionable in Southern Negro
cities to have diamonds set between or within them, causing
a brilliant and unexpected flash when the wearer smiled. The
practice has been dying out in recent years and has been considered a mark of barbarity by educated Negroes, but in the
demi-monde it may still be found, in company with the wearing of red lipstick on the eyelids and exaggerated or exciting
modes of dress that may be considered bad taste in more
select society, but which are worn with *élan* by women with
fine figures and poise.

90. I've got a woman stream-lined from her feet to her head,
     Now I've got a stream-lined woman from her feet to
      her head,
     If she should ever quit me she might as well be dead.

     Every time my woman smiles she shows the diamonds
      in her teeth, (*twice*)
     She wears fine clothes, and patent leather shows on her
      feet.

     Men's all crazy about her, she makes them whine and
      cry, (*twice*)
     She's a river hip mama and they all wanna be baptized.

In spite of the appeal of pearl-white teeth, the treatment of
decayed teeth in itself sets its own peculiar standards and
gold teeth have been much admired, suggesting affluence and
giving to the wearer a certain primitive splendour.

91. Now the woman I love got a mouth chock full of good
       gold,
    Now the woman I love got a mouth chock full of good
       gold,
    Every time she hug and kiss me she make my blood run
       cold.

The attractiveness of a "stream-lined woman" accords with
the concepts of feminine beauty common to White persons in
America, and the city Negro has been inclined to adopt
similar standards, but amongst folk Negroes the measure is
often very different. Instead of the slender, stream-lined
woman, they may sing of the "big, fat woman with the meat
shaking on her bone" with obvious delight and admiration.
The diminutive stature of a woman who is "li'l and low" is as
much admired as the girl who is "tree-top tall," as "tall as a
Georgia Pine," or in apparent paradox "long and tall like a
cannon-ball." By this is meant the *Cannon-ball Express* on
the Illinois Central line. A number of ancient folk phrases are
recalled in Willie Jackson's blues:

92. Well, a long, tall woman will make a preacher lay his
       Bible down,
    I said a medium-sized woman will make a jack-rabbit
       move his family in town,
    But a big, fat woman will make a mule kick his stable
       down.
    My baby will make a man take his coal-house down,
    And a long, tall mama will make a judge shake a court-
       house down,
    And my long, tall baby will make the mayor turn the
       whole town round.

Long legs are considered attractive, but so, too, are "big
bow-legs" though Blind Blake adds sourly:

93. There's one thing in this world I cannot understand,
    One thing in this world I cannot understand,
    That's a bow-legged woman crazy 'bout a cross-eyed
       man.

Doctor Clayton gives eloquent expression to the features
that he finds beautiful in the woman that he loves, and his

blues well summarizes some of the qualities that especially appeal to the folk Negro:

94. Well, I feel all right and everything is okay,
Yes, I feel all right, everything is okay,
It's the love of my baby, oh, makes me feel this way.

She's got ways like an angel, an' she's sweet like heaven
above, (*twice*)
She's got everything I want, everything I'm needing of.

She's got great big legs, and the cutest little feet,
(*twice*)
Says she's got a sweet disposition that worries every
other man she meets.

She's copper-coloured mama, Lord, her shape is a solid
dream, (*twice*)
She's the loveliest woman I swear I've ever seen.

In the eyes of the lover the features of the object of his affections are more beautiful than those of anyone else. Reflected in them is the love that they share: and the plainest of faces has beauty for him, the humblest of men is noble in stature to her. Occupying every thought, giving colour to every scene, the image of the lover remains. Sings Memphis Minnie to her husband, Ernest Lawler—Little Son Joe:

95. I see your face before me all through the night and day,
Oh—all through the night and day,
But I still love you in the same old way.

When you love me, Lord, I get such a thrill, (*twice*)
And when you put your arms around me, babe, I can't
keep still.

When you love me, love me a great long time,
Joe, I get everything else but you off my mind,
(*Spoken*) Play it, Son Joe,
Keep your mind on it now. . . . All right, Son, I'm look-
ing at you.

In their volume *The Negro and His Songs* Odum and John-son accounted for the "absence of the higher ideals of love and virtue" by telling the reader to bear in mind that these were the songs that represented only "what might be called the Negro lower class" (page 159). Presumably the depressed classes were incapable of spiritual love—a Victorian concept that one would imagine would have failed to survive the turn of the century, but Iain Lang was to declare in 1947 (*Background of the Blues*) that "among hundreds of blues" he had "come across only one celebrating loyalty based on affection rather than on physical attraction."

Song as a vehicle for the expression of the emotions and declarations of love is ageless and common to virtually all societies; with his tradition of song it is scarcely conceivable that Negro love songs did not exist in the nineteenth century; still less acceptable is the notion that they are non-existent in the present era.

During the Slavery period true marriage amongst Negroes was not unduly common. If two slaves on neighbouring plan-tations developed a love for each other they had little hope of being permitted to marry unless their respective owners were more than usually generous, but unions amongst couples on the same plantation were encouraged. Numerous instances of happy and faithful partnerships within the plantations have been perpetuated in the records, though the couples were never granted the blessing of the Church. Many well authenti-cated tragic and moving stories have survived which tell of the hardships endured by devoted Negro couples, many of whom suffered death for their affections, and touching accounts exist of slaves who worked for pathetically long hours after sun-down to buy themselves out of slavery so that they could be free to work for the purchase of the freedom of their loved ones.

Though the post-bellum years were marked by a period of great unsettlement for the newly emancipated Negroes, many settled down to married life or faithful unions with their women when there was no one to "read the book over them." In subsequent years large numbers of Negroes played their parts as responsible members of the community and, in so far as they were able, lived the lives of any other men: falling in love, marrying, raising children and enjoying the pleasures of family life.

Imitators of Negro song are frequently overtly sentimental but the Negro is himself seldom mawkishly emotional. To his folk song and in his blues the Negro has rarely applied a polished veneer of decorative words or elaborately turned phrases, but within this compass there are all the same innumerable examples of sincere and direct declarations of love and affection. When Odum and Johnson were publishing their works, a Dallas folk singer, Whistling Alex Moore, was singing with a simple but valid philosophy:

96. Like a ragin' storm and the captain on the deck, (*twice*)
    My poor heart's bleedin' and my mind's all wrecked.

    I think it's unfair to love and not be loved, (*twice*)
    I think it means beware when you kiss and cannot hug.

    There's no heart in life unless you understand, (*twice*)
    There's no heart in marryin' someone, just because you can.

    Hatred is self-punishin', forgiveness is better than revenge, (*twice*)
    There's no heart in buying love, or to lose and not to win.

Through the history of recorded blues runs a persistent vein of contemplative verses, viewed from the personal angle of the singer as is customary with the form, but having within them advice and counsel for others that stem from experience. Sometimes a series of pronouncements is made of conclusions resulting from knowledge that the singer has gained; they are also sometimes directed to a particular individual rather as the dedication of a book is addressed to one specific person though the contents have meaning for many.

97. You have to live and let live, you have to give and take,
    You have to make believe, you have to pardon me.

    You have to think it over, you have to plan it out,
    It's a proposition, worthwhile talking 'bout.

Those who make no mistakes, dear, don't do anything,
This broken heart needs a break, dear, whether or not
you care.

Words of endearment and declarations of love are fundamentally private, shared and understood between the lovers
themselves and having especial significance for them alone.
This does not prevent the poet from expressing his emotions
in verse, nor does it prevent the reader from sharing the sentiments therein, or from perceiving within them his own state
of mind and feeling a bond of sympathy with the composer.
In the blues a change from a general statement addressed to
the listener to a more personal one intended for the lover
alone is not uncommon.

98. The girl I love just as sweet as she can be, (*twice*)
And every time I kiss her cold chills run over me.

Listen here, little girl, my love for you is thoro', (*twice*)
And if you love me you won't do nothing wrong.

So there ain't no need to worry 'bout me babe, when
I'm out of town, (*twice*)
Because my love is for you and it can't be turned
around.

I was just sittin' down thinkin' babe, just a minute ago,
(*twice*)
What in the world made me love you so?

For the young lover or for the newly-in-love the complexity
of emotions felt is often greater and more confusing than any
experienced before and the combination of happiness and
despair, the hurt that is felt with the joy, the pain that is
always so inextricably interwoven with the pleasure has been
the source of inspiration for the songs, poems, books, plays of
centuries. In these the composer's conscious art is brought to
bear upon the theme and strand by strand the threads of the
lover's knots are untangled and examined. The blues singer
brings a basic simplicity of mind to the subject: he seldom
attempts to unravel the problem but states his condition of
heart in uncomplicated terms which in their sincerity lose little.

99. Don't leave me, baby, 'cause I am so down and blue,
    (*twice*)
    Deep down in my heart, baby, my love is only for you.

    You are the only woman ever got into my heart, (*twice*)
    Lawsy, how would I live, baby, if we were to part?

    I'm down and blue an' I'm as blue as I can be, (*twice*)
    Because your love, baby, means all this world to me.

Psychologically, biologically and anthropologically the belief
that the Negro is inferior to the White man and incapable of
the higher emotions is fallacious and insupportable. His
capacity for love, for devotion, for courage, for selflessness is
no less than that of the members of any other group, even if
conversely he is as prone to similar weaknesses of rapacity,
avarice, or hatred as are others. The patterns that have conditioned the growth of different societies and that have caused
them to adopt varying attitudes to the importance of religion,
of self-sacrifice, of romantic love or the autocracy of grand-
parents, for example, are exceedingly complex and reach far
back in time. But given equal social advantages and environmental influences the reactions of most races, with the excep-
tion perhaps of certain aboriginal groups, are very similar.
The North American Negro is culturally a part of the society
of the United States and that which he owes to the African
heritage has been reduced with the passage of time, the dilu-
tion of stock and isolation from the parent country to very
small proportions. In matters concerning the pure emotions
he does not react in a manner greatly different from that of
any racial group amongst his fellow-countrymen, though he
may express them in a less inhibited way. But he feels the
same distress when he falls in love with a woman who is not in
love with him, the same misery when his advances are rejected,
the same mixed feelings of desire and guilt when he finds
himself in love with one whose age is much below his own.

100. I'm afraid I love you and I've tried so hard not to,
    (*twice*)
    You are young and lovely, what more can a poor man
    do?

When I kiss you why do you tremble so? (*twice*)
I realize this is your first affair, but I just can't let you go.

There isn't any way in this world I can go on being
without you, (*twice*)
Your love is so true, that's all I ask of you.

The differences that exist between the behaviour of the
Negro and that of White Americans is largely due to their
relative positions in society as a whole; rich and cultivated
Negroes there are, poor and uncouth Whites there are too,
but in the main the Negro's social standing is substantially
lower than that of the Whites. His distress when left alone
and in love is no different; he is sufficiently aware of his lack
of privilege to realize the reason for his blunders.

101. Honey, my heart gets to beatin' like a hammer and my
eyes get so full of tears, (*twice*)
You only been gone twenty-four hours but it seems like
a million years.

Honey, if I ever mistreat you, God knows I don't mean
no harm, (*twice*)
Because I ain't nothin' but a little country boy, an' I'm
right down off the cotton farm.

Honey, I don't believe you think I'm nothin', you don't
believe I think I'm nothin' but a little clown, (*twice*)
Mmmmm—now when I was lookin' for you last night,
you was way out on the other side of town.

So the field-hand is left working in the vain hope that he
may better the fortunes of his family and himself. For the
share-cropper the desire to revolt against the virtual servitude
becomes the greater as he sees his woman bowed down by the
work she too must undertake, and many a man is driven to
violent and unlawful acts as a result. Torn in a conflict of
emotions he seeks angrily to choose between the woman who
can join him in a hopeless and unequal anti-social struggle—
the woman who can make her own decision to assert herself
—and the woman who can take the shafts of the plough,
guide the mules, and work beside him on the land.

102. I don't want none of these funny women if they don't
     know how to rob and steal, (*twice*)
     She workin' her po' self to death, in some po' farmer's
     fiel'.

     What do you want with a woman if she don't know
     "Yes" from "No," (*twice*)
     But what d'ya want with a good-lookin' woman if she
     don't know "Gee" from "Haw."

Undoubtedly the strain of continual work "from sun to sun"
in the endeavour to gain freedom from debt and serfdom
can kill the love in both heart and body. Husband and wife
labour side by side until all energies are sapped and the wife
who spends her days in the fields and her nights at the wash-
tub has little time for the expression of love. Determined to
gain independence for her family her labours may eventually
become obsessive and in turn a source of anxiety to those
who love her.

103. She's a cotton-pickin' woman, Lawd, she do's it all the
     time, (*twice*)
     If you don't stop pickin' cotton now, baby, I believe you
     sho' gwan to lose your mind. Yes yes. . . .

     She pickin' so much cotton, she even don't know where
     to go, (*twice*)
     She's leavin' in the mornin', sweet mama, honey, she
     gwan' from do' to do'.

     Oh Lawd, on my bended knee—yes I mean it,
     Oh Lawd on my bended knee,
     Pick so much cotton now, partner, will you forgive me
     if you please?

Then suddenly the strain proves too much; love dies and
with it the one reason for enduring the sweat and tears of excessive toil. Small disputes become magnified, minor troubles
become major ones. The bill of "furnishings" at the company
store has grown out of all proportion and when the customary
"figgering" has been applied to the sum earned during the
year, the inevitable debt means a future in harness. Comes

the day when all loyalties are severed, and trying to justify her actions by asking her husband to consider her dead—"to pin *crêpe* on his sleeve"—the woman leaves before her sanity leaves her.

104. I've been dogged and mistreated till I done made up my mind, (*twice*)
Gonna leave this old country, and all my troubles behind.

Get my ticket at the junction and flag the four-day train, (*twice*)
I'm goin' to leave this country before I go insane.

When I leave this morning, papa, pin *crêpe* on your sleeve, (*twice*)
Ain't comin' here no more, you can love just who you please.

When they all mistreat you, no need to think about me, (*twice*)
'Cos I'm leavin' this country blue as I can be.

If the blues kill me, tell everybody the news, (*twice*)
Here lays a woman died with the leavin' gal blues.

A bewildered and unhappy man watches the Texas-Pacific train as it disappears into the distance, knowing that his woman is being carried with every passing minute further away from the land that has brought them so much trouble. Staring down the line till his eyes get "green and sore," he calls softly and rhetorically to the driver of a train now long out of earshot.

105. I was laying in my window lookin' on ma baby's door, (*twice*)
She packed her trunk this mornin', did not even fixin' to go.

Say, the T.P. is runnin', smoke settlin' on the ground, (*twice*)

When the train was gone, couldn't find my easy rider around.

I ain't got me no more lover, no more baby now, (*twice*)
I said no more pretty mama to run me crazy now.

Engineerman, engineerman, please turn your train around, (*twice*)
I wanta speak one word to my baby, then she can let your window down.

I was standin' in my door, see that T.P. when she blows, (*twice*)
Takin' my baby away, she ain't comin' here no more.

In confusion he thinks back over their past years together, recalls the joys, the pain and the sorrows that they have shared and wonders miserably why the understanding between them no longer exists. When he prospered, he was loved; when his woman suffered, he was there to comfort her, but now that misfortune has come to him and he is most in need of sympathy and help, it seems that his woman has failed him.

106. Brownskin mama, what in the world do you want me to do? (*twice*)
You got my poor heart achin', I'm blue through and through.

I helped you when you were down and could not help yourself, (*twice*)
Now I'm down, you want to help somebody else.

You can go, do anything you want to do, (*twice*)
Some day you want me, honey, and I won't want you.

My mind's all torn up, that's why I'm all confused, (*twice*)
That's the reason why I'm moanin' these brownskin mama blues.

More Negro homes are broken proportionately than White, but the reasons are manifold: some homes are broken through the incompatability of the partners. In a number of Southern states persons are permitted to marry at a very young age—in Mississippi it has been legal until recently for girls to marry at the age of twelve. Owing to the pressure of economic stress upon their lives coloured children reach apparent maturity early in life and assume the physical responsibilities of adults —young girls nurse their younger sisters and brothers to relieve their mothers for heavier work, and young boys are soon "buck-jumping" in the cotton rows. Seldom do they remain at school after the age of eleven or twelve, and consequently many Negroes are free to marry when they are still emotionally and mentally immature and unable to bear the true responsibilities of married life, with the inevitable result that their unions are broken. The girl attacks her husband for his seeming incompetence whilst he suffers from her failure to cope with the management of the home.

107. All of this school and education didn't mean a thing to
         me, (*twice*)
      When I met a good-looking woman that was the end of
         me.

      This woman treated me so mean, she's the cruellest I've
         ever seen, (*twice*)
      This house is always dirty and her cooking I swear ain't
         clean.

      Now rambling with this woman caused me to be down
         so low, (*twice*)
      And now my dear old mother won't allow me round her
         door.

Inadequate facilities and the perennial break in education during periods of considerable agricultural activity have left many Negroes in appalling ignorance, and though some acquire a deep and wise philosophy from their worldly experience, others whose lives have been circumscribed are limited also in their abilities to deal with the problems of ill-disciplined children and slatternly mothers. Many resort to corporal means as the only method that they know to correct the wrongs that occur, though this may well aggravate rather than mediate their troubles. Few have been solved by wild thrashings given in unseeing anger.

108. I'm gonna get me a picket off a graveyard fence, (*twice*)
     Gonna beat you brownskins till you learn good sense.

     Tell me, brownskin, what is on your mind? (*twice*)
     Reason I ask you, brownie, you bound to run me blind.

An excess of spirits, arising out of a slight success, a desire to "raise a little hell" when things go wrong, or to give vent to suppressed feelings when circumstances make it inadvisable to express opinions, the need to expend unused energies in lay-off periods and the need for an escape when times are bad—these may make a nervous man violent, may make a powerful man "mean." His woman is the inevitable recipient of the release of his emotions and she becomes the butt of his misdirected feelings. Not infrequently these seek their outlet in excesses of physical love, giving to a man the feeling of mastery that is denied him elsewhere.

109. Ah, when I come home—think I'm doing well,
     Keeps me from being in trouble, just start to raisin' hell,
     That makes me evil, oh Lord, so evil,
     Yes, I get evil, baby, when my love comes down.

     You better wake up pretty mama, cause you can never tell,
     I may start out-swinging, cause I ain't doing so well—
     Yes, I get evil, oooh, evil,
     Well, I get evil, baby, when my love comes down.

To suffer violent man-handling from the man that she has loved and cherished for so many years is all the more distressing for a woman, no matter how his life may have conditioned his behaviour. Words of love once whispered seem forgotten now and all that is left is the pain of "mistreatment" at his hands. Through her tears she pleads for a little of the love that he once gave so freely.

110. I'm down on my knees, cutie, now to you,
    I say I'm down, cain't stand the ways you do,
    I can't stand the misery I've gone through.

    Now you know you have made me cry, (*twice*)
    An' you say you could see me die.

    You'll regret the way you treated me,
    I'm begging you to cure my misery,
    Before I go and jump into the sea.

It is now that the endearing words of another man who sympathizes with the unhappy woman seem sweet and desirable. The desire that once was in her heart for her husband burns instead for him and the thrill of clandestine meetings, the private excitement of the shared secrets and the seductive attraction of forbidden fruit fosters a passionate love. When her husband is out at work and when he is on night shift, she leaves a key for her "back-door man" to make his "'fore-day creep," finding all the excuses that she can to appease the guilt in her heart and to justify her actions to her own conscience.

111. I've got to have a daddy to tell my troubles to, (*twice*)
    One who knows how to love me and keep me from being
      blue.

    Loving night and day is the thing I crave, (*twice*)
    Give me lots of loving and I'll be your slave.

    Little drops of water, only grains of sand, (*twice*)
    Every sensible woman should have a back-door man.

Last to know of the infidelity of his wife is the cuckolded husband, for she has taken advantage of his faith in her and his confidence of her devotion to him. Perhaps he has taken her love for granted, perhaps he has failed in his duty to her, perhaps he has given rein to unreasonable anger and thought little of her feelings, but he still cannot believe that the woman that he has admired and on whom he has depended so much has taken a "creeping man," and given her love to a "mean-jumper." But the casual hints, the evasive answers, the slight changes in behaviour sow seeds of suspicion in his sub-conscious mind.

112.　I went to bed last night with nothin' on ma mind, (*twice*)
　　　I felt the good world—it was treatin' me kind.

　　　I dreamed I saw my mama tell me "Good-bye" (*twice*)
　　　Then around the back-door I saw her try another man's
　　　　size.

　　　Cain't no woman unbackdoor me, (*twice*)
　　　If I'm your one-an'-all or else your used-t'-be.

　　　I got up this mawnin', 'vestigatin' on ma min', (*twice*)
　　　I wanted to see if mama was the right kin'.

　　　Sometimes these dreams's just lak bein' away, (*twice*)
　　　I saw another man eatin' of my chocolate cake.

For the man who has struggled hard to try to secure for his wife a better home and standard of living, and in doing so has been forced to spend all his waking hours at work, "doubling" his jobs to secure extra pay, her unfaithfulness is especially bitter. Fundamentally, his neglect of his wife and his inability to give her the tenderness and love that she as a woman demands with her whole being, has been because her interests were uppermost in his mind. Knowing that he loves her, she never shares his love and in her frustration his woman exploits his weakness and gives way to her own—first in easy distractions, finally by giving herself to another man whose attentions are flattering and liberal because his responsibilities to her are negligible.

113.　I work all day long for you, until the sun go down,
　　　　I work all day long for you, baby, from sun-up until the
　　　　　sun go down,
　　　　An' you take all my money and drink it up and come
　　　　　home and want to fuss and clown.

　　　　I worked for you so many times, when I really was too
　　　　　sick to go,

I worked for you, baby, when your man was slipping in
my back-door,
I can see for myself so tell your back-door man I won't
be your fool no more.

I worked for you, baby, when snow was above my knees,
I worked for you, baby, when ice and snow was on the
ground,
Trying to make you happy, an' you chasing every man
in town.

It hurts to love a person that don't belong to you,
(*twice*)
'Cause when they found out that you really love them
and they don't care what they do,

They'll take your heart and they'll use it like a football
on a football ground, (*twice*)
And when they gits to playing with your heart and they
starts blackin' your heart around.

If the fickleness of women is proverbial, the temptations
cast before an attractive woman with time on her hands in
the flourishing unrestrained atmosphere of the Negro quarter
of a Southern town are enough to sway her loyalties. "Sharp-
clothed" gamblers and pimps with peg-top trousers, long watch
chains and sky-bonnet hats rub shoulders with muscular loggers in town with their "spending change," their brightly
decorated shirts open to reveal bared brown chests. Saloons
and barrelhouses rock to the music from the peacock-hued
juke boxes and the crap-shooters on the pavement pause to
admire the legs of the passing brownskin girl with the side-slit
"Mary Jane" skirt. When her man tracks her down on the
street corner she laughs in his face.

114. I've got a dreamy-eyed woman, lives down on Cherry
Street, (*twice*)
An' she laughs and chaffs with every brownskin ol' man
she meet.

So I told her last night and all the night before,
And I told her last night and all the night before,

"Say if you don't quit some of your struttin', baby, you
can't be mine no more."

Put both hands on her hips and these are the words she
said, (*twice*)
Said, "Big boy I couldn't miss you if the good Lord told
me you was dead."

When next he sees her she is leaning back in a sleek
Cadillac Eight, the arm of another man about her shoulders.
Whilst she is enjoying the pleasure of luxuries that he has
never been able to offer and her laughter still echoes in his
mind, he tries to convince himself that she will soon return.

115. I saw you ridin' roun', you ridin' a bran' new automobile,
    (*twice*)
    Yes, you was sittin' there with your hustler-driver at the
    wheel.

    Your face was tint' with powder, your lips was all full of
    rouge,
    Yes, your face was tint' with powder an' your face was
    full of rouge,
    Yes, but I know you was comin' home when you foun'
    out your driver didn't mean you no good.

Unable to sleep, unable to think clearly or to "give his heart
ease," the forsaken man only wants to have an opportunity
to clarify the situation in his mind. He cannot accept the fact
that their partnership has come to an end and in his confusion he seeks the strangely comforting solitude of the lonely
streets and the deserted railroad depot. In his thoughts he still
pleads with his woman and his tormented mind continues to
appeal, to plan, to dream of a reconciliation.

116. Yeah baby, yeah baby, why don't you quit your way?
    Oh, your time, now mama, be mine some ole day,
    Nobody make me believe that you'd treat me this a-way.

    Says I went to the station, went to the station, I sure
    didn't see no train,
    Didn't see my woman, no one to call her name,
    Take your time now, mama, be mine some ole day.

I says I'm beggin' you, mama, yeah mama, why don't
   you quit your ways?
Oh . . . your time now sugar, be mine some old day,
Eeh—nobody make me believe that you'd treat me this
   a-way.

I looked down the road, looked down the road, far as I
   could see,
Tryin' to find my woman, is she comin' back to me?
Take your time now mama; be mine some old day.

Still there remains a numbness in his mind; a chill, nerveless
part of his being refuses to react or respond to the truth of his
situation.

117. I got stones in ma passway and ma road seems dark at
      night, (*twice*)
   I have pains in ma heart, they have taken my appetite.

   I have a bird to whistle and I have a bird to sing, (*twice*)
   I've got a woman that I'm lovin', boy, but she don't
      mean a thing.

   Now you's trying to take my life, and all my lovin' too,
   You made a passway for me, now what are you trying
      to do?

   And kind mama, please, please let us be friends,
   And when you hear howlin' in my passway, mama,
      please won't you let me in?

As the extremes of mental capacity, of madness and genius
sometimes seem to converge, so too the extremes of emotion
seem closely allied. Outbursts of anger may come when the
heart is bursting with affection; pain and pleasure are inextricably interwoven; the deepest feelings of love may readily
turn to the cruellest hate. Humiliation, frustration, bitterness
and selfishness are bound up in the complex emotions that are
experienced by the lover whose partner has been unfaithful.

118. If I was cold and hungry, I wouldn't even ask you for
      bread, (*twice*)

I don't want you no more, if I'm on my dying bed.

At one time I loved you, but I sure do hate you now,
(*twice*)
Baby, you are the kind don't need a good man nohow.

Ev'ry man in town knows about your ornery ways,
(*twice*)
Cain't nobody change you now, 'cause you've been a
devil all of your days.

Marital unions are made and disengaged more freely
amongst Negroes than amongst the White persons from identical districts—particularly among the lower classes. This is
partly due to the fact that there is virtually no Negro moneyed
aristocracy in the majority of Southern towns and in only a
few is there a perceptible professional class. As a result there
is less need for conformity to conventional ideas of respectability and though the church exerts a powerful influence
upon its members, outside the church there is little stigma
attached to a union that is not legally contracted. This has
had the very beneficial effect that illegitimacy is not considered
a social barrier, but it has also permitted a somewhat easy
severage of family ties. Unions may be casually made, with
couples "batching up" with little ceremony, and they are
often as summarily and thoughtlessly broken.

119. My man left this morning, jest about half past four,
(*twice*)
He left a note on his pillow, sayin' he couldn't use me no
more.

Then I grabbed my pillow, turned over in my bed,
(*twice*)
I cried about my daddy, till my cheeks turned cherry
red.

In more thoroughly urbanized communities, and especially
those in the North, there is more attention to the official
registration and legalization of marriages, with the result that
separations are taken less lightly. Without public assistance
only a relatively small number of Negroes can obtain a divorce

but some are prepared in their bitter unhappiness to go to the expense involved. For those who are estranged, but for whom divorce is not possible, there are many hardships, for the woman as much as for the man. In the lower-class Negro communities the women are often self-supporting and have a certain measure of independence, some even taking pleasure in supporting their men in idleness. But their distress is no less when they are deserted.

120. Some black snake been suckin' my rider—hear me
        cryin', Lawdy, I ain't lyin',
      Some black snake been suckin' my rider some,
      You can tell by that I ain't gonna give him none.

      'Cause my left side jumps and my flesh begin to crawl,
      Oh my left side jumps and my flesh begin to crawl,
      Bet you ten to one dollar, 'neither mule kickin' in ma
        stall.

As a woman gets older and her physical charms begin to tire, as work and strain of bearing children take their toll on her face and body, she is less able to give her man the warmth and satisfaction that he desires. Too often fatigue makes her irritable and she has "her gimmies on." It is then that he becomes vulnerable to the attractions of another, younger woman, whose beauty has been unimpaired by arduous domestic employment and who has the freshness and desirability of her age. Forgetting the years of devotion that his woman has given him in the past, smothering his sense of shame with brutal talk, he packs his few personal belongings and leaves.

121. I got a brown across town, she's tall as a sycamore tree,
        (twice)
      Says she walked thru' rain and snow trying to ease that
        thing on me.

      I believe I'll pack my suitcase, leave my home, (twice)
      Yeah—'cos every time I see my li'l woman, she's got her
        gimmies on.

      Says don't blame me, baby, from talking out of my
        head, (twice)

Start worrying 'bout the movements you got, the springs
trembling on your bed.

She got a new way of trimming down a crazy man leave
his home, (*twice*)
Lord, the way she grabbed and turn you loose make the
flesh tremble on your bones.

A distraught woman is left alone with her misery, to cook
for no one but herself, to hear only her own footsteps on the
worn and knotted boards, and at night to soak the pillow with
her tears. The shortcomings of her own physical attractiveness
and the charms of the girl who has taken her man from her
plague her mind.

122. I woke up this morning, rolled from side to side, (*twice*)
I grabbed my pillow, Lord, how I screamed and cried.

Heaven made you, brownskin, the angels gave you coal
black hair, (*twice*)
A brownskin man get a good woman most everywhere.

Oh Lord, listen to my plea, (*twice*)
Please hear my cry and give me back my used-to-be.

No loss is greater than that of the lover who has lost his
partner to his best friend, for in losing one he has lost both.
Trusting both lover and friend, he welcomes into his home
and to his table the one person who by reason of his close
personal relationship is the last he suspects would wish to
break up his home. In the tight tenement communities of
Harlem and Chicago's "Bronzeville" women share sinks and
toilets, cooking facilities and dressmaking materials, but to
the woman who has generously shared her belongings and her
home, the realization that she has also shared her husband is a
stunning shock, and life seems to hold little for her now. Her
arms still feel the warmth of her husband's love, and his fond
words even as he betrayed her love still remain in her mind,
their sweetness now turned as bitter as gall.

123. I went to bed last night and the blues would'nt let me
rest, (*twice*)
'Cause I ain't used to sleepin' by myself.

Oh blues, oh blues, blues don't you see? (*twice*)
You are carryin' me down, blues you tryin' to kill poor
me.

Now blues and trouble walk hand in hand—have mercy
(*twice*)
I never had these blues, until my best friend loved my
man.

He put his arms around me like a ring round the good
Lord's sun, (*twice*)
Says he ain't had no woman to love me, Lord, like I
have done.

A woman who has been suddenly deserted, left without
support and with the house rent to pay, children to clothe and
food to procure, may well be left in desperate circumstances.
When other families are clamouring to obtain rooms, no landlord will accept promises of eventual payment; the individual
suffering of one coloured woman does not swell the bank
balance. In the over-crowded coloured quarters new work is
not always easy to obtain, and for an illiterate Negro woman
without references and encumbered with a family, the chances
of immediate employment are slender. Her pride and her destitution leave her "worried deep down in mind."

124. Can't read, can't write, gonna buy me a telephone,
(*twice*)
I won't talk to my man, till he comes back home.

I'm going away just to wear you off my mind, (*twice*)
And I know, daddy, a good man's hard to find.

Sitting on the kerbstone, worrying heart and soul,
(*twice*)
Just like a possum hiding in a ground-hog's hole.

Now the rain is falling, falling down from above,
(*twice*)
Lord, I want to be with the man I love.

Holding out as long as she can, she prays for news and if she and her man can write she may wait anxiously for a sign of his return. Stifling her pride she may eventually write to him for assistance, for a few dollars to help her to her feet.

125. Watching and waiting, to hear a bit of news, (*twice*)
Sighing and crying with these mail-man blues.

Run to the Western Union to send a telegram, (*twice*)
Try to get a favour from your one-time man in town.

Some folks are so deceiving, take friendship as a joke, (*twice*)
They'll whip you when you're up and you can't find them when you're broke.

Yes, disheartened and disgusted, mama's feelin' sad, (*twice*)
These old mail-man blues are the worst blues that I ever had.

Others, friends and relatives, are only too willing to offer advice if not material aid and to them she may turn for sympathy. Sometimes a temporary separation, that may well have ended in a reunion and a relationship made closer in the realization of the need for the other partner, can be worsened and even made permanent by the well-intended but misguided advice of outsiders who see only the surface effects and are unaware of the underlying complexity of emotions that have brought it about. But their words seem welcome at a time when the hurt of the separation is greatest and an irrevocable action may be made in ill-advised haste.

126. Lillie Mae wrote me a letter, these the last words she had to say, (*twice*)
She said, "J. B. the way you done you will be sorry one sweet day.

"Please don't call or write me, I don't wanna hear from you, (*twice*)

Darlin', I am my own boss, an' I know what I want to do."

She weighed a hundred and five pounds, she got long black curly hair, (*twice*)
Darlin', one thing I hate, people meddlin' in our affairs.

Many things may cause a man or woman to desert his partner—the awareness of having failed to provide an adequate home; the keen sense of frustrated ambition in a man who has no opportunity to improve his status or his family fortunes; the fear and humiliation of racial segregation; the lure of the cities and unknown districts where prospects promise to be better; the attractiveness of a lover and the deliberate shedding of responsibilities too burdensome to bear . . . these and many more: the outcome of personal tragedies and human failings.

Separation sometimes clarifies the mind, and their dependence upon each other becomes more evident to a married couple when they are apart than when they are permanently in each other's company. Maturity of mind can come with a major disaster in married life: it is then that a man may find himself for the first time. In the solitude of a lonely apartment, when his heart is "a thousand miles away," understanding may dawn of the wrongs of the past and with ever-growing wisdom he may resolve to prepare the way for a true and permanent reunion.

127. My, my mama tol' me, baby, I didn't believe it was true, (*twice*)
She said " Won't some sweet woman treat you just like I used to?"

But I seen my mistake after it was too late, (*twice*)
Well I tried not to worry, 'cause we're subject to mistakes.

It's your error, sweet mama, honey, but it's my mistake, (*twice*)
You just forgive me, I'll swing that up some day.

I'm out in this world to-day, wanderin' from place to place, (*twice*)
Trying to find some one, cook your blues mistake.

I'm down and I'm leaving, going far away, (*twice*)
You've got the business, sweet mama, I'll work up to
you some sweet day.

So he may learn that material things are not all that matter
in life and the desire for worldly gains that had seemed of
such importance was secondary to the love that had been so
readily sacrificed. A number of years may now seem wasted,
but the knowledge can be bought no more easily than the love
that was sold. Though he may still fail to realize it, the years
have not been expended entirely in vain.

128. Money is the root of all evil, look what it has done for
me, (*twice*)
'Cause me to leave my baby, now I'm living in misery.

But I'm gonna find my baby, if it takes me till the day
I die,
Yes, I'm gonna find my baby, if it takes me till the day
I die,
I should have never left my baby 'cos love is something
money can't buy.

Yeah, all of my money's gone, ain't got a dime to my
name, (*twice*)
Well, I been living here for quite a few years, ain't this
a cryin' shame?

With the ennoblement of character through hardship and
experience and the preparedness to assume the moral responsibilities of husband or wife or parent, are laid the foundations
of a family life based on true sympathy, understanding and
love. And with the eventual development of the truly adult
mind a man, Negro or White, is ready to play his part in the
corporate life of the community.

129. I'm going all round the world tryin' to find sweet Mary,
(*twice*)
I'm going to try to find out, oh Lord, what it is she's got
a sending for me.

I'm gonna build me a home in the mountains just for me
an' sweet Mary, (*twice*)
I swear it ain't but two of us now, oh Lord, soon it may
be three.

She ain't no bumble-bee, she can sure make some sweet
honey for me, (*twice*)
I swear I believe I'll lose my mind, oh Lord, if I don't
find sweet Mary.

Chapter 4

I'm a Rooster, Baby

OF ALL THE stereotypes that have been fabricated concerning the Negro in the United States—laziness, stupidity, animal cunning, childlike emotions, perpetual good humour and the others—there are none which are as persistent as the commonly held beliefs about his love and sexual life. White Amercans and frequently Europeans believe implicitly that the Negro is sexually promiscuous, that his morals are loose or non-existent, that he cares little for family life and accepts no family responsibilities. They believe that the Negro women are free with their favours, that the men are given to violent criminal assault and rape, and that they perpetually desire to violate the "sanctity of Southern White womanhood." It is held that the Negro does not recognize the institution of marriage and that the higher emotions of love mean nothing to him. Corroborative evidence they find in his songs and particularly in the blues which are considered as pornographic and libidinous. It would be wrong to dismiss these beliefs as being fabrications without any basis in fact; they are a complex mixture of fallacies and truths of which the foundations were firmly laid in the shameful years of Slavery and which have been buttressed in the course of time by circumstances which have been the outcome of the conditions in which the Negro has been forced to live.

Romantic love has had a turbulent and curious history, and

131

the Slave trade was a flourishing industry by the time the official legislations against "filthy dalliance" of the Puritans were being relaxed in favour of a more natural relationship between the sexes. This in turn was replaced by the Victorian concept of the role of the woman in matrimonial matters, but whatever the prevailing notions of the time as to the merits of love between man and woman, they were applicable only to White persons. Negroes were slaves and, apart from their work, they were required to beget more slaves; as the men laboured the women were in labour. Love played little part in this: couples mated at the orders of the plantation owner if they had not made their own unions. Negro slaves were officially classified below the level of cattle, and when they were sold at the auction block they had to undergo the most humiliating and dehumanizing examinations which were primarily designed to ascertain their strength and potential procreativity. With the "stud Negro" came the conception of the "big buck nigger" which inferred a distinctly subhuman status. Fecund mothers and fertile males were assets to the slaveholder who bred his slaves as he bred his livestock, the distinction of colour helping to justify his actions to his conscience. Liberation did not bring a new attitude to the Negro and the "animal concept" has persisted even to the present day; Negroes have themselves come to accept such fictions as the supposed "Negro smell" which sustains the notion of animal, sexual scents.

After years of encouraged sexual freedom the Negro did not immediately and voluntarily self-impose a strict code of morals on attaining his freedom, and during those perplexing and unhappy years the White Southerners could point to the social behaviour of many Negroes and find justification for their beliefs, never stopping to admit that these had been the root cause of the social disintegration. The strictures imposed by the Negro religious denominations were probably the outcome of rudimentary attempts to strengthen the moral codes, and the sexual drives were canalized into religious passion. With the establishment of some form of elementary society the desire to settle down and to assume the responsibilities of husband and parent was common to numberless coloured men, and as they worked their "forty acres and a mule" they found, as had their previous owners, that children were a material asset. When the problems of living became too great for them to surmount and families broke up, the Whites could point to the large numbers of fatherless children, the migrant, workless men and the women who shared their lives without the blessing of the Church, and saw ready support for their conception of the dissolute, debauched, immoral, feckless Negro. It took a strong mind and an impartial eye to examine the factors that had brought these circumstances about. Deeply ingrained in the conscience of the nation and particularly of the South is a complex problem whose sexual and social implications have immediate bearing on the fundamental problems concerning race relations, manifest at the most superficial in the perennial question: "Would you like *your* daughter to marry a Negro?"; at the most violent and disgusting level in the mutilations and lynchings by the Ku Klux Klansmen; and at the most shameful in the mute acceptance of these attitudes on the part of a large proportion of the population. Diverting and important as the examination of this problem may be with its many strange aspects—the pride of the White man who has a strain of American Indian blood, for example—and its world-wide issues of race and nationality, it is relevant but scarcely possible to discuss the subject in the present work. Nevertheless, these are factors which have influenced the prevailing attitude to the Negro; to his creative arts and to the blues, no less.

As the blues reflects the lives of the greater proportion of the Negro people, and in particular those to whom the stereotypes are applied, both the truths and the falsehoods are to be found revealed in them. Such are the conventions of American middle-class society that the blues may often appear to be shocking, and instead of being recognized as a genuine form of expression revealing its gaunt structure without a decorative façade, may be suspected of hiding even greater sins—as the larger of two icebergs in showing a greater mass above the surface than its fellow indicates a greater mass also below the surface. To apply to the blues the standards and to expect of the blues the conventions of popular music is to apply a false measure. In popular song and in particular the concoctions of 52nd Street euphemistic phrases are sung and winsome, sentimental, erotically evasive symbols are universally employed—as in the art of ballet, virile stories are emasculated by the use of conventional poses and movements, or in "polite" conversation the phrase "to sleep with" implies everything else in bed but sleep. Though metaphors are used in the blues, they are never evasive but are used as figures of speech should be used: to amplify the meaning by colourful comparison.

130. Now come along, mama, give me a hug,
  You got the world, I got the stopper in a jug, so—

  REFRAIN
  Freeze to me, mama, please don't let me roam,
  Freeze to me, mama, with both skin and bone,
  Freeze to me, mama, before I go home.

  Me and my gal we was side by side,
  She said, "Daddy, I would like to ride," I said—

  Freeze to me mama. . . .

As with all other subjects the blues, when dealing with matters of love and sex, is forthright and uncompromising. There is no concealment and no use of oblique references. It is this open declaration of subjects that the conventions of polite society have decreed shall be kept hidden from view which has caused so much offence and, incidentally, added the term "blue" to the English language as a word synonymous with "pornographic." During the twenties when the blues was first appearing on record there was much talk in sophisticated circles of "free love" and contraception, and the "flapper" enjoyed a new emancipation from the strict codes of the Edwardian era. But the fundamental Puritanical streak in American life persisted and the blues has remained in disfavour for its open "flaunting" of matters kept secret. Blues is a singular folk song in the Western world in that it deals with all aspects of life and death, of disaster and war, in which a common man, a Negro American man, may find himself participating. Not even the White folk songs of the "Okies" during the Depression were as all-embracing in their themes. With the passing of the last few decades there has been a certain return to a natural acceptance and understanding of sexual matters, though the potted Freudian knowledge shared by so large a proportion of the populace to-day has tended towards an over-intellectual, self-conscious awareness in which the impulses of adolescents and adults alike are interpreted in terms of psychological drives and complexes. With this has come a new tolerance that has had its most recent manifestation in an interest in the problems of the sexually maladjusted and in particular, the homosexual. More freely discussed in Great Britain than in America even to-day, this has been a post-war development in freedom of thought on a subject hitherto considered taboo. Not so in the blues, where this aspect of the lives of men with all its attendant difficulties has featured—not unduly prominently, but in proportion to its prevalence—since blues were first recorded.

Homosexuality is no crime, and the unfortunates whose natural sexual functions have been so misplaced are deserving of understanding. Sympathy is increasing but the hard shell of Puritanism is not easy to puncture and guidance for the Negro homosexual is slow in forthcoming. So he has been left with his problem, puzzled and unable to resist the disturbing features in his being. Nearly thirty years ago, when the homosexual was regarded in disgust and contempt if his existence was acknowledged at all, George Hannah sang in his high-pitched, feminine voice:

131. She call me a freakish man—What more was there to
      do? (*twice*)
      Just 'cause she said I was strange that did not make it
      true.

      I say you mix ink with water, you bound to turn it
      black, (*twice*)
      You run around with "funny" people, you'll get a streak
      running up your back.

      There was a time when I was alone, my freakish ways to
      treat, (*twice*)
      But they're so common now, you get one every day of
      the week.

      Had a strange feeling this morning, I've had it all day,
      (*twice*)
      I wake up one of these mornings, that feeling will be
      here to stay.

Amongst uneducated Negroes there is as little sympathy or understanding for the homosexuals as in any other group,

though they are accepted as part of the group. In the nomenclature that is applied to such unfortunate persons there is
ample evidence of the misunderstanding that is rife; the homosexual is a "freak," a "mellow," a "sissy," or a "drag." Especially vulnerable is the hermaphrodite who has the characteristics of both sexes—female breasts and male genitals. With
the characteristic combination of pithiness and pitilessness
that labels a legless man as "Halfy," the hermaphrodite is
known as "Peaches" or "Peach Tree." This abnormality produces complex emotions and passions that cannot easily be
controlled, and in the teeming communities of the Black Belts
it cannot be kept private. Apparently so afflicted, "Peach
Tree" Payne sang of his troubles, imitating the voices with a
rare facility that his unfortunate state had accorded him.

132. My home ain't here, it's down in Peach Tree land,
       (twice)
     Everyone at home calls me that Brownskin Peach Tree
       man.

     Why, even the li'l children says, "Mama, here comes
       that ole Peach Tree man," (twice)
     Your man says, "Where is he at? I thought you better
       get a bushel of his peaches if you can."

     You carry them in the spring-time, you eat them in the
       fall, (twice)
     The little girls say, "Papa, mama, says you carry his
       peaches strings and all."

     You oughta steal my peaches, slip in my doodla at night,
     You wanta steal my peaches, tip in my bed late at night,
     If I fix my bulldogs on you be careful and don't let 'em
       bite.

Homosexuality is no more prevalent amongst Negro persons than amongst White, taking the community as a whole,
though the references to a subject so shunned elsewhere gave
support to those who wished to contend that it was a common
aberration. In the overcrowded Northern Negro ghettoes this
social disorder tended to increase as did all others, for the lack
of privacy, the ease of soliciting, the difficulties inherent in

maintaining social order when young and old, male and female, criminal and virtuous are thrown into close and unavoidable contact were conducive to a lowering of moral standards. Latent tendencies which might otherwise have remained dormant were activated in Negro youths who were corrupted and forced into homosexual practices by the unscrupulous attentions of undoubted perverts and male prostitutes. Much marital misery resulted from the warping of young and vulnerable persons.

133. I dreamed last night I was far from harm,
      Woke up and found my man in a sissy's arms.

      REFRAIN
      Hello, Central, it's bound to drive me wild,
      Can I get that number, or will I have to wait a while?

      Some are young, some are old,
      My man says sissy's got good jelly roll.

      My man got a sissy, his name is "Miss Kate,"
      He shook that thing like jelly on a plate.

      Now all the people ask me why I'm all alone,
      A sissy shook that thing and took my man from home.

Not only the male homosexuals caused trouble in the homes; female homosexuals, though seldom castigated to the same extent by normal persons, can cause unhappiness in overcrowded districts where their aggressiveness and masculine tendencies cause embarrassment to the other women. Lesbians are known as "bull-dykers" in Negro areas, a term which hints at their bi-sexual characteristics, customarily abbreviated to "B.D. women."

134. Comin' a time, B.D. women, they ain't gonna do me no
          good, (*twice*)
      The way they treat us is a low-down and dirty too.

      B.D. women, they done laid their claim, (*twice*)
      They can lay their jive just like a nach'l man.

> B.D. women, B.D. women, you know they sure is rough,
> (*twice*)
> They have drunk up many a whisky and they sure can
> strut their stuff.

> B.D. women, you know they work and they make their
> dough, (*twice*)
> And when they get ready to spend it, they have no place
> to go.

Committed to live with his abnormality, the homosexual of either sex lives under great emotional strain and mental conflict. Either he can seek out the company of others in similar straits and accept the social ostracism that this generally brings, or he can attempt to suppress his abnormal sexual instincts which are aggravated by their unnatural character, and live with normal and happier persons. In spite of the difficulties involved some homosexuals do manage to achieve the latter compromise and even settle down to a comparatively normal married life. For Negro homosexuals there is less guidance and less assistance in taking this step, and the opportunities for conducting unrestricted social work into which White persons often sublimate their inclinations are few in number. Instead, some put their energies into Masonic or other secret organizations, or into the Church. A close relationship exists between religious and sexual ecstasy, and the devotion to the Church of those who are sexually frustrated is a phenomenon familiar to the psychologist. Unhappily, with the sincerely devout are also attracted to the Church occasional perverts and active homosexuals.

135. Say, you may not know my people, I will tell you who
they are, (*twice*)
Say, for mighty big devils, ooh, well, my mama saw
them servin' God.

Say, my daddy was a preacher, and my brother done
the same old thing, (*twice*)
Say, if you don't believe I like chicken, baby, ooh, well,
let me catch your wing.

Says I love my pullet, cause that meat's so tender and
  sweet, (*twice*)
Says I'm a rooster, baby, ooh, well, I can't stand rooster
  meat.

Knowing the homosexual proclivities of some persons associated with the Church, which in Negro districts includes
many unauthorized "sects" meetings in "store-front" chapels
at services conducted by unordained "ministers," the singer is
anxious to make it clear that he is not himself so inclined.
But his rejection of the homosexual, though lacking sympathy, is not a head-in-the-sand refusal to admit his existence
but an emphatic declaration of his own natural virility.

136. She is a Louisville woman, lives up in old smoke town,
       (*twice*)
     But I'm too good a man, to let one woman worry me
       down.

     Now don't get me wrong, because I am a real he-man,
       (*twice*)
     I don't go in for no funny business, I want everyone to
       understand.

The phraseology that he uses is not that of the popular
song; nor is it the language solely of the gutter. The language
used by many men in their own conversation would shock
them if they saw it in print or, indeed, heard it on record, but
the blues is not so hypocritical: the blues singer sings in the
language that he speaks. To those only accustomed to the
conventions of the printed and the recorded word, the blues
sometimes seems violent and coarse, but its expression is a
natural and uninhibited one. The songs of the college campus,
the baseball team, the barrack room and the stag party are
seldom less obscene, and considerably less healthy because
they are less honest in their declaration. The blues singer has
no intention of causing offence or even of shocking sensibili-
ties when he sings:

137. I stayed up for you all night, now baby, and I stayed up
       the night before, (*twice*)

> Well, its best for you to keep single, black gal, when
> you walks like a whore.

—for here he is making what is for him a simple statement of
fact: a deliberate, resentful criticism. In like manner a woman
may reject the advances of a would-be seducer in no uncertain
terms:

138. What's the matter with you, stop your whining around,
        (*twice*)
      Find some other place to lay your lazy bones down.

      You're too big to be cute and I don't think you are
        clean, (*twice*)
      You're the damnedest-looking thing that I have ever
        seen.

      What you got in mind ain't gonna happen to-day,
        (*twice*)
      Get off of my bed, how did you get that way?

      You'd better be gone when my man comes in, (*twice*)
      Stop shaking your tail, 'cause I don't know where
        you've been.

      Now a dog like you must have too much bread, (*twice*)
      Come out of my room, you can't sleep in my bed.

So the forthright, uninhibited language of the blues must be
accepted, and what is more, accepted without reserve or apol-
ogy, for it is a natural transposition of the everyday language
of both users and hearers. Nevertheless it must be acknowledged that the blues includes many sexual boasting songs that
are apparently aggressive in their use of phrases and images.
It has been contended that these are a form of protest song,
and there is a reasonable argument that they are designed to
shock and thus assert the personality of the singer. But just
as the blues includes all aspects of the lives of its creators, expressing themes which are seldom the subject of song, from
vagrancy and begging, to sickness and death by drowning, so
too the blues singer puts into his song the bragging of his sexual prowess that is customary in a virile man. His society is a

simple one and he boasts in the manner of members of other simple societies: Texas Alexander's words recall those used by the keel-boatmen of the Mississippi, the Texas cowboys or the Ohio backwoodsmen who cried that they were "half-horse and half-alligator, a little touched with the snapping turtle." . . .

139. I was raised on the desert, born in a lion's den, (*twice*)
Says my chief occupation—taking "monkey men's" women,

Says I never had a woman, couldn't get her back again, (*twice*)
Says I travelled over this country every kind of man,

The man who is proud of his sexual prowess, real or imaginary, takes pleasure in ridiculing the "monkey men": the West Indians and other Negroes that he despises whom he compares with the apes. He asserts his ability to achieve what they cannot and, in words that brook no argument, makes it clear what he demands of his women. That he is handicapped by blindness does not deter Blind Boy Fuller who feels when he cannot see.

140. I got a big, fat woman, grease shakin' on her bone,
I say, hey, hey, meat shakin' on her bone,
An' every time she shakes some man done left his home.

If when you boys see my woman you can't keep her long,
I say hey, hey, you can't keep her long,
I got a new way to keep her down, you "monkey men" can't catch on.

Baby, for my dinner, I want ham and eggs,
I say hey, hey, I want ham and eggs,
And for my supper, mama, I want to feel your legs.

Now you let me feel your legs, and they felt so strong,
I say hey, hey, and they felt so strong,
Baby, if you know what it's gonna be, baby, please don't let me know.

Though he despises the "monkey man" the blues singer frequently applies animal comparisons to himself: in all probability this is a legacy from slavery, an embittered acceptance of the lack of respect with which he has been held, causing him to take satisfaction from a violent assertion of those animal features of which he has been accused. So he becomes the "rootin' ground hog who roots both night and day," the "rattlesnakin' daddy who wants to rattle all the time" or the wild boar—the "tush hog."

141. Mama, can't you hear this tush hog rootin' roun' your
            front door? (*twice*)
        But if you give him what you promised him, mama, he
            won't have to root no more.

        I roots so long, mama, done rooted a hole through your
            door, (*twice*)
        But if you give me what you promised me, mama, I
            won't have to root no more.

        Mama, can't you hear this tush hog prattin' on your
            back door? (*twice*)
        But if you give him what you promised him, mama, you
            won't have to prat no more.

        Can't you hear this tush hog gruntin' all around your
            hole? (*twice*)
        But if you give him what you promised him, mama, he
            will soon be gone.

But when Champion Jack Dupree sings that he is the "black wolf that hollers," he is using a metaphoric animal image that is common in Western society at the present time.

142. When you hear this wolf howling, howling at every
            woman I see, (*twice*)
        Well, yeah, I'm only howling, well, well, for what belongs to me.

        So bye-bye, baby, this wolf going to take you to the
            woods, (*twice*)

Well I had been wolfing at you, oh well, but you don't
mean me no good.

It is of particular interest that the images used in the
blues are never based on tired and artificial, sentimental associations; lilies—even magnolias—do not figure in the blues of
love-making; no blues singer has a "love like a red, red rose."
He may be a "prowling tom-cat," he may wish to hear his
"panther squall" but he never expects his kitten to purr. This
is not to say that he has no sentiments nor that they are not
genuinely felt: the distress of a man who knows that his absence is causing the grief or the infidelity of his woman is no
less because he uses strong images to express it.

143. I went home last night babe, just about the break of
day,
I went and grabbed the pillow where my baby used to
lay,
I'm a rootin' ground hog, you gonna need me some
sweet day,
Well look at what Po' Joe done lost, eeh well, cause he's
so far away.

I'm a rootin' ground hog babe, and I roots everywhere I
go, (twice)
(Spoken) Lay it on me boy, it's bad!
I'm tryin' to keep my woman from takin' my lovin'; she
ended up givin' it to So-and-So.

Bovine comparisons are resented in urban White society
but those who live close to the land make their comparisons
with what they know best. When a Negro country singer from
the Mississippi Bottoms speaks of his "wild cow" he intends
no conscious insult nor crude comparison. Amongst simple
farming men cattle are held dear and such an image is sincerely meant, the charms of the girl being implied by the use
of hyperbole in his metaphoric descriptions. His is a tough
poetry, the natural poetry of a confessedly illiterate man.
Here the mixed metaphor "pigmeat heifer" underlines the extent to which the language of the blues is the language of the
Negro world, for the paradoxical image is readily comprehensible to the Negro who listens.

144. I been a mighty good bull cow, Oh Lord, but I got to
      go, (*twice*)
    I found me a pigmeat heifer, I can tell by the way she
      lows.

    She lows all night long, you can hear her for a solid
      mile, (*twice*)
    I can't stand to hear her low, I cried jes' like a chile.

    Whoa babe, your bull cow got to go, (*twice*)
    I can't stay here no longer, she calls me when she lows.

    Mama, I'm gone, with a horn long as your right arm,
      (*twice*)
    And when I get to hookin', I'll have me a brand new
      happy home.

    Good-bye, good-bye, an' I don't see you no mo',
    Good-bye, mama, if I don't see you no mo',
    Just remember me at night, when you hear mammy's
      heifer low.

From the country districts came other terms, and another
Mississippi-born singer requests:

145. I got a horse in Texas, pony all ready in Spain, (*twice*)
    I got a girl in Newport, got hair just like a mane.

    If you see my pony, please start her home, (*twice*)
    Babe, I ain't had no ridin' since my pony been gone.

But though his verse is similar it stems from different origins, for the pleasures of love are often figuratively called
"riding," and the male lover becomes the "rider," with "pony"
and "mare" as natural extensions of the same image. Sometimes the female partner by transference of the figure of
speech, herself becomes the "rider" or by the addition of a de-
scriptive adjective, the "easy rider." It is indicative of the importance of his guitar to the blues singer that the term "easy
rider" was widely applied by early blues men to their instruments, and whilst this undoubtedly derived in part from the
fact that the guitar was carried by a strap slung across the

singer's back, the use of a term which was widely applied to a lover, showed a close, if subconscious, psychological relationship between singer and instrument which is amply supported by the records made by the folk guitarists. In the towns the term "rider" has been employed almost as widely as in rural areas, but characteristically the image has changed and the singer who has lived largely in the city puts a new interpretation on the term.

146. Want to see my chauffeur, want to see my chauffeur,
　　　I want him to drive me, I want him to drive me down
　　　　　town,
　　　Says he drives so easy, I can't turn him down.

　　　Well I must buy him, well I must buy him,
　　　A brand new V-8, a brand new V-8 Ford,
　　　Then he won't need no passengers, I will be his load.

　　　Gwine t'let my chauffeur, gwine t'let my chauffeur,
　　　Drive me around the, drive me around the world,
　　　Then he can be my li'l boy, yes an' I can be his girl.

　　Not unnaturally the rhythms of love lead to many effective parallels which are made with the lusty bawdiness of an Elizabethan playwright, but in terms that are eminently of the present: the work of the auto-mechanic, the oil driller or the steamboat captain alike become the themes of songs, neither wholly innocent nor shamefacedly secretive.

147. Well, let me be your towboat and I'll tow you 'cross the
　　　　　pond, (*twice*)
　　　Well, I'll take you slow and easy, ooh well, it really
　　　won't take me long.

　　　When we reach th' Atlantic Ocean, the sea may be a
　　　little rough, (*twice*)
　　　But I will steady your boat, ooh well, 'cause I really
　　　knows my stuff.

　　　Now I've been captain on this towboat for twenty-eight
　　　years or more, (*twice*)

So just tell me how you want it, ooh well I'll tow you
'cross the floor.

Now blow your whistle, daddy, when you want a little
more speed, (*twice*)
Well, I am here to please you, ooh well, just tell me
what you need.

In the rhythmic ebb and flow of water the psychologist
recognizes a powerful sexual symbol and in the blues a sinu-
ous girl is frequently termed a "river hip" woman. Many of
the figures of speech used in such blues arise from the environmental or domestic circumstances in which the singer
finds himself. The man who has worldly goods can only offer
these to the woman whom he admires, though in doing so he
may also attach to them a metaphoric significance.

148. When I went out hustlin', tryin' to do the best I could,
(*twice*)
I knowed you were broke and hungry and I tried to
chop some wood.

I got wood in my wood-house, and I've got coal in my
bin (*twice*)
'Cause my fire went out, Lord, since God knows when.

Now woman, don't worry, cause my heater's always
hot, (*twice*)
'Cause good wood and coal is all I've got.

An exhaustive study of Negro sexual symbols used is long
overdue, indicative as they are of his modes of thought and
his reaction to the popularly held stereotypes of his behaviour. Among domestic metaphors culinary themes are especially common, which a brief examination of one stream of
associations will serve to illustrate. Arising simply from the
motions of sexual intercourse the term "jelly roll" is a familiar
one which has been in use for more than half a century. In
the blues it occurs frequently:

149. Jelly roll, jelly roll ain't so hard to find,
There's a baker shop in town bakes it brown like mine,

I got a sweet jelly, a lovin' sweet jelly roll,
If you taste my jelly it'll satisfy your worried soul.

I never been to church and I never been to school,
Come down to jelly, I'm a jelly-rollin' fool,
I got a sweet jelly to satisfy my worried soul,
I like to have my jelly and I like to have my fun.

The term is correctly applied to a jam (jelly)-rolled and lightly baked confection and in consequence the references to baking "nice and brown" have an added punning significance. So a lover admires his "jelly bean" and the way she can "jello" and prides himself on being a "good jelly roll baker." But the baker makes not only jelly roll but also other foods. Crisper than the jelly roll, the biscuit is well-baked, and a desirable young girl is consequently called a "biscuit," whilst the good lover is a "biscuit roller." Significant in both female and male applications the term is used by the folk Negro in genuine endearment:

150. An' I woke up this mornin', same thing on my mind,
     (*twice*)
     You know I tho't about that woman have treated me so
     nice and kind.

     Don't your home look lonesome, biscuit roller gone?
     (*twice*)
     You know I ain't got no doggone feelin's baby even
     bein' alone.

Contrasted with these confections mere bread is a commonplace, and of breads, cornbread from maize flour is considered one of the poorest. Though "cornbread" may imply lovemaking that is coarse, whilst "jelly roll" suggests love-making that is sweet, some singers may refer to "cornbread rough" as a desirable quality, unconsciously accepting the idea of crude libidinous relations.

151. Some of these women I just can't understand,
     All you women I just can't understand,
     They cook cornbread for their husbands and biscuits
     for their man.

In order to make his confections, the good cook must have the necessary equipment and the singer boasts of having "a good range in my kitchen" and wants no one to cool his ardour by "turning his damper down." Certain of the phrases that have arisen in this manner have passed freshly into the Negro language. Thus the prostitute becomes the "kitchen mechanic."

152. Women talk about me, they lies on me, calls me out of
         my name, (*twice*)
     'Cause their men comes to see me just the same.

     I'm just a workin' gal, poor workin' gal, "kitchen
         mechanic" is what they say, (*twice*)
     But I'll have a honest dollar on that rainy day.

Many valid and pithy metaphors are thus derived from the process of cooking and others are closely related culinary terms. Some have double, treble significance: "sugar" as a word of endearment has the added associations of wealth, for money is sweet to possess and is likewise called "shug" or "sugar." The "greenback"—the dollar bill—by virtue of its colour became known as a "leaf" and a wad of greenbacks became "cabbage." Further terms were added to the growing vocabulary of love-making, when such delights, as sweet to own as money, also became "cabbage" and the phrase "greasy greens" for much-handled dollar bills was aptly applied to the licentious lover. The colour of individual Negroes themselves inspired other related terms. A light-skinned Negro is "honey"-hued, a shade deeper may be called "coffee" with the result that a lover may be a "bumble-bee," a "honey-dripper," a "coffee-grinder."

153. Bought me a coffee-grinder, got the best one I could
         find, (*twice*)
     So he could grind my coffee, 'cause he has a brand new
         grind.

     He's a deep-sea diver with a stroke that can't go wrong,
         (*twice*)
     He can touch the bottom, and his wind holds out so
         long.

He boiled my first cabbage and he made it awful hot,
(*twice*)
Then he put in the bacon and it overflowed the pot.

Many of these are sweet, even slightly flattering terms but
in the use of the term "pigmeat" a deliberate acknowledgment
of the low status accorded the Negro in the past may be detected. It must be remembered that the pig, most "unclean"
of animals by Biblical standards, was rated of more importance to the planter than the slave and the Negro still remains
conscious of being "treated like a hog." So he prides himself
on being a "rooting ground hog," even a "dirty ground hog"
in challenging self-abasement. At the same time bacon, chit-
terlings, hogs' maws, pig feet, pig ankles and pig ears, ham
and other meats are particular delicacies, sweet, appetizing
and cheaply obtained—and the Negro speaks of himself as a
"sweet papa pigmeat."

154. Look heah, papa, you don't treat pigmeat the way you
should,
Ooh, don't treat pigmeat the way you should,
If you don't believe that it's pigmeat ask in the neighbourhood.

I ain't so good-lookin', I ain't got no great long hair,
Ooh, I ain't got no great long hair,
But I don't have to worry, I know it's pigmeat any-
where.

You can carry me to the mountain, I mean and will be
pigmeat there,
Ooh, it will be pigmeat there,
Raise a cold in China, stand to catch us anywhere.

It is not possible here to pursue further the many symbols
used in the blues. As love is the most potent, the most profoundly moving of all human emotions, it is fitting and to be
expected that blues on the themes of love should be richer in
symbolic imagery than on any other subject, as in all probability are love songs in every other folk music. Those terms
that sprang spontaneously from the theme and which passed
smoothly into the language of the Negro are often used with

scarcely a thought for their value as metaphors, but in the course of everyday speech. The man who wishes "to pick her tomatoes," who is "wild about her yellow yams" and who complains that the "niggers run around her potato vine" wishes to taste the fruits of love and he expresses his desire in phrases readily understood and appreciated by the subject of his affections. His words are no more direct, and his images scarcely less poetic than those of the ancient Arab desert songs of love that were loosely bound together to become the Song of Solomon though one doubts whether they would ever be the subject of interpretation as Christian symbolism.

155.   Your peaches look mellow hanging way up in your tree,
       Don't them peaches look mellow hanging way up in
           your tree,
       I like your peaches so well, they are takin' effect on me.

       I'm gonna get my step-ladder, babe, I'm gonna climb
           up on your top limb, (*twice*)
       If I'm gonna monkey your yaller peaches, it's gonna
           be too bad, Jim.

       Every time I climb your tree, babe, I wonder what
           make you smile, (*twice*)
       You want me to climb up your tree ever since you was
           a chile.

But such terminology is prone to misinterpretation. To Odum and Johnson it was impossible to print a great mass of the material that they collected in the first quarter of the century because of its "vulgar and indecent content. These songs," they added, "tell of every phase of immorality . . . and filth; they represent the superlative of the repulsive." The principal theme was that of sexual relations and there was no restraint in expression. Admitting that they shortened many of the songs "by the omission of stanzas unfit for publication," the authors contended that no other form of folk song was as indecent as that of the Negro. It would seem, however, that most forms of folk song have their counterparts elsewhere, though the uncompromising declarations of the blues have been placed on record, whereas those of all but the most primitive peoples have seldom been recorded, though their existence is not questioned to-day. There is no denying that many Negro songs are frankly pornographic and amongst the blues there are many that fall in this category, no more and no less meritorious than those in any other branch of song. Certain examples have a particular significance, however, and especially those known as the "Dirty Dozens."

The precise origins of the "Dozens" will probably never now be known, but it is a well established fact that Negro slaves used their work songs to sing the insults and comments to their overseers that they could not say outright to their faces, and the practice has continued to the present day on the State and County Farms and amongst the share-croppers on the larger holdings. Similar insulting songs are chanted by the Italian rice-workers and others have been noted in various countries. In the group song there is a certain anonymity, the individual offender being lost in the team, and punitive measures are seldom taken against the singers. Furthermore the overseers and straw bosses are well aware that anger or humiliation that gains an outlet in song is less likely to seek one in physical violence. Related to this habit has been that of singing blues and insulting songs apparently directed at inanimate objects; at mules, farm animals or at other persons in a Negro community, but as all concerned are well aware, referring obliquely to officials and White persons in authority. These often take a strong and offensive form, many being of a pornographic nature, but they serve to give vent to frustrated emotions. In turn this has led to the similar type of song which is specifically directed against other members of a Negro society—the "Dozens." "Putting in the Dozens" developed as a folk game in the late nineteenth century. A number of persons would gather and endeavour to exceed each other in the insults that they invented with a view to goading someone present to eventual wrath. In the process many obscene and scandalous inferences as to the ancestry of the individuals concerned would be made. Sometimes the anger of persons who had received unfair treatment or who were the victims of racial prejudice would be so dissipated, but at other times the "Dozens" were sung with intent to hurt and to provoke. If a particular person was the subject of enmity in a Negro folk community the offended man would "put his foot up"— in other words, jam the door of his cabin with his foot and sing a blues that "put in the Dozens" at the expense of his enemy, "calling him out of his name." This was the "Dozens" with vengeful intent but often youths would "play the Dozens" to work off their excesses of spirits in harmless and cheerfully porno-graphic blues singing competition.

156. I like your mama, I like your sister too,
I did like your daddy, but your daddy wouldn't do,
I met your daddy on the corner the other day,
You know about that he was funny that way.

157. REFRAIN
So he's a funny mistreater, a robber and a cheater,
Slip you in the "Dozens," your pappy is your cousin,
And your mama do she Lordy—Lord. . . .

Now, now, boys say you ain't actin' fair,
You know about that you got real bad hair,
Your face is all hid now your back's all bare,
If you ain't doin' the bobo, what's your head doin' down there?

Now you're a dirty mistreater. . . .

Frankly libidinous, the "Dozens" survives to-day; inten-tionally evil, it takes its name from the dice throw of twelve, the worst in crap-shooting. But though the "Dirty Dozens" is in part improvised, it is somewhat on the fringe of the blues. There is reason for the "Dozens" and some justification for it, as there is in the pornographic blues that occasionally appear. In general the blues has no need for pornography for its candour of expression obviates any necessity for secretive and allusive songs. The greater the tendency towards the "point number"—the song with sexual hints and dig-in-the-rib suggestiveness, the closer to the sophisticated night-club song and the further from the folk form the blues becomes. But it has its measure of *double entendre* and ribaldry for it is sung by all types and conditions of men and makes no pretence at purity. There is good-natured humour, and bland insolence, openly expressed desire and swaggering bragging in the blues.

158. If you want to live happy, go back home with me;
       (*twice*)
     I will sing you songs . . . such as "Nearer My God To
       Thee. . . ."

     I got a brand new sofa and a great big feather bed,
       (*twice*)
     You won't have to worry about a place to rest your
       head.

     I've got nice clean linen, and easy ridin' springs, (*twice*)
     But it don't mean nothin' if you can't shake that thing.

     And they call me "jelly" 'cause I rolls all in my sleep,
       (*twice*)
     I will roll your jelly and also grind you deep.

     I got a jazz-playin' piano and a great big rockin' chair,
       (*twice*)
     You can rock in rhythm by the music that you hear.

But for the Negro as for any other member of the community the physical aspects of love are primarily the expression of the emotions of love. When he is separated from his woman he feels the burning of desire for the one that he loves and is happy to declare the passion that he feels in honest and uninhibited terms. In Bo Carter's voice there is no hint of salaciousness, only the rough warmth and longing of a lonely man when he sings:

159. Red hot mama, meat shakin' on her bones,
     Think about your lovin' when I leave town,
     I got ants in my pants, baby, for you.

     Every time I meet you on the street,
     A funny feelin' from my head to my feet,
     I got ants in my pants, baby, for you.

     I'm gonna hug you, baby, hold you tight,
     Now love me, baby, like you did last night,
     I got ants in my pants, baby, for you.

Chapter 5

The Jinx is on Me

FOR THE MOST PART the blues is strictly secular in content. The old-time religion of the Southern churches does not permit the singing of "devil songs" and "jumped-up" songs as the blues are commonly termed, and it is not an expression that is natural to the church member. Music and song, he considers, must be for the purpose of praising the Lord, and though "holy dancing" is permitted by many Negro churches, "sinful dancing" is strictly forbidden. To the outsider the distinction may be a fine one, but within the church it is clear enough: spontaneous dancing which is the result of religious ecstasy is the only form acceptable. Often the Negro cultist churches are even more strict in the application of their codes of behaviour than are the orthodox Baptist and other denominations, and the segregation of the sexes, even to the exclusion of conjugal union between married couples, is not uncommon. Going to the movies, smoking, alcohol, even wearing the dresses above the ankle are innocuous forms of behaviour that the strictures of the cult churches rigorously ban. Though "conversion" may come to the blues singer, membership of such a group is not for him if he continues to sing the blues. Some blues singers—Georgia Tom Dorsey, Sarah Martin, Virginia Liston, Bertha Idaho and more recently, Little Richard, to mention a few, eventually gave up the blues and were embraced by the Church to which they devoted their talents as singers and composers. A number of other blues singers worked also as singers of spirituals, amongst them Blind Boy Fuller—under the name of Brother George—Blind Gary Davis and Brother Son Bonds, but they were somewhat exceptional cases. They kept their blues and religion strictly apart and though the influence of blues phrasing and instrumental accompaniment is to be noted in the work of some Gospel singers and, more recently, the passionate expression of the Gospel singer has been detectable in developments of the secular form, blues that is performing a specifically religious function may scarcely be said to exist. The worldly blues singer does not use his songs for hymns of praise, though an occasional reference to religion may be found.

160. I cannot do right, baby, if you won't do right yourself,
      (*twice*)
      Lord, if my good gal quits me, well, I don't want
      nobody else.

      Now you can read out your hymn-book, preach out
      your Bible,
      Fall down on your knees and pray the Good Lord will
      help you.

      'Cause you gonna be, you gonna be, my help some day,
      Mama, if you can't quit your sinnin' please quit your
      low-down ways.

In its bare realism the blues is somewhat bereft of spiritual values. The lower-class Negro has had to decide often whether he shall accept with meekness the cross he must bear in this world and join the Church with the promise of "Eternal Peace in the Promised Land" or whether he shall attempt to meet the present world on its own terms, come what may. The blues singer has chosen the latter course.

Victimized by circumstances over which he has no control, facing adverse conditions with no conception of the events that have brought them about, witnessing friends and relatives falling sick and dying with no cause that he can comprehend, the primitive and uneducated man falls readily into superstition. Observing a sequence of events or noting the coincidence of happenings strange or unexpected in themselves, he will satisfy his desire for understanding and seek to quieten his disturbed mind by drawing illogical but acceptable relationships between them. Frequently it is the lack of even a rudimentary education rather than inferior intelligence or intellectual capacity that causes a man to invent or to accept such superstitions as a substitute for knowledge. He may be well versed in "folk-lore," having a considerable fund of such beliefs on which he may draw and with which he advises others, and by intuitive rather than scientific or rational deduction he may on occasion draw conclusions that are largely accurate. Varying trends of the weather he may attribute to the behaviour of a flock of birds and thus successfully forecast a climatic change: his observations correct but his deductions inaccurate though they lead to the right conclusion. At other times such superstition will have no basis in fact or fiction but the force of tradition and the desire to be safe when an element of doubt arises accounts for the persistence of unsound beliefs. Even in the most educated of Western societies the horoscopes and the astrologist's forecasts are followed avidly by the lonely and the nervous; touching wood, stepping aside from ladders and black cats, avoiding speech of the devil or a tally of unhatched eggs are "precautions" that are taken by a high proportion of the community. Few persons are without private superstitions though these may be simply born of reluctance to break established habits of behaviour.

In the South the Negro has seldom benefited from an education that in any way has abided by the principle of "separate but equal" facilities and standards. Often the annual expenditure per Negro child in a county or State has been but a tenth that of the expenditure *per capita* on White children. Compulsory attendance at schools has seldom been enforced and it has been part of a policy that has had its origins in slavery that the Negro be very sketchily educated lest he should become aware of the extent of the injustices he has suffered, or becomes "uppity" and exceeds his "station." Windowless, draughty, ill-heated and ill-equipped Negro schools stand within sight of White schools built at a hundred times their cost, in areas where the coloured population is equivalent to that of the White. Even in an area such as Madison County, Mississippi, where Negroes own some ninety per cent of the land and pay an equivalent proportion of the taxes, the county revenue is administered by the Whites with the inevitable anomalies rife when the educational accounts are drawn up. There are opportunities for Negro teachers in the South, but they must accept low standards of living and working conditions and must be motivated by a strong sense of mission. Many teachers in Negro rural schools are therefore unqualified and often of scant education themselves; they must be prepared to lose their classes when cotton picking or the demands of the parents on the labour of their charges draw their pupils from school. Though marked strides have been made towards integration and non-segregated education with the resultant raising of standards that they must bring, these are comparatively recent developments. Under the system that has obtained for so long it is no source of wonder that Negro children in rural communities have grown up in surroundings circumscribed by the superstitious beliefs of their fathers, and have accepted them in lieu of any better informed instruction.

In his folk beliefs the Negro's social position is often reflected, as in his fear of black articles; the black butterfly that heralds bad news and the dreams of black water that foretell evil happenings are eloquent indications of his awareness and resentment of his colour. With punning reference to both animal and human being, Ma Rainey sings:

161. Black cat on my door-step, black cat on my window-sill,
     (*twice*)
     If some black cat don't cross me, some other black
     cat will.

     Last night a hoot owl come and sit right over my door,
     (*twice*)
     A feelin' seemed to tell me I'd never see my man no
     mo'.

     I feel my left side a-jumpin', my heart a-bumpin'. I'm
     mindin' my P's and Q's,
     I feel my brain a-thumpin' and I've got no time to lose,
     Now I'm just superstitious, tryin' to overcome these
     blues.

Much significance is attached to the behaviour of animals and birds under various circumstances, and these are looked upon as omens and portents of good or evil. The events anticipated by the hooting or screeching of owls may only be allayed, it is believed, by turning the pocket inside out or putting a shovel in the fire. The lowing of cattle in the "early dark" or the midnight call of the whip-poor-will foretell a death; a rabbit crossing the path brings bad luck, a rat running towards one brings good luck; whilst a spider on one's shoulder is a sign of fortune. Old beliefs die hard.

162. Why do people believe in some old sign? (*twice*)
      You hear a hoot owl holler, someone is surely dying.

      Some will break a mirror, and cry bad luck for seven years, (*twice*)
      And if a black cat crosses them they'll break right down in tears.

      To dream of muddy water, trouble's knocking at your door, (*twice*)
      Your man is sure to leave you and never return no more.

More deeply seated in their implications are the strange relationships that are thought to exist between apparently unconnected actions: the pinning of a hair-grip to a tree which brings a letter in the next post; the wearing of a hat backwards that counteracts evil; the insanity that results when a hair that has fallen from the head is used by a bird to build its nest. As old as history itself is the practice of interpreting dreams, and modern psychiatry has substantiated at least a small proportion of the conclusions drawn by the seers when they interpreted his intentions or his desires from the dreams of a man. Still, black or muddy water is a sign of trouble for the dreamer, but if he dreams that the ill-omened water is running it is a sign that his bad times will eventually pass. The meanings of many dreams are interpreted as the direct opposites of their content—a belief which does have some psychological justification when it is concerned with conditions of the mind. Watching where he places his feet, taking care not to break the spider's web that crosses his path, turning the pictures to the wall when there is a death, burning the sassafras wood only outside the house—the folk Negro of the older generation is bound by strictures and superstitions that govern his everyday behaviour. Amongst the more sophisticated Negroes such beliefs have been partially discarded with improved education, but many who migrated from the Deep South to the Northern cities took their beliefs with them: the permanent "blues what am." In his blues of this name Jazz Gillum repeats old folk beliefs: that a coffin will turn when peanuts are brought into the house; that someone must leave the home if the dogs howl or the lamp dims. He fears to be touched with a broom, he is alarmed lest his brother should put his bare feet in his own shoes, seeing bad omens in these seemingly harmless actions. The Negro who accepts such superstitions is resigned to the effects of their power over his life.

163. I stubbed my toe against the kitchen door, (*twice*)
       And now my hens won't lay no eggs no more.

       I went to church, sat in the thirteenth row, (*twice*)
       Next day my landlord said I had to go.

       I suppose there ain't no use in shedding tears, (*twice*)
       I'm gwine to have bad luck for seven years.

It is tempting, but facile, to attribute the Southern Negro's beliefs exclusively to his African heritage. They have much that is common to superstitions of peoples from Scandinavia to the Philippines: in other words, the growth of such ideas is a familiar phenomenon amongst simple and uneducated persons of all nations. Many clearly have Anglo-Saxon origins, absorbed from the culture of the plantation-owners, and the "poor Whites": the itching ear that means that somewhere one is under discussion; the irritating foot that warns of a forthcoming trip; the smashed mirror and the umbrella opened under the roof that mean misfortune. Others have an elementary symbolic significance: the corn grains that will bring fertility and the hatchet that will cut the pains of childbirth have their parallels in a multitude of primitive cultures. Some Negro folk-lore has an indisputable similarity with beliefs current amongst West African tribesmen whose peoples were seriously depleted during the centuries of slave traffic. A definite connexion seems very likely in many instances but others may have been born of the new conditions experienced in the New World.

Well established and documented is the survival of African magic in the Americas and particularly in the West Indies. Dahomean "religion" was brought over by the slaves imported by the French and has remained largely intact until the present day in the French possessions. Especially does it flourish in Haiti where "voudun" or "voodoo" is the dominant magical-religious practice amongst the Haitian Arada Negroes. In Cuba, similarly, many African religious have survived in modified forms with ancestry traceable to the Congo and the Niger River regions and these flourish through the medium of cults and secret societies. Here the influences are from the Kimbisi and Abakwa tribes as far as has been determined, though connexions with smaller groups have been identified, whilst the influence of the great Yoruba tribe and its worship of Shango the thunder god is to be found extensively in Trinidad. Elsewhere in the West Indies and the coastal regions other clear influences from Africa may be traced with spirit worship, snake cults, and other manifestations of African magic readily discernible.

In Louisiana and related regions in the South of North America the French brought large numbers of slaves drawn from these areas and from Haiti following the revolution in 1803 of the Negro King Christophe. George Cable's oft-quoted and exceedingly discerning article in the *Century Magazine* of February 1886 identified Negroes from some eighteen tribal sources in Africa and singles out for special mention the "voudou"-worshipping Aradas. In North America the newly imported slaves were expected to adopt the Roman Catholic religion. Its mysticism appealed to them and many unexpected parallels between the stories of the saints and aspects of their own still-remembered religion were drawn in their minds. From this confusion of religious beliefs developed the Southern black arts of "voodoo"—or as the Negro prefers to call it, "hoodoo," with its practitioners centred in the French South and above all in Louisiana.

164. Believe I'll drop down in Louisiana just to see a dear old friend of mine, (*twice*)

You know maybe she can help me 'bout my hard, hard time.

You know they tell me in Louisiana there is hoodoos all over there, (*twice*)
You know they'll do anything for their money, murder anyone I declare.

Now Miss Hoodoo Lady, please give me a hoodoo hand, (*twice*)
I want to hoodoo this woman of mine, I believe she's got another man.

In Louisiana and Alabama there are undetermined numbers of men and women versed in the lore and beliefs of voodoo who practise their arts for both good and evil in "white" and "black magic." These are the "conjures" or "conjure ladies," the "root doctors," the 'hoodoos' and the "gipsies" whose occult powers are believed to be extensive and who are consulted by the crossed-in-love, by the bereaved and by the murderously inclined alike. The conjures who devote their powers for good often prepare their spells and offer their services free; those whose abilities are put to more evil use exact fees relative to the undertaking. Both are widely respected and feared. So considerable is the faith that many folk Negroes have in the pronouncements of the voodoo men and women that frequently their assurance and encouragement is sufficient to ease their troubled minds.

165. Well, I went to the gipsy an' I laid my money on the line, (*twice*)
I said, "Bring back my baby, or please take her off my mind."

That gipsy said, "Don't worry, everything's gonna be all right some day, (*twice*)
That girl she really loves you but she just can't stand your ways."

Conjures are called upon for a variety of purposes to work spells that involve careful preparation and selection of materials for the charms used, and the study of many portents for favourable signs indicative of the appropriate time and circumstances of their application. The "two-headed doctors" are called in at the birth of children to ease the birth and to prepare spells that will help to ensure a good life for the newcomer. Barren women seek their advice and purchase their charms so that they might also conceive, and when death comes, the spells of the voodoo doctor smooth the journey of the departed and safeguard the lives of those who remain. On the doorsteps of the brothels they sprinkle Good Luck Dust and from roots and animal fur, ashes and hair they fabricate charms that will bring fortune to the gambler. Among the most potent weapons are High John the Conqueror Root which must be gathered before September 21, and Goofer Dust, the latter being powdered earth gathered from a grave, preferably that of a child, which will bring death to the victim when it is sprinkled on his pillow.

166. Don't tell me no story, don't tell me no lie, (*twice*)
    Now you's a good-lookin' woman but you bound to die.

    I'm gonna sprinkle a little goofer dust all around your
      nappy head, (*twice*)
    You'll wake up one of these mornings and find you will
      be dead.

As in English folk-lore the rabbit foot is a powerful charm for protection, but the strongest charm to bring back the wayward lover is the Black Cat's Bone. It is a costly and valued charm whose scarcity is largely due to the elaborate ceremony which attends its preparation. Zora Neale Hurston attended such a ceremony, having first starved for twenty-four hours, subsisting only on one glass of wine at four-hour intervals. A black cat was captured in the dark after a heavy fall of rain—not an easy task in itself—and hastily taken deep into the woods where in a ring protected by nine horseshoes a new vessel on which the sun had not been permitted to shine was filled with water and brought to the boil. Into the water was thrown the cat, three times cursed as it screamed in agony. At midnight the remains of the cat were drawn from the boiling water and its bones passed through the mouth until one was found which tasted bitter—the Black Cat's Bone. The ceremony was attended by a state of tension and terror that she found almost indescribable but in the morning she returned with the precious bone in her hand. This most prized of voodoo charms is sure to bring back home a lover who has left, or to secure the love of the person against whom its power is directed, and belief in its effect may cause many a man to attribute to it the influence that his own infatuation exerts upon his actions.

167. I feel like jumping through the keyhole in your door,
       (*twice*)
       If you jump this time baby, you won't jump no mo'.

       I believe my good gal has found my Black Cat's Bone,
       (*twice*)
       I cin leave Sunday mornin'; Monday mornin' I'm sittin'
       back home.

Amongst the Louisiana and Alabama Negroes the power of "gris-gris," "jujus" and "hands" is greatly respected. Such "mojo hands"—the African terms "gris-gris" and 'juju" have largely been discarded—are made with great care from personal fragments and from natural objects. Hair from the armpits or pubic region, finger-nail parings, pieces of skin are considered especially effective in love charms as, too, are fragments of underclothing, of a menstrual cloth and other closely personal effects. Combined with parts of night creatures, bats or toads, and with ashes and feathers from sources selected for a symbolic significance relative to the purpose for which they have been prepared, they are tied into small "conjure-bags" or put into an innocuous-looking receptacle and either carried to exert their power upon the victim when contact is made with him, or buried beneath his doorstep, or hidden in his bed or hearth.

168. I'm going down in Louisiana, baby, behind the sun,
       (*twice*)
       Well, you know I just found out, my trouble just begun.

       I'm going down in New Orleans, hmmm—get me a
       mojo hand, (*twice*)
       I wan' show all you good-lookin' women just how to
       treat your man.

Traditional centre of voodoo in the Southern States is New Orleans where the fame of many of its conjure women and voodoo doctors has spread far. Negroes who have strong faith in their abilities both for good and evil travel long distances and part with not inconsiderable sums of money in order to consult them, and purchase their preparations and "hands." Not always does the mojo prove successful, for every preparation has a counter-spell which can nullify its effects if used in time. But the victim who finds that he has been "hoodooed" bows to its powers.

169. Oh, the mojo blues, mama, crawlin' 'cross the floor, (*twice*)
Some high-life rascals done tol' me I ain't here no more.

She went to the hoodoo, she went there all alone, (*twice*)
'Cause every time I leave her I have to hurry back home.

Some people tell me, honey, them high-brown blues ain't bad, (*twice*)
That must not have been them low-down things they had.

Most famous of the conjure women was the celebrated Marie Leveau, the daughter of Cristophe Glapion, whose birth was registered in the St. Louis Cathedral, New Orleans, on 2 February 1827. A Creole quadroon, she studied under the earlier Doctor Alexandre and for more than half a century practised her magic at her houses in St. Anne Street and Bayou St. Johns. Subsequently her work was carried on by her reputed nephew, Luke Turner, and many other conjures with wide reputations in the mysterious underground world of voodoo. But though New Orleans and, to a lesser extent, Mobile were principal centres on the Gulf Coast, there are many other hoodoos and seers in other parts of the South. One of the most famous of these was Ida Carter, known as Seven Sisters, who practised in Hogansville, Alabama. Her fame was almost as great as that of Aunt Caroline Dye, whose name appears in blues songs from the earliest days of their recording. Aunt Caroline Dye lived in Newport News and continued to spin her magic until her death in 1944.

170. Yes, I went out on the mountain, looked over in
     Jerusalem, (*twice*)
     Well, I see them hoodoo women, ooh Lord, makin' up
     in their low-down tents.

     Well, I'm going to Newport to see Aunt Caroline Dye,
     (*twice*)
     She's a fortune-teller, oh Lord, she sure don't tell no lie.

     And she tol' my fortune when I walked through her
     door, (*twice*)
     Says, "I'm sorry for you buddy, but your woman don't
     want you no more."

Apart from the more celebrated practitioners, there are
many who enjoy strong local reputations and who eke out
meagre livings with "conjuration." Simple Negroes may be
inclined to attribute to the conjures all forms of misfortune
and the inhabitants of little known areas get stigmatized
for being hoodoos to a man, much as suspicion falls on Cajuns
that they are all murderously inclined.

171. When you get down to Smoky Holler, put your money
     in your shoe,
     These Smoky Holler women sho' put a med'cine on
     you.

     Now I'm feelin' so bad, I'm feelin' so sad,
     I ain't had a drink for so long—why I'm feelin' so bad.

     Lord, but I'm going to Tallahassee, I got the Tallahassee
     blues,
     When you get the Tallahassee women put a med'cine
     on you.

Voodoo is illegal, even in New Orleans, and because it is
an undercover activity the extent of its practice is not easily
determined. Some indication may be gained from the Negro
popular press which carries in every edition advertisements
for Easy Life Mixture, for Black Cat's Oil, Heifer Dust,
Lovin' Powder (at twenty-five cents) and Extra Fast Lovin'
Powder at a slightly higher price. With them go fantastic

guarantees, and beguiling phrases which are designed to suggest to the police that the powders and philtres sold are mere novelties but which still give to the intended market the assurance of success. Their sale is widespread and the advertisements appear on the backs of many record lists intended purely for the Negro market. Nor is the belief in voodoo confined to the South; it is extensive in the North where "gipsies" ply a highly lucrative trade, claiming at the same time some connexions with the South in their origins and the source of the roots and charms that they sell.

172. I went to the hand-reader just to have my fortune told, (*twice*)
  He said, "You need a cash policy—doggone your bad luck soul."

  He give me some Good Luck Tea and said, "Drink it before it gets cold." (*twice*)
  He said, "Drink it all day, doggone your bad luck soul."

  And he give me some pills just to drive my blues away, (*twice*)
  He said, "You bad luckin' rascal, drink it three times a day."

  Bad luck is in my family, an' there ain't nobody home but me, (*twice*)
  I was a fool for thinkin' that my happy days would ever be.

Amongst the more sophisticated of the Northern Negroes, belief in voodoo or related superstitions is considered to be a matter for some shame and a throwback to the days of servitude in the South. So it is with a ribald sense of humour and a studied disrespect for the beliefs of the older generation that Peter Clayton—calling himself Doctor Clayton—sings his *Root Doctor Blues*.

173. I'm a first-class root doctor and I don't bar no other doctor in this land, (*twice*)
  My remedy is guaranteed to cure you, pills and pains ain't in my plan.

You claim your regular doctor makes you feel like a
a real young girl, (*twice*)
Doctor Clayton's root treatments make you feel like
an angel flyin' round in another world.

After you receive my special root treatment, women
please don't start no signifyin', (*twice*)
Don't cry because some woman beat you to my office,
Lord, or I'll have to work overtime.

Amongst the voodoo doctors the principal book of magic
is a reprint of the *Book of Dream and Mystery* accredited to
the medieval exponent of the White and Black Arts, Albertus
Magnus, which enjoys a wide sale in Harlem, though banned
in Haiti. But the Black Arts have always received much
stimulation from Christianity and the Black Mass is an inver-
sion of the true Mass, with obscene substitutions for the symbolic wine and bread, and lewd incantations for the Creed. The
saints have proved to be allies to voodoo and the Bible has
been given strange and unintended interpretations. The Feast
of St. John is almost as much voodoo as it is Catholic and St.
Anthony of Padua, St. Mary Magdalene and many other
saints have been incorporated into its ceremonies. Voodoo
does not only appeal to the superstitious: it also satisfies the
need for protection, and acts as a form of escape, particularly
when coupled with spiritualism with which in the cities it is
often inextricably bound. Many Negroes seek the protection of
secret societies and cults, and the illegality of voodoo together
with the air of mysticism that surrounds its rites has a great
appeal. This has been loosely linked with African cults and
tribal societies, but to conclude that the connexion is a
powerful one is somewhat superficial, for whilst there exist
half-forgotten echoes of Africa in voodoo ritual, the desire
for the comfort and intrigue of the cult is natural to mankind
of all societies: it has been noted that in an ordinary
American community of some seventeen thousand souls,
more than eight hundred independent organizations exist, a
pattern of behaviour far from uncommon in the United
States as elsewhere.

Charlatans and criminals who exploit the beliefs of the uneducated Negro disillusion many who put their faith in the
voodoo cults. Whilst this effect is not wholly bad, it has often

brought misery and insecurity to those who have been unable to turn to orthodox religion for comfort. Religious cults of a non-voodoo, non-spiritualist nature that nevertheless have a high degree of mystical content or, conversely, the strictest rules of conduct that have a purgative effect upon the mind have thrived as a result of this. The Peace Mission of Father Divine; the Church of Bishop "Daddy" Grace—the United House of Prayer for all People; Bishop Ida Robinson's Mount Sinai Holy Church of America Inc., and the Moorish Science Temple of Timothy Drew are among the more important and influential religious cults of this character.

174. Pepper on the table and my good gal can't be found, (*twice*)
  Some man must have caught her 'cause she's the biggest shark in town.

  Since my gal went to New York, my house done changed, (*twice*)
  She don't like the boogie woogie and you can't tell her a doggone thing.

  I ain't no washfoot Baptist, and I can't do the Holy Roll, (*twice*)
  I joined Father Divine and it gave me peace that satisfies my soul.

Though some of the religious cults are undoubtedly suspect, a large number take a curious but on the whole far from unsavoury form and canalize to good ends of mutual benefit and comfort the resources of their members. With congregations often numbering only a score the little "store-front" churches which have been adapted from converted shops, and the larger "temples" which were once theatres, picture-houses or warehouses satisfy the spiritual needs of large numbers of the populace and provide the mystique that affords the sensation of protection for the socially insecure. Embracing the ritual and the rules of the Church the new member renounces sinful pleasures—and with them the blues. There are, nevertheless, many groups which purport to be of a religious nature but which are in fact successful methods of turning the sincere convictions of innocent Negroes to the profit of a few unprincipled criminals. Accompanied by fake ceremony and ritual especially designed to appeal to folk Negroes recently arrived from country communities, the services are conducted with a view to the extortion of sums of money in the form of bogus "collections" for the Church. Baptismal waters and holy oils are sold by the bottle for twenty-five cents and higher grades for double the sum, both within the church and in the street from the perambulators of wandering vendors.

Negro superstition is the subject of highly lucrative exploitation by the vendors of charms and love philtres, and cheap pseudo-religious votive ornaments and accessories alike, but it is in the systematic organization of the Numbers Racket that the most relentless and deliberate exploitation takes place.

The Numbers Racket reputedly comes from Cuba where it was known as Bolito. A successful method of earning large sums of money for a small number of people, it was introduced into Harlem and subsequently into Negro urban districts throughout the States during the years of economic depression when it was organized by "Dutch" Schultz. Bets are placed on combinations of numbers in groups of three, and the winners receive prizes of dazzling size in proportion to their modest bets. A return of fifty dollars may be received from a single cent played on a number, but the proportion of winners is exceptionally small—perhaps one in a thousand. Nevertheless the large prizes possible from low stakes invite many players on the numbers game and hundreds of thousands of Negroes play policy every day. As a result of the successes that Negroes who might otherwise be absolutely destitute have gained, the policy racket has wide support and the fact that it is illegal deters very few from placing their stakes. Those who played and won remain in the mind whilst those who played and lost are soon forgotten.

175. Me and my friends played a number, just as happy as
      happy can be,
  Everybody got paid for that number,
  Everybody got paid but me.
  (*Spoken*) I lost my stake.

     The jinx is on me, the jinx is on me,
     I don't have no luck at all, the jinx is on me.

For many Negroes the Numbers Racket becomes an obsession and they depend for their living entirely upon their winnings in the play. Inevitably they put great store on possible combinations of numbers that would seem to be well-omened, and on the numbers that occur in dreams. So the Numbers Racket, called by some Negroes by a curious mental twist "Playing the Races," continues to thrive at their expense.

176. I go on, go on playing the races all the time, (*twice*)
     You know she ain't good for nothin', she broke most all the time.

     Dreamed a number all the last night, yes, yes, and my baby did the same, (*twice*)
     My baby got up this morning and she played it the same.

     I come home every Friday, throw my check down on the bed, (*twice*)
     My baby takes all my money, puts it all on 5–6–2.

To exploit this superstition the policy racketeers publish "dream books" which give lists of numbers which are supposed to have a mystic connexion with aspects of human experience, with objects natural and man-made, and with every conceivable circumstance that may arise that may possibly be so used. Daggers and dogs, stars and strangers, Christian names and Christian symbols, connexions obscure or obscene are all given their number codes, and the policy player, upon experiencing a particular event, happening upon an unusual object, encountering a feature which he believes significant, or dreaming of any of these, consults his book to guide him in playing. Many omens of good luck are the reverse of the expected association and therefore accord with popular superstition. Folk beliefs are carefully noted and commonly held notions are perpetuated and employed to the benefit of the racketeers. To tread in excreta is commonly believed to be a sign of good luck and to dream of fæcal matter likewise. The fæces are assigned the combination 3–6–9 (or three, six and nine) and this is considered a number of especial fortune.

177. Going down to the office and get a numbers book, (*twice*)

So I can catch a gang of clowns like a fish a fishing hook.

I've got me a book, I got it from a numbers man, (*twice*)
I can't play all the numbers but I'm sure gonna play my hand.

I'm going down in Georgia and write some on the farm, (*twice*)
If I ever hit on the book, I'm gonna bring that money home.

I acted like a fool, I wouldn't play on 3–6–9, (*twice*)
Just think of all that money in that numbers book of mine.

It is of interest to note that the most famous Negro regiment is the 369th, which has had a distinguished record of service though it has had poor treatment. This particular number combination may have come from such a source. As the Numbers Racket is illegal the "office" is a euphemistic term. It may be a drug store, a saloon or a beauty parlour that acts as a "drop" for the racketeer. Others may operate from a street corner, but whatever the drop, its position is carefully and jealously protected by the racketeers. The positions are known by colourful names: "Bootleg," "Red Devil," "Streamliner," "Black and White," and the books issued from the particular drops contain slips of identifiable colours. Numbers may be bought in groups of three, or a succession of numbers which operates both from left to right and in reverse order may be bought for an additional sum by the customer who specifies when purchasing that he is playing the numbers "saddled" instead of "straight." Policy grosses some twenty million dollars a year of which half at least goes into the pockets of the racketeers and their four thousand minions, from the "big shot" down to the "numbers runner" who collects and issues the numbers in the street. He walks quickly, the numbers runner, keeping a wary eye for the police. By a code of winks and raised eyebrows, by flickering fingers and muttered words as he rapidly passes he collects the orders and indicates the winning numbers.

178. Got the number runner's, got the number runner's, got
     the number runner's blues,
   Got the number runner's, got the number runner's blues,
   And every time I see a policeman, I almost jump out of
     my shoes.

   Standing on the corner, standing on the corner, wasn't
     doing nothing wrong, wrong,
   Standing on the corner, wasn't doing nothing wrong,
   Oooh, that policeman was looking, he grabbed me by
     the arm.

   When I got a hearing, when I got a hearing, the judge
     looked at me a short while,
   When I got a hearing, the judge looked at me a short
     while,
   He said, "I believe that you' guilty," give six months on
     that hard rock-pile.

   Working on that rock-pile, working on that rock-pile,
     like I done a terrible crime, crime,
   Working on that rock-pile, like I done a terrible crime,
   And when I left that rock-pile, I didn't have a single
     dime.

   Scared to run the numbers, scared to run the numbers,
     scared to run the numbers now,
   Sacred to run the numbers, scared to run the numbers
     now,
   But if I keep on getting broke, going to run those num-
     bers anyhow.

For many a criminally inclined Negro the attractions of being a numbers runner outweigh the risks involved, for the returns are considerable and assured. The bigger racketeers may
bank a hundred thousand dollars a week and the sale of the
pitches and drops when the agent is temporarily put away by
the police or squeezed out by "muscle men" of a rival faction
also brings in large sums. "Dutch" Schultz was suppressed in
Harlem for a while by Governor Dewey, Chicago's "Jones
Boys" were squeezed out of their holdings, but they did not

mind: they had made their millions and were able to open a silk factory in Mexico City on the profits. To-day the Numbers Racket in central Harlem is controlled by a six-foot, fourteen-stone Negro called "The Lamb," one Bumpy Johnson. And whilst the policy racket flourishes the simple Negro in the street buys his numbers book from the "Big Train," consults his dream book, burns a phial of incense to find the three lucky numbers in the ashes, and prays for a hundred-to-one win on the phallic "Big Dick"—fifteen-sixty-seventy-five.

Chapter 6

Let the Deal Go Down

IN THE NEGRO underworld the most important members are the numbers racketeers whose success, whilst partly due to the exploitation of superstition, is primarily dependent on the Negro's fondness for gambling. Of indictable offences for which Negroes are convicted, illegal gambling provides a large proportion. It is exceedingly doubtful whether any racial group has an inherent propensity to gamble, but the Negro's fondness for betting is born of the culture which has evolved from his place in the American social structure. Economic instability and low social status cause him to gamble in the hope that he may better his financial position and be able to afford the clothes, the Cadillac Eight and, if possible, the home, that are marks of the position to which he aspires, in a society where status is measured in terms of prosperity rather than culture. Lack of opportunities to achieve positions of responsibility denies him the right to make important decisions or to exercise his initiative, thus refusing him sources of mental stimulation. Playing his hand, staking his chips, rolling his dice, he gains the thrills that his work does not afford him. Pitting his wits against other gamblers he exercises his intellect. From the turn of the cards he may experience the sweet, cruel delight of victory or the knife-thrust of failure when he loses: he gains pleasure from them both. He does not have to suffer the indignities of the Jim Crow "Nigger Heavens" in those theatres where he is permitted to attend shows at all, in seeking this entertainment; the street corner, the backyard or the parlour are the scene of his play. And he has the time to play.

Six days of labour, and the seventh a Day of Rest—but not for the man on relief, for the man who has been laid off from his work, nor for the man whose work is insufficient to keep him active throughout the year. Raising cotton provides less than two hundred working days in the year; for half the year the share-cropper is idle unless he can find some other employment or has been able to obtain for his own purposes a plot of land that he can cultivate. So the unemployed, the laid-off and the temporarily idle have plenty of free time: time that hangs heavily in which there is little to do. The woman raises the children, stitches the clothes, washes and sweeps. The man repairs the tools, cuts back the wood, fashions staves, shoots a little, fishes, hunts. When there is nothing else to do he joins his fellows to tell "lies," "put in the Dozens," sing the blues. Or gamble.

179. I love to gamble, gamblin's all I do, (*twice*)
      And when I lose, it never makes me blue.

      I gambled away my money, I gambled away my shack, (*twice*)
      Same way I lost it, same way I get it back.

      I won a woman in a poker game, (*twice*)
      I lost her too, win another just the same.

      Sometimes I'm rich, sometimes I ain't got a cent, (*twice*)
      But I've had a good time, every way I went.

It is the excitement of gambling and the belief that a run of bad luck is bound to change sooner or later, that keeps a man playing the games when it would be wisest to leave off. Gambling acts as a drug on the senses, stimulates and intoxicates. Whilst mild games cause little distress, the inveterate gambler is apt to play for higher and higher stakes and to lay down all that he possesses in the hopes of winning a high return. For these reasons gambling can be demoralizing and add considerably to the suffering of a Negro family, for the man who stakes heavily is causing damage not only to himself but to his dependants if he loses. Once in debt to a calculating player who has played a deceptive game of losing for a while until the stakes run high, he may be forced to borrow, beg or steal money in order to pay off and is almost inevitably drawn into further games in the desperate attempt to recoup his losses. His excuses and vain hopes are unlikely to appease his woman.

180. I gets my money from an ole lady, she says, "Son, give it to the Poor," (*twice*)
She says, "Don't shoot dice an' play Coon-Can, an' don't give my money away."

Ain't no use my sayin' bad luck is in my hands, (*twice*)
I been playin' all night long, an' your daddy win the first game.

When you lose your money, please don' lose your mind, (*twice*)
Because the best of gamblers, mama, gotta lose, sometime.

When I ran aroun' tryin' to gamble, Lawd, I caught myself up here, (*twice*)
Stayin' out late at night, sleepin' with women I slept with before.

I even been down on the track, playin' horse-races,
I even been down on the track, playin' horse-races, ain't no good,
You give me so much trouble, I had to move from your neighbourhood.

A true gambler accepts the rough with the smooth, the losses with the gains. His fortune may depend on the turn of a card, on a timely manœuvre or an outrageous deception. As he plays his game of poker he must weigh carefully the improvement percentage of his hand with the relative value which he is to call or bet compared to the size of the actual or likely jack-pot. If he plays his hand faultily or his bluff is called, he accepts his losses philosophically without rancour or betrayal of his feelings. Maybe he is broke now; the next game he may win.

181. I lose all my money on a point last night, (*twice*)
I set down a four flush and a trey comes by.

I lose all my money—got all my clothes in pawn, (*twice*)
Now you gonna be surprised when you see me with my good clo's on.

When I was down why did you let me lay? (*twice*)
For every man's subject to a losing day.

My gal's a gambler, she plays both night and day, (*twice*)
She hollers, "Jack!" in the game, when ace to jack and trey.

I don't shoot dice, strictly don't play no pool, (*twice*)
Because I sell to my ace—don't think I'm nobody's fool.

Poker is a favoured game amongst Negro gamblers, especially in various modifications such as Florida Flip—Five Card Stud in which each new card is served down so that the players may elect which card to turn up before every interval. One of the oldest card games associated almost exclusively with Negroes is Coon-Can, a form of gambling rummy in which the dice are also employed. Because it needs only two hands to form a game it is widely played and extremely popular.

182. Well, they call me Coon-Can Shorty, the man from Coon-Can Land, (*twice*)
Well, now I will play with any man, ooh well, well, the game they call Coon-Can.

My dice won't pay—'cause it's the only game you see, (*twice*)
And every chump in town, ooh well, seems to fall down on me.

My babe give me money—Coon-Can Shorty is my name,
  (*twice*)
But before I lose her money, ooh well, I must spread
  the news I'm in town again.

But some day my dice gon' pay and my money gonna be
  on the wood,
Ooooh well, my money gon' be on the wood,
And every chump in town, ooh well, they ain't gonna be
  no good.

Some say they will Coon together—if you chain 'em
  down, (*twice*)
But now you know I got it there—ooh well, well if you
  come in this town.

But the favourite game is Georgia Skin, fast and open to
innumerable methods of cheating by experienced players. Two
players act as "principals" and take it in turns to deal, alternat-
ing when one or the other loses—or "falls"—on a card. Each
"piker," as the player is called, is dealt a card and as a player
"falls" a further deal is made. After the deal, the players sing,
"Let the deal go down," as the principal flips the cards from
the top of the deck. Bets are placed on the cards as they drop
but a player may "scoop one in the rough" by selecting any
card from the deck on payment of an additional sum to the
principal. Some of the fortunes and the atmosphere of the
game are recalled by the gravel-voiced Georgia singer Peg Leg
Howell in his *Skin Game Blues*:

183. Said you better let the deal go down,
       Skin game coming to a close,
       And you better let the deal go down.

     When I came to the skin game last night, thought I'd
       have some fun,
     Lost the money I had, baby, pawn my special gun,
     Pawn my special gun, pawn my special gun, loving baby,
     Pawn my special gun.

     Better let the deal go down, skin game coming to a close,
     An' you better let the deal go down.

(*Spoken*) Hold the cards, dollar more, Deuce beat a
nine. Half more too. Put up more, Nigger!

Gambled all over Missouri, gambled through Tennessee,
babe,
Soon as I reached Georgia, the Niggers carried hand-
cuff to me.

Said you better let the deal go down,
Skin game coming to a close,
And you better let the deal go down.

Much depends on the turn of a card and inevitably superstitions as to the nature of certain cards have developed, some
being considered as lucky and others as ill-fated ones to have
in the hand. Because the Negro is called a "Spade" by some
contemptuous Whites, the Spades suit is sometimes considered
ill-favoured. Adapting the word by a popular form of jive
slang, in which the vowels are repeated with unrelated consonants separating them, to "Spagingy Spagade" certain Negroes may even take an inverted pleasure in this, or boast to
be the "King of Spades." In similar fashion the Mississippi
blues singer, B. K. Turner, called himself the "Black Ace"
singing, "I am the Black Ace, I'm the bold card in your hand,"
with challenging pride. Spades, Clubs and Hearts have various
symbolic meanings to the Negro. Most favoured is the Diamonds suit and the favoured card the Jack of Diamonds with
which players sometimes associate themselves.

184. Jack of Diamonds, you appear to be my friend, (*twice*)
But gamblin' gonna be our end.

Gee, I've travelled the whole round world through,
(*twice*)
There's nothin' in this world I've found that pleases you.

I love Jack of Diamonds but he was a cruel man, (*twice*)
He could play dice and cards and he was King of old
Coon-Can.

Jack of Diamonds, in fact, is a deceptive card that can be
of great service if played correctly, but "Jack of Diamonds is

a hard card to play." He can turn your "money green"—in other words he can make coins into "folding money," into paper dollar greenbacks. But Jack of Diamonds can also make a slave of the player.

185. Jack of Diamonds is a hard card to play,
      Jack of Diamonds is a hard card to play,
      Jack of Diamonds is a card sent many a poor boy to his
          grave,
      Jack of Diamonds is a hard card to play.

      Put this Jack with the Queen and it'll turn your money
          green,
      Jack of Diamonds is a hard card to play,
      Jack of Diamonds is a hard card to play,
      Put the Jack with the Queen,
      Jack of Diamonds is a hard card to play.

      I'm gonna tell you like Dirty Butter tol' Natty Chin,
      Keep on playin' boy, you're bound to win,
      Jest take the Jack with the Queen,
      And it'll turn your money green,
      Jack of Diamonds is a hard card to play.

In the fortunes of this card more than any other the Negro sees reflected his own situation and it has a code significance in his blues which is not lost on his listeners. Thus when bad luck comes, it turns money green in quite a different sense: loving the play on the words the blues singer refers now to the coin proving to be false, turning bad in the hands. By such means is the blues used as a form of protest and a vehicle for sentiments that could not be more openly expressed.

186. I said dices are dices, please, don't you agree on me?
          (*twice*)
      'Cause I'm just broke and hungry as any gambler can
          be.

      My buddy played a Jack when he gave me that heart-
          luck Queen, (*twice*)
      They were the unluckiest cards that a gambler has ever
          seen.

Jack o' Diamonds, Jack o' Diamonds will turn your
money green, (*twice*)
Unluckiest card that a gambler has ever seen.

Apart from gambling with cards, the Negro likes best to
"Roll the Bones"—to shoot craps with the dice. The game is
simple, and can be virtually interminable, and other names
by which it is known—Memphis Dominoes or Mississippi
Marbles—are evidence of its popularity in the South. The
"crap shooters" lay their money on the wood to make betting
good, and "keep it in sight to save a fight"—staking their bets
on the throw of the dice. Best numbers are seven and eleven,
the worst throws are two, three and twelve, when "up jumps
the Devil." The rattle of the dice on the wood and the chant-
ing of the players lures the gambler to the game, which may
soon change, with the addition of an extra die, to "chuck-a-
luck." Whether he is trying to "buck the tiger" at poker,
sweep the deck in the skin game or shake off the jinx that has
caused his run of bad luck in the past, the player prays that
the scales will tip in his favour and that his nickels and dimes
will turn to dollars. The stakes are not always high in the
terms of the professional gambler but a man's fortune is his
total wealth and the loss of a few dollars when they are all
that he possesses can be for him as great a tragedy as any
enacted before the croupiers in a Riviera Casino.

187. People, people, I'll tell you the way it seems, (*twice*)
You can only get a favour when your money is green.

I'll bet my last dollar, swear an' I ain't no gamblin'
fiend, (*twice*)
Folks, I'll just take a chance, tryin' to make my money
green.

Gambling is illegal in most of the states—the only truly
"wide-open state" is Nevada—but this does not mean that
there are not gaming-houses in abundance, though they may
operate as a result of dubious manipulations of the law. In the
"tonks" and gaming dens of the Negro sectors few of the
casual workers from the tobacco factories or the oil refineries
succeed in making their fortunes, for here they meet the professional Negro gamblers. Against the fuzzed shuffles, the

fixed decks, the crimped and pricked cards that are detected only by the extra-sensitive, sand-papered finger-tips of the professional, the logger who tries to triple his pay has little chance of winning. But though he—or she—may prefer to shoot craps with his buddies the temptation to enter the bigger games is hard to resist, and he falls an easy sucker to the invitation of the sharp cat with the skybonnet, diamond tie-pin and a "mouthful of gold."

188. My baby she found a brand new place to go, (*twice*)
    She hangs across town at the Monte Carlo.

    She likes my money, tells me she goin' to the picture-
        show, (*twice*)
    But that girl's been throwin' ma money away at the
        Monte Carlo.

    (*Spoken*) Monte Carlo is one of the biggest gambling-
        houses in town.
    If you stick it's bound to carry you down.

    I heard she had a boy friend and they called him Buddy
        Joe, (*twice*)
    He's a big shot across town, runs a game at the Monte
        Carlo.

Big-time gamblers keep to the cities for most of the year, playing amongst themselves for truly high stakes. Tens of thousands of dollars may pass amongst them in a single bet. But in the early fall the gamblers appear from Memphis, St. Louis and Chicago in Clarksdale or Jackson. They come up from New Orleans and Mobile and visit the cotton and rural areas of Mississippi, Georgia and Alabama. For this is the time of the year when the Negro farmer is relatively flush with money; he is excited as the end of the season comes, and the fall-money paid out for his crops burns in his pockets. In districts where wages are paid on a day-to-day basis as crops are weighed in, the worker is happy enough to spend his income as it comes; in those areas where the share-cropping system still operates he is paid in a lump sum at the conclusion of the harvest. The big-time gamblers wait for him. This is the time of the "Skin-ball" and the games of Skin are established in every roadside juke-joint. In their thousands the croppers and the field-hands appear at the gaming centres and, hoping to turn their year's returns to a fortune, may stake their entire earnings on a turn of the card. Others are more cautious, but it is a time of considerable excitement and infectious gaiety, when caution is cast aside. When the small-time players, the croppers and workers of field and factory, have been cleaned up, the noted gamblers amongst the local Negroes move in and the play is earnest, with numbers and liquor concessions, property and heavy sums staked, lost and won. Meanwhile the field-hand returns to his dog-trot cabin, temporarily wiser but protesting his right to use his time and his money as he wishes.

189. Some o' these women sure do make me tired,
  Gotta handful o' gimme, mouthful of much obliged.

  Well, mama, don' allow me to fool roun' all night long,
  Now I may look like I'm crazy, poor John, do know
   right from wrong.

  Now, drop down, babe, and let your daddy be,
  I know just what you're trying to put on me.

  Well, mama, don' allow me to, foo-ol roun' all night
   long,
  Now I may look like I'm crazy, poor John, do know
   right from wrong.

It is not only the gamblers who appear in the South in the early fall, at harvest time and immediately after. For this is the period when the travelling entertainments appear: the circuses and tent shows—Silas Green's from New Orleans, the Georgia Smart Set, the Rabbit Foot Minstrels or Irvine Miller's Brownskin Models. Gaily decorated trucks drive slowly through the townships and laughing, dancing jugglers high-step on their "Tom Walkers" or stilts, drawing the children and their parents from the doorways, to follow in cheerful procession to the show-grounds.

A visit from a travelling show is a big event in the small Southern communities. It brings a period of gaiety and abandon during which moral codes tend to be relaxed. Side-stalls and amusements commence to operate as the tents are erected. In the bigger centres there are fairs and circuses and Negro hands content for the time being with their earnings travel comparatively long distances to attend them, camping out in the vicinity of the show until the gay season is over or their money is expended. Some of their number who have instrumental and vocal ability join the shows in a temporary semi-professional capacity as blues singers, travelling from town to town and village to village, freely sharing the loose, unrestrained and riotous living that the brief stops afford. So a singer such as Gus Cannon or Ben Covington would leave his home district during the cotton-picking, corn-husking, cane-cutting, tobacco-harvesting season and entertain with the shows as they toured through the South and mid-West— though in the case of Texas Alexander, to some disadvantage:

190. I carried my woman to the St. Louis Fair, (*twice*)
    She got stuck on a man that was in the fair.

    I brought her back to Dallas with a travelling show.
    (*twice*)
    She had men hanging round her like a circus show. . . .

At this time the travelling vendors of cheap patent medicines also exploit the comparative affluence of their country cousins. Few of the medicine men sell creditable wares; usually they are concoctions of their own devising which act as strong purgatives. They realize that the Southern folk believe that "the more you're sick the more you needed it," and make sure that their brightly coloured, foul-tasting "medicines" have the desired effect of causing their purchasers to retch violently. To advertise their arrival many medicine salesmen employ blues singers—Joe Lee Williams or Sonny Terry for example—to put on a "medicine show" which attracts a crowd to whom the concoctions could be sold. The appeal of such shows was immediate, for ready-made entertainments were few. In those districts that sported a theatre of some form, Negroes were not generally admitted to it, but the majority of the townships were without such refinements. So the Negro in search of amusement goes to the "juke" where he can carouse, dance, and join in the rough entertainment that the establishment affords. A timber-framed shack, with a low veranda and gaudy advertisements decorating the exterior, the juke is often closed during the week and comes into rough and noisy activity on a Saturday night. But during the lay-off season, when there is little else to do, the juke is open every night and the pleasure-seekers "barrelhouse" in wild, sweating dances to the music of guitars or piano. It is "low-down" stuff and the participants are condemned by the "do-gooders"—the strict church-going folk. Singing the blues and "stomping 'em down, bedslats and all," the "sinners" do not care. They need an outlet for their unspent energies and know few others. In a deep, gritty voice, "Mr. Freddie" Spruell sang of the only life he either knew or wanted in the Delta:

191. In the lowlands of Mississippi, that's where I was born,
(*twice*)
Way down in the sunny South, Lord, a man grows cotton and corn.

I'm lookin' for a low-down woman who's lookin' for a low-down man, (*twice*)
Ain't nobody in town got as low-down as I can.

I like low-down music, I like to barrelhouse and get drunk too, (*twice*)
I'm just a low-down man, always feelin' low-down and blue.

White square-dances and cotillions had been adapted in the slavery period to suit the less formal tastes of the slaves and from these the "breakdowns" of later years and spontaneous open-air dances called "sukey-jumps" evolved. To mark the conclusion of corn-husking, the raising of a house, a wedding, or indeed any social event that merited some form of celebration, "play-parties" were held which lasted until the dancers and celebrants dropped from exhaustion and liquor. Banjo, fiddle, guitar and piano rags provided the music, but when the early morning light was breaking over the hills and the energies of the dancers were beginning to flag, the musicians dropped into the blues, slow, interminable blues, and the couples "slow-dragged" across the floor.

192. My feet is so sore, cain't hardly wear ma shoes, (*twice*)
Out last night with wild women and it give me the big
night blues.

I grabbed ma baby, I danced till the clock struck
twelve, (*twice*)
I had to rassle with my good gal, an' I ain't feelin' so
well.

I'm going back to that party, get with the wild women
again, (*twice*)
Well I'm goin' leave ma home, gonna order me a quart
of gin.

At the jukes and honky-tonks provided by the companies
for the workers on the "jobs"; at the breakdowns held in the
back-of-town taverns in the Southern villages or in the rough
dance halls of Shreveport and Memphis, Atlanta and Nashville, the dances were not characterized by their refinement,
and any grace that might be observed in them was born of
freedom of movement rather than studied dance figures. Yet
new dances were constantly being evolved by the strutting
Negroes. From Florida came the Swamp Shimmy, in which
vigorous undulations of body, hips and limbs made up for
lack of forward movement. From the desperate Negro quarter
around 4th Avenue, Nashville, known as the Nashville
Bottoms, came a new "twister" with hand-claps and hops—
the Black Bottom, the punning significance of its name doubt-
less appealing to its inventors. In its original form it made few
concessions to respectability but when it entered the White
dance halls many of its frankly erotic features were modified.
Other dances such as the Texas Twist and the Georgia Crawl
also indicate their place of origin. Echoes of folk amusements
were to be found in the many dances that mimicked animal
movements: the Grizzly Bear and the Elephant Squat, the
Buzzard Lope and the Turkey Trot, the Eagle Rock and the
Turtle Twist, the Bunny Hug and the Fishtail. Holding the
Mule, Walking the Dog—the Southern Negroes brought their
dances from the Mississippi jukes to the back parlours of
Chicago's South Side and New York's Harlem. From the
South they also brought the "Rolling Blues"—rapid, twelve-

bar blues played on the piano with six or, more commonly, eight beats to the bar to which the pianist half-sang, half-spoke his instructions to the dancers:

193. I want you to pull up on your blouse, let down on your skirt,
      Get down so low you think you're in the dirt. . . .
      Now when I say "Boogie!"—I want you to boogie;
      When I say "Stop!"—I want you to stop right still. . . .

It was the ill-fated Clarence "Pinetop" Smith, who was killed by a stray bullet in a fracas when he was twenty-three, who first used the term "boogie woogie" on record. Known as the Fast Western to the Southern Negroes, he re-christened the style after the "boogies" or parties on the South Side where the loud and rhythmic blues-based piano music was popular. Too Tight Parties and Too Terrible Parties, Chitterling Rags and Calico Hops, Juggles and Struggles, Skiffles and Scuffles, Breakdowns and Shake-me-downs, Stomps and Boogies—essentially they were one and the same thing, informal, reckless gatherings and dances, as popular in Atlanta as they were in Detroit. The blues guitarists and pianists arriving from the South found that their music was ideally suited to the wild assemblies that were even more a part of Negro life in the immediate post-war years than they were among the Whites. In the confined space of a tenement parlour there was as little room for freedom of movement as there was on the congested, sand-strewn floor of the juke, and the dancers evolved their "shimmies," their "shakes," their bumps and grinds that recall the *danse du ventre* of the Oul'd-Naïl in which the dancers shrugged their shoulders, fluttered their fingers, traced and retraced the seams of their trouser legs, twitched and rippled and did the belly-rub, "dancing on a dime." The blues pianist or guitarist may not have called the gathering but he was the most important member of the throng, giving his orders, demanding his liquor and his women, shouting the blues, "whipping" his guitar "to a plank" and his piano "to a jello"—directing the dancing:

194. Say, you li'l girl with the black dress on,
      Come over here, stand by me.
      Let me show you how to do the Head Rag Hop!

Now let's git it! Shake it; Shake that mess!
That's what I'm talkin' about.
Baby, you strawin' yo' mess now!
I thought you tol' me you didn't know how to do that
    Fishtail?
You doin' that Head Rag Hop now!

Spirits were high and the spirit flowed; tempers would flare
into burning quarrels on the instant, to be decided with shiv
and steel blade on the back stairs. To some Negroes the
parties became notorious as "razor-drills" or, in cynical recognition of the insensibility of the dancers by the morning,
"flop-wallies." But they continued, partly because the strain
of living in the overcrowded Negro ghettoes caused an over-
welling of emotions that needed some form of release, partly
because they solved at least one aspect of the housing problem. When rents could not be paid, a man would throw a
party providing jugs of liquor and platters of pig-ankles and
engaging a blues pianist to provide the music. By charging a
levy on his friends of some fifteen or twenty-five cents he thus
gathered enough to meet the demands of his landlord, and
mutually assisted his friends when their own turn came. So
the House-Rent Party became an established institution in
Chicago, Harlem and Washington and, to a lesser degree, survives to-day. A rather pathetic pride and a desire to suppress
the bad reputation of the parties inspired the euphemism,
Social Whist Parties, and in Harlem for many years a lonely
Negro known as the "Wayside Printer" pushed through the
streets a barrow mounted with a small printing machine. Its
platen was small, but it was big enough to print invitation
cards with such a legend as:

Wear your dress above your knees
And strut your stuff with who you please.

SOCIAL WHIST PARTY

at Slamfoot and Mama Jackson's. 3rd. Apt.

or bearing some other apt quotation from a favourite blues
recording, that belied the dignity of the name by which the
party was known. So successful were these functions that

Good-Time Flats which were informally run on semi-permanent lines became popular. A piano and a stool or two for the guitarists and mouth-harp players, who would drop in when their shifts were over, took care of the music, and a table in the hall with favoured Southern dishes made the "Buffet Flat," whilst the "Barrelhouse Flat" had a row of barrels with a plank counter above them to turn the parlour into an illicit saloon. Good-time girls who were free with their favours for little pecuniary reward frequented the Flats and back rooms were used both by them and by the gamblers. Operating outside the rackets controlled by the beer barons and big-time gangsters who had the police in their pay, unable to meet the sums required for "protection money" which ensured freedom from molestation for the more expensive "speakeasies," the owners of the Flats were hard-pressed to keep their premises open. But in the close-crowded tenements the domestic "front" afforded some protection and addresses could be changed without attracting too much attention.

195. I've got a barrelhouse flat in Detroit and one in St.
　　　Louis, too, (twice)
　　But my barrelhouse flat in Detroit really just won't do.

　　I'm gonna build me a little barrelhouse flat way out on
　　　Dago Hill, (twice)
　　Where I can get my beer and whisky when it's fresh
　　　from the still.
　　(Spoken) Police sergeant just won't let me be, he tries
　　　to find my whisky everywhere I hide it.

　　I got a barrelhouse flat in Chicago, it's fifteen storeys
　　　high, (twice)
　　I get all these high-yellers and play these babies dry.

　　Those babies like my good whisky, and they drink my
　　　sherry wine, (twice)
　　If you want good time, come and try this barrelhouse
　　　flat of mine.

Precautions were taken to keep the Flats from the knowl-edge of the enforcement agents and the police, whose raids were feared by the bell-hops and kitchen mechanics, truck drivers and domestic cleaners who frequented them and who could ill-afford to lose their jobs. If the demands for protection money could not be met, the police raided the flat and forced it to close. Boards would be nailed across the windows, a padlock placed on the door and a police seal affixed, and for a time the proprietor was out of business until he—or, as often as not, she—opened again elsewhere.

196. Cain't sell no whisky, I cain't sell no gin,
Cain't sell no whisky, I cain't sell no gin,
Ain't got no money to buy my way back home,
Cain't save a dollar to save my doggone soul.

I can't keep open, I'm gonna close the flat,
I can't keep open, I'm gonna close the shack,
The Chief of Police tore my playhouse down,
No use in grievin'—I'm gonna leave this town.

Paradoxically it was the introduction of Prohibition that caused the marked increase of alcoholism in the United States during the twenties and the many evils that were associated with it. Prohibition came early to some of the Southern states where it was introduced as a measure intended to safeguard the White population from the danger of "liquor-crazed" Negroes. As early as 1881 Texas filed its first Prohibition referendum; and in 1908 Georgia had voted to be a dry state and within the space of a year Alabama and Mississippi followed suit. Tennessee was almost a hundred per cent dry at this time—but not surprisingly, Memphis, Nashville and Chattanooga remained "wet." At this time there were more than two thousand saloons in New Orleans alone and liquor was freely available to Negroes. When Prohibition was introduced in Georgia the convictions for drunkenness dropped initially by half and believing that the danger from drunken Negroes would be minimized by similar action a further half-dozen Southern states and three firmly Protestant states also voted to be dry. When, in 1920, the Eighteenth Amendment came into force, thirty-three states already had the voluntary Prohibition laws—the unexpected reaction was a marked increase in the production of illicit liquor: when the fruit was forbidden it bore an ever greater attraction. Early figures certainly showed a decrease in the number of incidents of drunkenness punished by the courts, but now drinking was carried on in greater secrecy and probably to greater excess. In stills hidden in the back-woods and in the mountains, raw alcohol was produced under conditions which were scarcely conducive to the production of pure spirit. The "bootlegger" —so named from the belief that he carried a flask of his wares in his boot—made substantial profits from his illegal produce and went to more pains to avoid detection and capture than he did over the preparation of his liquor.

197. There's the whisky on my back and the sheriff on my track,
I'm going to make it to the woods if I can.

REFRAIN
If you can, if you can, you better make it to the woods if you can,
If you want to have to leave home, you just mess with a bottle of corn,
You got to make it to the woods if you can.

You may think they're doing you wrong, but they'll take you to the county farm,
You better make it to the woods if you can,

When you go out for a load, sheriff will stop you on the road,
You'll have to make it to the woods if you can.

It's a real surprising thing, just to hear those .44's ring,
You'd better make it to the woods if you can.

Crudely distilled and prepared under unhygienic conditions in bath-tubs and zinc bowls, the liquor was often extremely dangerous. Raw wood alcohol with sufficient cheap sherry added to hide its true nature would be sold as whisky, and liquor purporting to be Bourbon or gin has been made from any vegetable matter that will rot and ferment. Plugs of tobacco, shots of methylated spirits have been added indiscriminately and the alcohol withdrawn from bottles of Sterno used as a foundation for crude drinks. "Rot-Gut" whisky, gin and other drinks prepared in these ways have colourful names that adequately sum up their properties and their "kick": "White Mule," "Mammy," "White Lightning," "Splo," "Alki," "Red Horse." Many deaths have been caused by "moonshine" liquor of this type and the police made and continue to make vigorous attempts to check the production. Some states made a compromise in permitting the consumption of beer but not of hard liquor, but the production of moonshine could only be checked by rigorous offensives on the part of the Law.

198. I have made every beer tavern, I done stopped at every
       liquor store, (*twice*)
    So I tried the alley and stopped by the bootlegger's
       door.

    The bootlegger told me, "Stop! These G-Men have been
       around, (*twice*)
    And broke up all the moonshine and poured the mash
       out on the ground."

    So I'll get plenty women, see, if my pal follows me
       around, (*twice*)
    So we'll take it soft and easy, get it a little farther down.

    We've got to run a new racket, people, we've gotta find
       a better rule,
    An' if we can't get decent whisky, we will take a drink
       of mule.

During the twenties, when Prohibition was at its height, vast fortunes were made by gangs of criminals who profited from the nation's aggravated thirst by supplying immense quantities of bootleg liquor. Gangster Al Capone was netting a hundred million dollars a year—of which thirty per cent was spent on graft. The criminal fleets of Spike O'Donnell and Johnny Torrio, Big Jim Colosimo and Al Capone floated upon spiritous seas. Between them the gang wars raged for the control of the liquor trade. Even the biggest of the Negro gangsters were very small craft among them, though the Negro population consumed a considerable proportion of the liquor. The depredations of the Chicago crime machine eventually came to an end with the Depression, when money became scarce, and with the repeal of the Eighteenth Amendment. An effective reduction to the extent of bootlegging if not of drinking habits occurred with the abolition of Prohibition in many states, for the re-introduction of hard liquor at competitive prices made it an uneconomic proposition, with the liquor companies giving maximum support to the police in their drive against the illegal manufacturers.

199. Bootleggin', bootleggin', bootleggin' ain't no good no more, (*twice*)
    Bootleg whisky twenty-five cents and you can get good whisky for twenty-four.

    I'm a real good bootlegger but I done fell poor, (*twice*)
    Since good whisky been in, bootleggin' ain't no good no more.

    Now I been bootleggin', bootleggin' six years or more, (*twice*)
    But now I'm a real good bootlegger, a good bootlegger that done got poor.

    (*Spoken*) Lord, I gotta get me another racket when I do my time.

    I done lost my corn and I ain't got a dime, (*twice*)
    I'm just a good bootlegger, that's gotta go and do his time.

Liquor laws vary from state to state; restricted hours of consumption, limitations on the nature of the drinks dispensed, and discriminatory practices apply in some states, whereas others permit the free sale of alcohol but may exert heavy penalties for drunkenness. In most Negro communities legal or illicit gin-mills, barrelhouses and beer taverns continue to operate: in tent and shanty saloons for serving the lumber-camps of Tennessee and Arkansas or the turpentine-camps of Florida, maintained by the very companies that employ the men who spend their money in them; in the all-Negro townships of Mount Bayou, Renova and Wyandotte; on Davis Street in Mobile, Alabama, or Farish Street in Jackson, Mississippi, and in a multitude of Catfish Rows and Blackbird Hollows from the Gulf Coast to the Great Lakes. They afford temporary escape but they create problems rather than diminish them. The men and women who habitually frequent the dives are quick to shed their responsibilities and the rough saloons where sweating, lurching, quick-tempered men from the "jobs" jostle to reach the bar make their contributions to family disintegration and are a breeding ground for crime.

200. When the sun was shining I did not stay,
    I went to the beer tavern, I throwed all my money away.

    I went to the beer tavern, ma baby tol' me not to go,
    Come back home, ma clo's was thrown outdoors.

    I took a gal to the beer tavern, things was lookin' hot,
    But ma ole lady took her pocket knife and cut out ma
      baby's heart.

It is the beer tavern which provides an opportunity for social contacts and a measure of self-made entertainment. In the South particularly, one of the principal sources of discontent and crime is the lack of entertainment or profitable means of occupying the long periods of leisure. At these times, when the burden of the hours hangs heavy, the beer tavern becomes a natural meeting place where the young men laugh and abuse each other and the old men who have lived beyond their age of usefulness can reminisce and talk and drink.

201. Grandpapa got drunk this mornin' and it made grandma mad, (*twice*)
    'Cause he done lost all the money, Lord, that he ever
      had.

    Now there's no use to worry, there's no use to grieve and
      moan, (*twice*)
    Now just go ahead and be happy, try to carry ma good
      works on.

    Now you too old to marry, and the law won't let you
      divorce your wife, (*twice*)
    Now you go ahead and try to be happy; grandma might
      take your life.

Now listen here grandpapa, grandma said, "Sit down and
  be yourself!" (*twice*)
For that day that she quit you, you can't get nobody else.

For the disappointed and the frustrated liquor can bring
temporary oblivion. If Splo and White Mule, bootleg and pro-
prietary brands of whisky and gin prove too expensive, they
turn to Sneaky Pete and the other cheap wines whose names
suggest their insidious attacks on the reason. Negroes are
rarely suicidal; the suicide rate amongst coloured people is
far below that of Whites, but the percentage of Negroes convicted of liquor offences is some eight times that of Whites
pro rata, and accounts for nearly half of the total number of
arrests of this nature. These include violation of the various
liquor laws applying in the different states, but a large proportion are convictions for drunkenness, brought about by
deliberate consumption in the attempt to obscure the memory
of a failure or a tragic event.

202. Heard somebody knocking, wondered who it could be,
  (*twice*)
Nobody but the mail man bringing me misery.

He gave me a letter, here's what the letter said, (*twice*)
Come home at once, your baby's almost dead.

Say, I went to the river, got drunk as I could be, (*twice*)
To forget my baby and all my misery.

Say, I liquored up there, but it done the trick, (*twice*)
Make me forget the blues and my do–de–lee–do.

Amongst women the proportion of drunkenness is relatively
low in the Southern rural communities, greater in the cities,
particularly in the North. In the South the Church exerts its
influence upon the women members who form the bulk of
the congregation, but the disrupting effects of the migratory
move to the North with the violent tearing of family roots,
the hopes of a newer and better environment and eventual
disillusion have broken the spirit of many a woman who no
longer has the Church on which to lean for condolence and
comfort. Insanitary living conditions where one broken toilet

serves a dozen families, and a number of women have to share the same meagre cooking facilities, the horrors of the hot bed apartment and the fruitless search for a better home cause her to lose her self-respect and her pride in her appearance and, in a sudden reversal of her past behaviour, to develop insensate yearning for the severance from her surroundings that liquor addiction brings. When the strain is no less great for man or woman she is fortunate if she receives sympathy and understanding for her condition.

203. I don't want to discourage you, I don't want to give
     you a bad name, (*twice*)
     The way you are breaking my heart, it's a doggone
     shame.

     You start to drinking at 29th Street, drink on down to
     the 1st, (*twice*)
     You finish up a dollar trying to satisfy your thirst.

     You won't go to the hairdresser, mama, you can't keep
     clean no more, (*twice*)
     You ain't cooked a decent meal since you been in
     Chicago.

     I don't want to leave you, wants to give you one more
     break, (*twice*)
     Just to see, kind mama, what kind of woman you will
     make.

She is more likely to get a brusque reception and a timely reminder that her habits are bringing her relationship with her partner to a rapid conclusion.

204. She comes home this mornin' with her stockings rolled
     down,
     Hair all nappy, and her face full of frowns.

     REFRAIN
     You been drunk, yes babe, you been drunk,
     You been drunk, mama, I believe you been drinking gin.

     I opened the door, you were lying in the hall,
     Your breath smelled like you been drinkin' nach'l
     alcohol.

(*Spoken*) I don't want no woman that stays out all
night, you know when you get drunk, baby, and stays
out all night, you know you don't do things that's
right·so I know you been drunk! Stay sober if you
want to get along with me!

Only one thing that makes me mad,
Breath smells like something the buzzards had.

I come home this mornin' 'bout half past ten,
You'll be hospital bound, won't you say where you've
been.

She woke up this mornin' with a bottle in her hand,
Say, "Look here, daddy, turn on the electric fan,

'Cause I'm drunk, yes, babe, 'cause I'm drunk,
I'm drunk baby, I been out all night drinkin' gin."

Habitual consumption of low-grade or bootleg liquor has a
poisonous effect and rapidly causes addiction to alcohol with
ultimately fatal results. The addict who "swills the lush" soon
becomes known as a liquorhead, a wine-o, a whisky-headed
man or woman. There are numerous terms, for amongst the
poor there are many persons so addicted, for whom life can
hold few prospects. They drink to deaden the pressure of their
thoughts, and weak-willed though resorting to such a means
may be, it seems to the man or woman who attempts to break
the habit that he is rejected, unwanted and ill-fortuned. With
minds less alert and faculties dulled, their resistance is immeasurably weakened. Clara Morris declaims the excuses and
underlines the acute misery of a whisky-headed woman.

205. I drank so much whisky I staggered in my sleep, (*twice*)
Soon every morning, I'm staggering down the street.

I cain't get no whisky—dear me, I go home and whine,
(*twice*)
The way I keep from worryin' I stay drunk all the time.

When I ain't got no liquor, look like everything I do go
wrong, (*twice*)

That's when I get evil, me and the devil cain't get along.

It was so-bad whisky, made me lose my best boy friend,
(*twice*)
But I can't help it, I will drink until the end.

Up to the present there have been few satisfactory methods
devised to bring about the cessation of this blight on the Negro
life. Addicts tend to resent the attempts on the part of the
Churches to break them of the habit and the work of associations inaugurated with the specific intention of steering them
back to normality, though laudable and frequently effective
where applied, is on too small a scale to cope with the extent
of the vice. Operating with every bit as much vigour and on
a far greater scale, are the manufacturers of the cheap gins,
wines, and alcoholic drinks purporting to whiskies, who ensure that the liquor is available and in large quantities. Every
year tens of millions of moonshine gallons are distilled and the
bulk of this illicit output goes to those in the lowest income
groups who can afford no better—amongst whom Negroes
form a disproportionately high percentage. Advice against the
dangers of consuming this crude alcohol is given to addicts
when possible, but many are too weak-willed or too stubborn
to relinquish the habit.

206. Lord, I won't have no more trouble, mama, and I
won't have no more worried ways, (*twice*)
Because I started to drinkin', Lord, and it's cuttin' off
my happy days.

Whisky, whisky, whisky, you used to ease my troubled
ways, (*twice*)
Lord, now you turned on me, Lord, you shortnin' down
my days.

Straight whisky, straight whisky, straight whisky,
mama's killin' me, (*twice*)
Lord, I don't know what I'm gonna do, mama, in a
lonely graveyard I will be.

Lord, the doctor tol' me to stop drinkin', Lord, I cain't
control my mind, (*twice*)

But the woman that I'm lovin' keeps me worried all the time.

Liquor is the resort of the unfortunate, the depressed, the discontented, the workless. The vice will not disappear until the social evils that are the fundamental causes of addiction have been removed. With a pathetic catalogue of humble vices, the Atlanta street beggar, Blind Willie McTell, explained why he had "got the blues." When the circumstances of his own life were examined the ultimate effects of his indulgences seemed of little importance.

207. I done walked these blocks till I gotta go buy me some shoes, (*twice*)
And that is why Mr. McTell has got the blues.

I got drunk last night, mama, and the night before, (*twice*)
An' if ma luck don't change, Mr. McTell won't get drunk no more.

Cigarettes is ma ruin, whisky is ma crave, (*twice*)
Some of these nice-lookin' women gonna carry me to my grave.

Less prevalent than might be supposed is addiction to drugs, though evidence of drug traffic is frequently to be found in coloured areas, and Negroes are often associated with it. White drug-peddling organizations prefer to have their headquarters in Negro districts where they can "lose" themselves more easily and where their traffic is less readily observed. But Negroes are employed in the traffic itself and a number of criminals make large incomes from it.

Few Negroes can afford to pay the sums demanded by the "dope" racketeers for shots of their drugs and narcotics, and the victims are more readily found amongst middle-class White youths and girls who are sufficiently impressionable. Easily influenced to partake of the drugs initially, they are able to meet the heavy demands for money when forced by their own suffering to continue to purchase them. Popular amongst Negro addicts is opium, and Negro "junkers"—so named from the Oriental origin of the drug—indulge in "kicking the gong around." Unable to afford the fresh opium, called "mud" in the trade, they purchase the yen shee which is the opium equivalent to the butt end of a cigarette: the cinder left when the opium pill has been burned. A teaspoonful broken up and mixed with water makes a pellet which the addict can chew. It causes festering sores, but it provides the desired relief. Drug-taking habits are difficult to break. Most despised of criminals, the dope peddlers know this and for a while supply the opium free, fully aware that once the habit has been formed they will reap dividends for a lifetime—the lifetime of the addict.

208. They call me, they call me a "junko" 'cause I'm loaded all the time,
　　I don't use no reefers, I'd be knocked out with that angel wine.
　　Six months, six months ain't no sento' and one year ain't no time,
　　They got boys in penitentiary doin' from nine to ninety-nine.
　　I was standin', I was standin' on the corner with ma reefers in ma hand,
　　Up steps the sergeant, took my reefers out ma hand.
　　"My brother, my brother used a needle, and my sister sniffed cocaine,
　　I don' use no junk, I'm the nicest boy you ever seen."

　　My mother, my mother she tol' me, an' my father tol' me too,
　　"That junk's a bad habit, why don't you leave it too?"

　　My sister she even tol' me, an' my grandma tol' me too,
　　"That usin' junk, pardner, was goin' be the death of you."

Only a small number of Negroes are "snowbirds" going "on a sleigh-ride" by sniffing cocaine. The effects of the drug are terrible, causing acute physical distortions and inducing at least temporary insanity. The commonest drug used by Negroes is marijuana, a form of hashish which can be cultivated under back-yard conditions and is consequently cheap. Known variously as "the mezzes," "muggles," "tea," or "weed," it is smoked in the form of cigarettes called "reefers" which are peddled in the streets, in clubs and dance halls. "Vipers"—as addicts of marijuana are called—can obtain brief spells of elation and dreamy forgetfulness without suffering markedly deleterious effects. The drug has the peculiar property of destroying a sense of the passage of time and a smoker may remain in a state of apparent consciousness whilst he experiences the illusion of limitless time. It is therefore favoured by improvising jazz musicians and features more prominently in their parlance and in the titles and content of their tunes than it does in the blues. Because of its cheapness many Negroes seeking "kicks" will "get high" through its use, but the pleasures are temporary and may leave the addict more depressed than hitherto.

209. When my head starts achin', I grab my hat and go,
      'Cos cocaine and reefers, can't reach my case no more.

   REFRAIN
   I gotta find my baby, I declare I wouldn't lie,
   I ain't had no real good loving, since that girl said
      good-bye.

When he dances away the hours at the juke the Negro is seeking an entertainment that does not bring with it reminders of Jim Crow discrimination; when he spends long periods laughing and "lie-telling" at the barrelhouse he is hiding from himself his uselessness and inactivity in the endless days of the "lay-off"; when he frequents the Good-Time Flats he forgets for a while the realities of the congested ghettoes of the city; when he goes to the Rent Party he aids a member of his race whose plight is similar to his own and who will soon be called upon to perform the same service. He gambles in the hope that he may augment his meagre income; he drinks or falls a victim to the dope habit in order to build an artificial screen between himself and his environment. But none of these measures solves any fundamental problems. They do not bring an end to segregation nor occupy his time to the profit of his mind or his pocket. They do not relieve the internal pressure of the Black Belts nor minimize the exploitations of unscrupulous landowners. Ultimately he realizes that as solutions to his problems they are of little value to him.

210. I used to live in New Orleans, it's been a good many
     years ago, (*twice*)
   But since I been up North I been sleepin' on the bar-
     room floor.

   I been on relief in Chicago and soup-lines in Kokomo,
     (*twice*)
   But I'm going right back down South where I won't be
     driven from door to door.

   I ain't gonna shoot no more dice, I ain't gonna play no
     more Georgia Skin, (*twice*)
   There's so many ways to lose and only one way to win.

   All I want is some overalls and a grip that fits just right,
     (*twice*)
   My baby can cook me cornbread and cabbage, and I'm
     New Orleans bound to-night.

Chapter 7

Evil and Mean and Funny

SOCIAL EVILS IN DEPRESSED areas are the indirect result of numerous environment deficiencies: insufficient work, low rates of pay, long periods of inactivity, lack of opportunities for advancement, lack of forms of entertainment, inadequate living conditions and overcrowding. In Negro districts the external pressure of racial discrimination and the internal pressures of class and social group aggravate the situation. As the Negro population ratios in the South and North have altered and as the urban areas have grown, so these social problems have increased in the towns and cities. Better chances of obtaining rewarding work have attracted Negroes to the cities, but their migration has brought its own problems. The coloured people who already live in the cities resent the arrival of the newcomers and are openly hostile to them. When a man arrives from the country he finds few welcoming hands extended to him, and more competition than he had imagined:

211. And Dallas is hard, I don't care how long you wait, (*twice*)
     There will be somebody covering on your pay-day.

     Well, don't never make Dallas your home, (*twice*)
     When you look for your friends they will be gone.

In the height of the Negro flood-tide to the Southern cities and to the North, the housing situation arising from the influx became acute, and has become even more extreme as the years have passed. The White population resisted with determination, and often with arms and explosives, any inroads into their districts made by coloured people. Negro areas did not grow in a rate commensurate with the increases in population, and frequently did not expand at all. They only became more congested. White fears at the rapid increase in the coloured population of the cities ignited terrible race riots that flared up in sudden bursts of violence. Many Negroes were massacred in July 1917 when such a riot occurred in East St. Louis, but although scores of Negroes were arrested there was not a single arrest of a White rioter. Two years later a similar riot occurred in Chicago.

212. East Chicago is my native home, (*twice*)
Come to Chicago, people, and it won't be long.

Mama, in Chicago I had my good rags on, (*twice*)
Now in this town, now my suit's in pawn.

East Chicago is on fire, East St. Louis is burnin' down. . . .

In Washington the same year a Negro was brutally manhandled during a race riot in the very shadow of the White House without so much as a whisper of protest being raised. Though these districts, and others that had suffered similarly, eventually settled into uneasy silence, the strain between the incoming Negroes and those already resident continued to increase. As the numbers grew in Negro districts which could only expand into the poorest White areas where the property had long been condemned, deplorable slums developed.

Chicago's Negro population in 1900 was a little more than thirty thousand. By 1925 this figure was quadrupled, and the numbers have steadily increased between the wars with the result that some four hundred thousand Negroes now live there; only a score of cities in the United States have a higher total population. The residential area did not expand in proportion and more and more Negroes were crammed into the congested South Side. Restrictive covenants as to race still control the tenancy of three-quarters of Chicago's residential areas. New York had its own particular problems. The area known as Harlem formerly housed some eighty thousand persons but by 1927 this population had increased by a further two hundred thousand—most of them Negroes. The coloured population has more than doubled since. Landlords made fortunes by purchasing old tenement buildings and letting them at exorbitant rents to Negro tenants, though they were bitterly fought by such organizations as the Hudson Realty Company which bought the property and evicted the coloured tenants. Most remarkable was the instance of Detroit where eight thousand Negroes lived in 1915. In a decade the coloured population had multiplied more than ten times. Most of the Negroes had come from the South hoping to escape the housing conditions that they had suffered there. In Mississippi and parts of Georgia eighty-five per cent of Negro families had homes without toilets or privies, and similar conditions prevailed in Texas and Louisiana. Those who had worked on the "jobs" and had lived in company-owned towns had lived often under terrible conditions. Of 423 towns comprising approximately fifty thousand dwellings examined at this time, nearly forty per cent had no bath, toilet, running water, gas or electricty. Small wonder that they left these areas for the promised luxuries of Harlem, Chicago and other Northern cities.

Slums that were long reputed to be the worst in the world, worse even than those in Naples, were to be found in the Negro quarter of Philadelphia, the "City of Brotherly Love." The block on Lenox and 143rd is unique and the congestion is without parallel; and still the numbers have increased so that to-day there are six hundred thousand Negroes in New York as a whole. Where did the people live in a district which had multiplied its population six times in a score of years? Ten thousand of them could be found in basements and converted cellars with virtually no light or ventilation. They divided and subdivided their rooms and partitioned them yet again, whilst they paid as much as twenty-five dollars for the use of a single room. Two dozen or more families might share a single toilet on Chicago's South Side and six families live in an apartment built for the use of one. Some there were in the South who distrusted with good reason the invitations of the enlistment agents and who preferred to stay in their home towns rather than risk the conditions that, it was rumoured, existed in the North. New Orleans, for example, was a superficially glamorous French town whose beguiling architecture, wide-open disregard for the law, and colourful reputation closed the eyes of many to the squalor that existed "back of town."

213. Have you ever been down South in dear old New
    Orleans? (*twice*)
    It's an antique town—got things there that you never
    seen.

    Canal Street's of diamonds, St. Charles Street's made
    of gold (*twice*)
    But when you go "back of town" bound to see nothin'
    but old Creoles.

To go "back of town" in New Orleans led one eventually into the American District where, as a result of the rigid caste system of colour, the darker "American" Negroes lived in their tumble-down, tar-paper-roofed shacks. Roads so deep in mud as to be unnegotiable by a wheeled vehicle alone served them and the entire population of a street relied upon a single pump for their disease-infested water. Yet there were some Negroes who were still prepared to endure these conditions rather than face those that they had heard obtained elsewhere. Genevieve Davis amongst them:

214. New York's a pretty city and the lights do shine so
    bright, (*twice*)
    But I'd rather be in New Orleans walkin' by candle-
    light.

    "The streets here are money"—that's what I'm told. . . .
    (*twice*)
    Well, when I'm with the man I love I think they're
    paved with gold.

    Did you ever dream lucky, wake up cold-in-hand?
    (*twice*)
    And you didn't have a dollar to pay your house-rent
    man.

Louis Dumaine and the members of his band who accompanied her remained in New Orleans but other jazz musicians joined the migrating millions to spread their music in the North. Theirs was a move which was numerically small though far-reaching in effect. The emphasis that is placed upon the closing of the Storyville red-light district, and the evacuation of the musicians, has tended to give an unbalanced impression of the total move at that time. Similarly, their arrival in Chicago and points East brought a new and exciting music, and for many of them considerable lucrative employment which was not shared by all their fellows. Later, when the Depression set in, many were to live and die in miserable circumstances, but their interest as personalities and as creative musicians has drawn attention from the plight common to so many of their race. Even the Rent Parties have been chronicled more as colourful devices for overcoming a financial crisis, which had the fortunate effect of perpetuating the boogie woogie piano style, than as manifestations of the calamitous conditions of living.

Through the thirties the congestion in the Black Belts was aggravated, and the occasional housing schemes, though very laudable, were on too small a scale to alleviate the acute distress to any marked degree. For the working-class Negroes who formed the majority of their population, living in the Bronzevilles was squalid, insanitary and corrupting, but any attempts to move or to find better accommodation were met with open and frequently active hostility not only from the White populace, but also from any Negroes who had already been living there.

215. Me and my wife run all over town,
Everywhere we'd go people would run us down.

REFRAIN
Lawd, in the bourgeois town, ooh the bourgeois town,
I got the bourgeois blues, gonna spread the news aroun'.

Me and Marthy we was standin' upstairs,
Heard a White man say, "I don't want no niggers up there."

Me and my wife we went all over town,
Everywhere we go the coloured people turn us down.

White folks in Washington, they know how—
Chuck a coloured man a nickel just to see him bow.

Tell all the coloured folks t' listen to me,
Don't try to buy no home in Washington D.C.

Those who had a home, though it might only be a one-roomed "kitchenette" apartment or even the corner of an apartment partitioned with a sagging curtain, held on grimly to their quarters and paid the avaricious landlords—of whom in Chicago some eighty-five per cent are White. Those who sleep over the street gratings envy even the tenant of the "hot-bed" apartment for his place to rest. The "hot-bed" is an apartment which is rented to three separate groups of tenants each of whom use the flat for eight hours of the day or night. When their period of tenancy is up for their part of the day they relinquish the bed and the gas ring to the next tenant who climbs on to the still warm mattress and tries to make the best of his rent. Meanwhile the streets team with the homeless, the rejected and the evicted, and the lines of cars give a false air of prosperity to the district. For many Negroes their car constitutes their sitting-room, even their bedroom. One can be purchased for a sum equal to a few months' rent, but many are too poor to afford even this means of providing a "home." In the flats the Negro who has difficulty in meeting the rent fears the notice telling him he has to quit: there is another Negro waiting on the doorstep.

216. It's a sign on the building, yes I mean, you hear me
       sing,
     There's a sign on the building, we all got to move right
       away,
     I ain't got no money, no rent that I can pay.

     It soon will be cold, you hear me sing, yes I mean,
     It soon will be cold, I ain't got no place to go,
     I'm going back South, where the chilly winds don't
       blow.

Such overcrowded conditions of living where men and women, boys and girls of all ages are forced to spend their days and nights with little or no privacy have given rise to the gravest moral turpitude. Absconding fathers, husbands and family partners, low wages, and high rents, the depredations of ruthless elements in the communities, have together broken down moral standards. Corruption is rife, corruption that is hard to resist.

217. Day is comin', days go, but my work is never done,
(*twice*)
I have to get up every morning with the rising sun.

That road is narrow and crooked, leads to you don't know where, (*twice*)
It's hard for an honest girl to make her way up there.

All these neat and pretty men, please take 'em away,
(*twice*)
All they want to do, lead some poor girl astray.

Some are like jelly-beans, so cute and sweet, (*twice*)
I carry carbolic acid for every one of them I meet. . . .

In Negro segregated areas it is often impossible to find a residential street that does not contain a brothel, and does not have its parade of street-walkers both night and day. To bring up a Negro child without immediate contact with prostitution is therefore difficult. There is sympathy for the prostitutes, for frequently they are girls who have been forced to resort to the only method left to them to obtain a living, but the Negro family strives desperately to emulate the respectability of the White middle-class and their presence can be an embarrassment to the professional Negro who resides in the same district. White land and property owners find that renting buildings for purposes of prostitution is lucrative and does not affect them personally. Recruits are drawn from the many young girls who have found themselves homeless and workless in the city, and from those who have come straight from the country and are attracted by the glamour and bright lights of urban life, beguiled by the smart clothes and smooth manners of the town-dwelling men. Such a girl is flattered by the attentions she receives and looks back with scorn on the simple manners of the country boys.

218. Yeah, a country gal, man, have wrecked my life to-day,
       (*twice*)
       For I didn't stint myself, my poor girl she throwed it
       away.

       You can buy a country gal in my home, man, she
           wanna sleep on a spring mattress every day, (*twice*)
       When the poor thing ain't used to nothin', people, but
           sleepin' on cotton and hay.

       Ooooh, a country gal think she smart when she lovin'
           every man in town, (*twice*)
       When the poor thing ain't doin' nothin', people, but
           tearin' her reputation down.

One of the results of the all-pervading depression and the meagre opportunities for satisfying work with good opportunities of promotion and responsibility has been a deterioration in the attitude of many Negro men to legitimate employment. They feel that they are being duped and exploited and in many urban districts the man who obtains a good living without working, who relies upon gambling or a "racket" for his income, is admired, envied, even esteemed. The pimps—or "P.I.s"—with their pointed, patent leather, two-toned shoes, their "sharp" clothes and diamond pins have solved the problem of obtaining money without labour; they live by their wits and their power over women; they show their peculiar strength over other men's weakness, and so they are grudgingly or openly admired. Overcoming any initial resistance with "sweet talk," they ply the girls with brightly coloured clothes and flashy jewellery, and afford them protection from the attentions of undesirable characters and other procurers, their razors concealed in the lining of their lapels. This is living on "easy street," without dirtying one's hands with manual work. It is the ambition of many a Negro to find a woman who will support him by prostitution or by more legitimate work, and the curious society that arose in the twenties in which many Negro women who worked as housemaids, domestic servants, yard girls and kitchen mechanics had better chances of retaining their employment than had their menfolk, caused many of them to take a pride in supporting a man. They were even prepared to share him with other women for the protection that he afforded them and the love that he could give.

There are, of course, just as many Negroes who bitterly resent the "easy lifers" that rely on women for their support. Seeing beyond the glamour and the cheap attractions they can recognize the immorality of such a way of life. But at the same time, many who work long hours at hard and ill-paid labour feel keenly the apparent injustice in so poor a reward for trying to earn an honest living, whilst others exist in comfort and ease from so base a means.

219. What makes the rooster crow every day before day,
　　　　(*twice*)
　　　To let the pimps know that the workin' man is on his way?

　　　We're up before sunrise slavin' sixteen hours a day,
　　　　(*twice*)
　　　We pay a house-rent and grocery bill and the pimps get all the rest of our pay.

But the pimps remain untroubled for they are primarily concerned in obtaining and vetting the clients that their women serve, protecting and if necessary fighting on behalf of their girls as the occasion arises, seeing that they are not double-crossed and keeping the police quiet. Attempts to keep the soliciting of prostitutes in check have been perfunctory and the girl "on the turf" who is accused of stealing when entertaining a man, or who has been brought in on a similar charge, is given a "shakedown"—in other words she is required to pay a sum to the police officer for protection and is then free to ply her trade. Her "P.I." meets the sum and goes her bond if necessary.

220. I was walking down Morgan, just on Maxwell Street,
　　　　(*twice*)
　　　I asked the desk sergeant what police thought my gal ain't awfully sweet?

I stood an' talk to the desk sergeant, "Tell me where
can she be,
Hey, hey, where can she be?"
'Cause I knew my mama got arrested on Maxwell Street.

Lawd, I'm talkin' bout the wagon, talkin' bout the police
court too, (*twice*)
The Maxwell Street was crowded on Sunday, an' it's
hardly fair too.

There's Maxwell Street Market, Loudwater Street Market too, (*twice*)
If you ain't got the money, the women got nothing for
you to do.

In the Negro sectors of every large town are the infamous
tenderloin districts—some of which having been romantically
perpetuated in the public memory, in the titles and themes of
jazz and popular song; Basin Street and Rampart Street in
New Orleans with the splendid mansions which excluded Negro clients in the one and the pathetic hole-in-the-wall cribs
of the other; Nashville's Black Bottom and Fourth Avenue.
In the language of its underworld Cecil Gant sings:

221. Have you ever been to Nashville, down on Fourth Avenue? (*twice*)
They got something new there, they call it owl stew.

Well I've been to Chicago, points East, North and West,
(*twice*)
But the stew in Nashville, it really is the best.

It's not so very high, and the price is very low, (*twice*)
If you get it once, you gonna want some more.

Memphis has its colourful and corrupt Beale Street, and its
Gayoso too, less widely known but no less vicious; Chicago
its Maxwell Street Market, Shreveport its Fannin' Street, Jackson its Farish Street, Detroit its Hastings Street and Dallas
its Elm Street.

222. Ah Billiken, these Ellum Street women don't mean you
    no good, (*twice*)
    When your back is turned they're with every man in the
    neighbourhood.

    These Ellum Street women, Billiken, do not mean you
    no good, (*twice*)
    If you wanta make a good woman, have to get on Has-
    kell Avenue.

Leaning from low-silled windows, lounging in doorways or
standing on street corners, dark-skinned girls, eye-lids coloured
with lipstick and gold teeth flashing, seduce the passer-by with
promises of their favours.

223. I come to you, sweet man, and I'm falling on my knees,
    I come to you, pretty papa, and I'm falling on my knees,
    Say if you ain't got nobody, come and take me please.

    'Cause I'm a mighty tight woman, a real tight woman,
    I'm a real jack of all trades,
    I can be your sweet woman, also be your slave,
    I can cook things so good till you swear that I won't
    have.

    I've got all the men cryin', I'm a broad that never feels
    blue,
    I hear everybody sing that I'm tight in everything I do,
    All I want is a good man to make him happy too.

    If you're a married man you have no business here,
    When you out with me, I might make your wife shed
    tears,
    'Cos I'm a mighty tight woman, there is nothin' I fear.

Many of the women who made their living from prostitution earned for themselves considerable reputations in their
own districts, and men fought for their favours and for the
rights to be their pimps. Half a century after they were active
many of the more notorious women who worked in the New
Orleans brothels—Mary Meathouse and Coke Eye Laura,

Mary Jack the Bear and Bird Leg Nora, or the strong-arm women who haunted Dearborn Street and Armour Avenue in "Levee" of Chicago—Lizzie Davenport, Florrie Moore and the twenty-five-cent "zooks" of Bed Bug Row are still remembered. They had a less distinguished clientele than Cora Pearl, Kate Cook and Mabel Grey of mid-century London but their favours and their vitriolic personalities have impressed themselves no less in a colourful but sordid history. The women who sought to keep their menfolk feared the boastful claims of the brazen "hustling gals."

224. Women cry in danger, but I ain't raisin' my hands,
   (*twice*)
   I got a way of lovin' they just can't understand.

   I can strut my boody, make my sweet pigmeat, (*twice*)
   'Cause I know my onions that's why I always beat.

   Well I love my coffee, crazy 'bout my china tea, (*twice*)
   But a sugar daddy is sweet enough for me.

   They call me over, they said that I'm red-hot, (*twice*)
   They said that I've got something the other gals ain't got.

boasted Nellie Florence from Atlanta, and as she sang the demoniacal laughter of Barbecue Bob—or Laughing Charlie? —could be heard in the background.

Next to the gambling rackets the commercialization of prostitution constitutes the most lucrative form of crime in the United States and is operated on a syndicated system that is nation-wide. Big-time racketeers control the brothels and see that the receipts are canalized into their own pockets. The girl receives relatively little, though her standard of living may be higher than if she were not so employed. Of her total earnings as much as half may go to the landlord, a percentage to the mobster who introduced her to the syndicate, protection money must be paid to mobsters, police and politcians, and her final income is passed to her pimp who protects and provides for her takings. The racketeers exploit the belief that the Negro is basically sensual and immoral and establish a large number of the brothels in Negro sectors where White males seeking a "good time" will gravitate. Proportionately the number of coloured prostitutes far exceeds that of White girls—more than a quarter of all women so engaged being Negro. In some districts the precentage is much higher and though statistics of arrests do not necessarily give an accurate impression, in New York some fifty-four per cent of all arrests of prostitutes are of coloured girls, a rate that is ten times that of White women in proportion to the population figures.

Social workers try to help the girls and advise the young men, but lonely, dissatisfied, unhappy men, husbands or unfaithful wives, boys wishing to appear manly in the eyes of their fellows, provide an endless clientele.

225. Well, the sun going down, moon begin to rise in blood, (*twice*)
    Well, now life ain't worth livin' if you ain't with the one you love.

    Well, the preacher's round the corner, trying to save your boy's soul, (*twice*)

    We steppin' round the corner tryin' to find some jelly roll.

    Well, I try to explain to you, baby, everything that was right, (*twice*)
    But when I knowed everything, you was going out and spending the night.

Inevitably the prevalence of prostitution in Negro districts causes the spread of virulent social diseases, and in particular syphilis and gonorrhœa. How tragically widespread were these diseases became apparent in 1940 when it was discovered that of the first hundred thousand men drafted into the armed services the number of Negro sufferers from syphilis was proportionately eight times that of the Whites, one in every four Negro draftees showing a positive reaction to the Wassermann tests applied to them (see page 296). Large numbers of these men had not contracted the disease through their licentiousness, but through the hereditary passage of the virus and contacts with the disease caused by the deplorable, insanitary conditions in which so many lived.

226. I wonder why fast life keeps on follerin' me, (*twice*)
Well, it seems like ole fast life ain't gonna let me be.

Fast life is killin' me, stiff-dead on my knees, (*twice*)
Fast life is a misery, that is awful hard to please.

It don't pay nobody to live this life so fast, (*twice*)
Just take it slow and easy as long as it will last.

More sinister perhaps than the prevalence of prostitution is the commercialization of male sexual aberrations. One of the most unsavoury aspects of the exploitation of sexual misplacement is the "freak show," unhappily common in Harlem, where crude exhibitions and perverted stage displays are presented. Similar, and peculiarly common in the twenties, were the Drag Parties or dances where males present dress in female clothes and assume female characteristics. Such functions are illegal in many states and so is open soliciting in the streets by homosexuals. For the homosexual the arrival of the police wagon, arrest and ultimate imprisonment is welcome, for sexual perversion is rife in American prisons where extreme overcrowding in highly unsuitable premises creates conditions conducive to immoral behaviour. Young offenders are expected to share cells with hardened "three-time losers" and vagrants; petty thieves and perverts are frequently forced into close association, producing highly undesirable results. Supervision is hindered in many instances by inadequate staffing and heavy, solid, cell doors, whilst minor prison officials, ill-paid and sometimes unprincipled, are apt to exploit the situation to their own gain. A situation far from uncommon in the North is rampant in the Southern county jails and on the prison farms. There the Negro prison society with its own crude and cruel codes of behaviour is divided sharply between the "wolves"—those who seduce and corrupt other prisoners —and the "gal-boys" or young prisoners who are forced to accept a female role. Such corruption is everywhere widespread and likely to prevail until the prison system is modernized and made humane. Advances have been made in certain prisons in the North and West which have enlightened governors with a sense of mission and a determination to institute penal reforms. Their work has proved worth while in every instance though sometimes they have been hindered by the ignorance of other, less progressive authorities and by the suspicions of the prisoners themselves. Humane treatment of sexual offenders has produced encouraging results and progress is being made in the extremely difficult task of correcting the anti-social tendencies of the seasoned criminals who exploit them.

227. I live on a young man to make my living the easy
     way, (*twice*)
   But since I have been locked up in jail, ooh well, well,
     I found out it did not pay.

   I laid in jail all night long with my closed eyes to the
     wall,
   I laid in jail all night with my closed eyes to the wall,
   Thinking that cute little way, ooh well, well, was the
     cause of it all.

   I had the easy-way blues from my head down to my
     feet, (*twice*)
   I had to send for Mister Bud Mellow, ooh, well, well
     to come and put my feet on the street.

   Do you know how I felt when the news come back?
     (*twice*)
   "Since you're not in town, ooh well, well, now he's out
     on the old race track."

   He put my feet on the street, but this is what he said:
     (*twice*)
   "You go get yourself a good girl, oh well, well, cut out
     that easy way."

Homosexuals who take the female part in perverted relationships often affect the mannerisms of women, take particular care of their manicure and may even attempt to use smuggled make-up. Their "husbands" lavish presents upon them to the best of their meagre resources, use feminine pronouns when referring to them, and show the same feelings of jealousy that they would display over women in normal relations. The jealousy that a man feels for his partner frequently leads to violence in the prisons, in the wire-fenced road camps, in the shack towns on the "jobs," and in the city warrens where the taut, strained atmosphere causes the disintegration of the nerves. Such conditions make these areas breeding grounds for crime. Driving a man to the point where his self-control suddenly snaps, the importance of a number of incidents of little significance in themselves becomes inflated in the total effect; tempers flare on the instant and an irrevocable crime is committed. Where White men will use fists and thus perpetuate no crime in the eyes of the law, a dispassionate examination of cases reveals that Negroes more frequently resort to the use of knives with the result that indictable offences are committed. Very often jealousy on the part of a man or woman is at the root of such impetuous crimes.

228. I've got a two-by-four, and it just fits my hand, (*twice*)
    I'm goin' ta stop all you women from runnin' around
    with my man.

    I don't want to hurt that man, just goin' to kill him
    dead, (*twice*)
    I'll knock him to his knees, go back to the man I once
    have had.

    When I leave home, your other woman is knockin' on
    my door, (*twice*)
    I'm going to stop so much talkin' and raise heck with
    my two-by-four.

Double-bladed, and the width of the hand, the "two-by-four" clasp knife is favoured by the prostitute who can conceal it in her kimono without difficulty; broken and jagged-edged, it becomes a "froe" and still has its lethal uses. Longer is the chib, keen-bladed and deadly in the hands of an irresponsible person, who can manipulate it with the upward thrust that makes disarmament far more difficult. It is the weapon of the "strong-arm woman" who seduces a man and when he is in her arms, robs him and cuts him "every way but loose." It is the weapon that killed blues singer Charlie Jordan on 9th Street, St. Louis.

229. When I get drunk I'm evil, I don't know what to do,
     (*twice*)
     Guess I'll get my good chib and get something good
     for you.

Less likely to cause death, the razor permanently scars a
victim and the razor-slashing attacks and fights have arisen
from the grimly vicious determination to leave a recognizable
signature of a man's revenge. With the handle removed, the
spur of the blade lies back along the hand and the blade
projects a fraction between the fingers: a couple of swift
slaps and the victim is unaware that he has been cut until
he feels the blood upon his face.

230. I got cut all to pieces, aah-aaah . . . about a man I love,
     (*twice*)
     I'm gonna get that a-woman, just as sho' as the sky's
     above.

     Now when my man left me, I was half-dead, lyin' in my
     do', (*twice*)
     I was sufferin' and a-groanin', "Oh, daddy, please don't
     go."

Tools of trade often make dangerous weapons: the cotton-
hook with which the roustabout man-handles the cotton bales,
the cleavers of the abattoir workers on "the killing floor"; the
knives of the cane-cutters. Amongst the railroad and telegraph
men, the street cleaners and builders, the ice-picks which are
used to break up the accumulations of freezing snow during
the hard Northern and mid-Western winters become tools of
murder, and the small size of some of these, coupled with
their excellent balance and penetrating bills, make them a
favoured weapon.

231. I tho't my woman had the blues, she looked so worried
     and sick, (*twice*)
     Only to find out in her bosom she's carrying an old ice-
     pick.

     But she wasn't sick—I could see trouble in her eyes,
     (*twice*)

She wanted to stick me with that ice-pick, Lord, and I
don't know why.

Half-a-pint in one hand, cigarette between her lips,
(*twice*)
Trying to get that ice-pick out with her finger tips.

Why don't you go to bed, woman, and put that old ice-
pick down? (*twice*)
From room to room squabbling, every night in your
gown.

Most victims of a razor-slashing attack survive; those who
have been attacked with an ice-pick seldom do, for the sharp
bill that has been designed to break rock-hard ice penetrates
the skull of the attacked person without difficulty. The blues
singer, Sonny Boy Williamson, died as the result of such an
attack, as he came home after singing at the "Flame Club"
in Chicago on a bitter evening late in 1947. His week's wages
were in his pocket and for this sum he lost his life at the hands
of a member of his race, a desperate street "mugger" lurking
in the dark shadows of a doorway. The mutilated body is
robbed and the "bloody carpet rags" in the harsh venacular of
the Negro underworld—is picked up by the all-night prowl
cars, whilst the "roundheels" have disappeared in the shadows
of the slums. "Muggings" were originally aimed at White men
who came into the Negro districts seeking coloured women, but
the desperate form of protest was soon directed at other Negroes in blind and futile anti-social acts. Sometimes such rob-
bers work with a girl as a decoy. Standing in a position from
whence they can see her every move as she goes up the street,
they wait until she has successfully solicited a man. As she
brings him back past the alley or side entrance to the building
where he is hiding, he springs upon the unsuspecting man and
"jumps" him, beating him senseless and swiftly robbing him.

232. I got a mind to ramble, I got a mind to rob and steal,
(*twice*)
I got a mind to hijack, people, you don't know how
I feel.

I can stand right here, look over on to the avenue,
(*twice*)
I can see everything my li'l ol' baby do.

With the attacker lies the advantage of surprise and the odds that he will succeed in his intentions are vastly in his favour. Felonious assaults of this nature are all too frequent in Negro urban districts of the lowest category. Persons who live within the districts are known and to some degree protected by the codes of behaviour that operate in the underworld; the girls who work regular beats are able to pass unmolested, for their pimps have made working arrangements and safeguard their interests. It is the girl who penetrates on another's beat and the racketeer who attempts to "muscle in" on another's territory who are immediately marked as prospective victims. But above all the attacks are made upon those who are alien to that part of the Black Belt, who are seeking amusement, illicit pleasure or the novelty and thrill of visiting a notorious area, or who are newly arrived from the country and unfamiliar with the ways of the city slums.

233. I'm a man from the gutter, women in your dive at night,
     (*twice*)
     I'm evil and mean and funny, so don't come back with
       that line of jive.

   I met a woman from the Delta, grabbed her and I held
     her,
   Squalled like a panther, still that didn't help her,
   She was in the clutches of a drunkard, a man from the
     gutter.

   She waggled and she twisted, boy, she was two-fisted,
   But I was working the jive that evening,
   I let nothing slip by.

   The woman I'm loving, got eyes just like a snail, (*twice*)
   But I'm a man from the gutter—he'll really have your
     way.

Underworld organization is complex and delicate; aspiring criminals do not "break in" easily. Crime is less organized in Negro sectors than elsewhere in the cities and violent incidents tend to be more spontaneous. Negro gangs do operate effectively in the gambling and drug rackets though some are answerable to larger criminal organizations that control the

underworld of a whole state. An especial problem is raised
by the Negro gangs led by youths in their very early 'teens.
In clothes, in manner, they emulate the big-time racketeers,
but the greater irresponsibility of youth, the desire to be
esteemed by their companions, make them more desperate in
their depredations. Ten times as many Negro children as
White in proportion to their numbers are slain in fights and
disputes between such gangs or individuals. The acute housing problem forces them on to the streets and the large numbers of broken homes throw many on their own resources.
They are joined by the thousands of homeless children, the
vagrants who have hopped the trains, slept in the jungles and
have become skilled in stealing, fighting and fending for themselves. For these tragic children there are all too few organizations providing aid, security and guidance in adjusting
themselves to play a constructive role in a society in which
they are at present only parasites. Instruction by way of example comes from the "ramblers," the criminals, whose mode
of life, whose authority and swift vengeance attract by their
glamour and their ruthlessness. To preserve his position as
the sole, undisputed leader, the gangster must be unrelenting,
merciless and coldly, unemotionally concerned with all that
happens in his district. Those who attempt to oppose him
must do so with methods even stronger and more violent, or
expect the inevitable, violent suppression.

234. I am gonna take you for an easy ride,
      Drop you off by the riverside.

      REFRAIN
      I've got the gangster's blues, I got the gangster's blues,
      I've got the gangster's blues, boys I am feelin' mean.

      I'm gonna bind your mouth so you can't talk,
      Tie your feet so you can't walk.

      You can start your screaming but must give in,
      I'm gonna tear you to pieces and put you back again.

During the Depression when men were workless in their
millions and the distress drove them to brutal, selfish acts the

crime rate rose alarmingly. At this time, some two-fifths of all homicide and assault offences in the United States were committed by Negroes—a figure unquestionably related to their more severely distressed circumstances. The squalid, rat-infested shacks that make up the Negro section of Pine Bluff, Arkansas, between the old river bed and the railroad tracks; the homes of the roustabouts and stevedores who live along Vicksburg's Catfish Row and its adjacent streets where twenty-three thousand Negroes are crammed together; the M. & O. Bottoms of Tuscaloosa lying in the lowland delta between the railroad and the Alabama River; the teeming ant's nest of Jackson, Mississippi, with its coloured population of nearly fifty thousand of whom almost half do menial unskilled labour—these are inevitable centres of violent crime. Rock Town and Bush Bottom in Nashville; Buckeye Quarters and Ram-Cat Alley in Greenwood—the very names are suggestive of the nature of these moral plague-spots. Hopeless congestion, malnutrition and disease, rotting timber walls and un-paved roads littered with decaying vegetable matter ultimately numb the senses, destroy values and dull initiative to stunned, unthinking stupor—or they provoke unreasoning anger. Blind fury turns the protesting mind and a sane, simple individual becomes violently anti-social, discriminating neither between colour nor class.

235. Want to set this world on fire, that is my mad desire,
I'm the devil in disguise, got murder in my eyes.

Now if I could see blood runnin' through the streets,
(*twice*)
Could see everybody lying dead right at my feet.

Give me gunpowder, give me dynamite, (*twice*)
Yes, I'm gonna wreck the city, gonna blow it up to-
night.

These were the conditions that made Memphis the "murder capital of America." In the 1870's the town was a veritable pest-hole where yellow fever was rife. White landowners deserted the town but the Negro menials and the poor Whites, short of food, without money and ignorant, were left behind. Of the mere twenty thousand persons who were left in the town some seventy per cent were Negroes and for some years until the cotton industry was reestablished the criminal element flourished. Its home was to remain in the Negro sector where every kind of vicious behaviour continued unchecked, in the "Underworld Block" from Hernando Street to Fourth Street. Its nerve centre still remains the celebrated—or infamous—Beale Street which extends for a mile from the De Soto Fish Dock on the Mississippi Waterfront. Here could, and still can be seen the gamblers and the gangsters, the pimps, the ponces and the prostitutes, the crippled and the corrupt. Cuttings and shootings amongst the roustabouts, loggers and fieldhands in town on a spree were a nightly occurrence in the early part of the century and the low premium on life caused others to take the law into their own hands in the Negro sector of a town, where the dictatorship of Boss Crump made little of official law enforcement. Sang a Memphis Negro, Furry Lewis:

236. I believe I'll buy me a graveyard of my own, (*twice*)
I'm gon' kill everybody that have done me wrong.

If you want to go to Nashville and ain't got no fare, (*twice*)
Cut your good gal's throat and the judge will send you there.

I'm goin' git my pistol, forty "round the ball," (*twice*)
I'm gon' shoot my woman just to see her fall.

I'd rather hear the screws on my coffin sound, (*twice*)
Than to hear my good gal says, "I'm jumpin' down."

Many other cities have Negro sectors with reputations almost as unsavoury and it is undeniable that these are the result of adverse environmental conditions. Second only to Memphis is Atlanta where the murders exceeded an average of a hundred a year in the 1940's. That Harlem and Chicago's South Side have similarly alarming figures will scarcely cause surprise. A survey made in 1939 showed that there were eighty-seven thousand more Negroes in Chicago's Bronzeville than the lowest acceptable living standards would permit. During the war the population increased by a further sixty thousand and the influx has continued during the past dozen years. But the South Side, though bulging at the seams, has not increased in area, and the crime rate shows little sign of decreasing.

Of the tens of thousands of slum-shocked persons living under these conditions, many are almost irrevocably lost to society: men and women whose consciences have been obliterated and whose moral codes have been abandoned. They are feared by those who live with them and reveal in their aggressiveness to outsiders a cold, open hostility even to those who sympathize with them.

237. You' a cold-blooded murder' an' I can't look in your
        face, (*twice*)
    Now you got blood in your eyes, you got low-down
        dirty ways.

    Now you got me in between the Devil and the deep,
        blue sea, (*twice*)
    When I try to love you I keep trembling in my knees.

    You's a cold-blooded murder' an' I'm still in love with
        you, (*twice*)
    We cain't get together, no way I try to do.

Some of the homicides committed by Negroes are cold, brutal slayings by "bad niggers" or "mean niggers" as the Negroes, using a double-edged form of abuse, themselves call them. But the majority of murders are probably *crimes passionels* committed in fits of jealousy over the infidelity of partners. Indiscretions made possible by the lack of privacy in the towns, the rivalry for the affections of notorious women, and the esteem that goes with having won and held them, make such affrays all too frequent, and the frontier spirit of admiration for the man who settles his dispute with finality leads to swift retribution. Passions may be so violently disturbed as to hinder clear thinking:

238. I looked out of my window, just 'bout the break of day,
        (*twice*)
    Just in time to see another man taking my best gal away.

> An' I looked for my pistol but I found I had the safeter on, (*twice*)
> But before I could shoot it, that man had my best gal and gone.

But the cuckolded man is unlikely to let the incident happen twice He waylays his rival with his "hard-shootin' pistol"—a "forty five" or that favourite amongst Negroes, the more accurate and equally deadly weapon in close quarters, the "thirty-two–twenty, built on a forty-five frame." Not by nature a killer, as mild perhaps in ordinary affairs as his hard life permits, he is not to be compromised in an affair of honour and prestige, as Big Maceo Merriwether explained to his friend, Tampa Red:

239. I walked all night long with my thirty-two–twenty in my hand, (*twice*)
Looking for my woman, well, I found her with another man.

When I found that woman they was walkin' hand-in-hand, (*twice*)
Well, she didn't surprise me when I found her with another man.

She started screamin' "Murder!" an' I never raised my hand, (*twice*)
Tampa, she knew I had them covered 'cause I had the pistol right there in my hand.

I ain't no bully an' I don't go for the baddest man in town, (*twice*)
When I catch a man with my woman I usually tear his playhouse down.

Statistics drawn from Uniform Crime reports of the U.S. Department of Justice reveal that Negroes account for a quarter of the total number of convictions for prostitution, some forty-four per cent of the convictions for assault, more than thirty per cent of those for robbery, and forty per cent of the convictions for homicide. These are alarming figures which must give at least an approximate indication of the proportionate crime rates in these categories. They do not include the large numbers of gang crimes which remain unpunished through fear of further consequences or the hope that the gangs will eliminate each other by their own means. Such figures do not account for the many crimes against Negroes committed by White persons which are never brought to court or which are deliberately hushed up: the numerous acquittals "for lack of evidence" or on the grounds of "self-protection" which have allowed trigger-happy armed bus drivers, and veritable lynching parties operating under a different guise to go free. Nevertheless, between 1911 and 1935 the rate of homicides amongst Negroes was seven times that of White persons between the ages of twenty-five and thirty-four, and ten times that of Whites amongst adolescents. Substantially the same relative proportions have continued since, causing a terrible and fearsome problem which must be faced.

In other fields the Negro is held to be almost exclusively responsible for the violation of segregation laws, according to the numbers of arrests made, though in violently prejudiced areas a White person who shows sympathy to Negroes may be punished outside the law. Negroes are precluded from committing the crimes that go with the accumulation of wealth: tax evasion, financial exploitation of the public, embezzlement, fraud, counterfeiting, and others that require higher social and professional position for their success. The crimes for which they are punished are less pre-considered and, to the public, more sensational.

It is incontestable that the crimes of Negroes are the immediate results of their environment. This has been well demonstrated in Chicago where fifteen hundred families from the worst slums of the South Side were rehoused in a new, clean and spacious district where modern but economical apartments known as the Ida B. Wells Homes were constructed. Living in a healthy community where trees line the streets and children had room to play, the families became models of social behaviour: in five years only one family gave rise to complaint and even the minor crimes were virtually unknown. Only when the Negro achieves equal status with other members of the community; when the slums are cleared and decent homes fit for human beings to live in are built; when segregational laws and Jim Crow covenants are abolished; when true equality of educational facilities and opportunities for work are available; when, in fact, the Negro is permitted to play his part in American society without discrimination, will Negro crime diminish until it is no better perhaps but certainly no worse than that of the rest of the nation.

Chapter 8

Goin' to Take a Rap

FROM THE MOMENT of their capture and incarceration in the floating hell of the slavers' ships Negroes have known violence. Shackled in the slave coffles, laid head to toe in the 'tween decks of the vessels in their hundreds to suffocate or survive in the fetid heat and the stench of their own fæces; jettisoned when storms broke or ships of the line appeared; sold at the block, to the highest bidders, they suffered unspeakable privations. The history of slavery is a long and dismal one in which the succession of brandings and burnings, dismemberings and flayings is only brought into more stark relief by the all too infrequent contrast of occasional humanitarian treatment. In 1724 the Black Code laid down the punishments that could be meted to offending Negro slaves by their owners. Looking back to medieval times in their brutality, recalling the savagery and the cold-blooded nonchalance of the torturers in a panel by Gheerhardt David, or an oil painting by Peter Breughel of the treatment of the Flemish during the Spanish Domination, they included the slitting of noses, the severing of limbs and the hamstringing of legs for the most trivial of crimes. A third attempt at escape from slavery meant death— by breaking on the wheel. For a century and a half the Black Code persisted, to cease officially only with the Civil War.

No more hundred lash for me, no more, no more,
No more driver's lash for me,
Many thousand gone. . . .

sang the slaves freed from bondage. But the barbarism of the
Code was ingrained in the soul of the South and could not
cease with the stroke of the pen. Catholics and Negroes alike
were terrorized by the Ku Klux Klan whose incantations,
Kleagles, Grand Wizards, religious hypocrisy and declarations
of knightly behaviour did not—and do not—hide the underlying horror and brutality of a murder society; the hooded night-
shirts echoing the garb of the Inquisition hide individual
identities, but they have never concealed the shame of the
iniquitous masquerade. Ostensibly the floggings, lynchings
and castrations perpetuated by the Knights of the Klan were
punishments meted to murderers, rapists and other criminals.
But they were punishments outside the law, committed by
insensate White men who judged and condemned without
giving the accused a trial. That many of the Negroes who were
lynched were innocent of the crimes that they were supposed to
have committed is established beyond dispute; their guilt
would not justify the murder at the hands of a blood-lusting
lynching mob. The Klan was revived in 1915 by William Sim-
mons, a Methodist preacher, and numbered amongst its members police officials, state governors, a Supreme Court judge,
politicians and professional men as well as a cross-section of
the entire community, respectable and rabble. Four out of
every five Southern politicians during the twenties and thirties
had been members of the Klan and have added their money
to its eighty million dollars capital. Since 1880 over four
thousand men and women—three quarters of them Negroes
—have been burned to death in the kindling fires, have swung
as mutilated and violated corpses from cotton-wood limbs,
have been charred with blowtorches, torn to pieces with
corkscrews. The fingers of lynched Negroes were displayed
in butcher's shops and disgusting "mementoes" stood pickled
in the Klan museums. The tentacles of the Klan stretched to
every state and it is no source of wonder that although its
speeches were available on gramophone records, examples of
recorded blues about Klan activities and the lynching mobs
are not to be found. A singer could recall his experiences on
the Georgia chain gang when he had escaped to the North

and was safe from retribution; but he could not be sure that the Klan would not seek him out.

A seven-week filibuster in 1938 succeeded in ousting a proposed anti-lynching Bill and the several attempts at passing such a Bill through Congress since have all been quashed by Southern senators. Although the "protection of Southern womanhood" has frequently been the excuse for a lynching, less than a quarter have been punishments for rape or even the suspicion, genuine or faked, of the crime. Many have been for attempting to vote, for trying to defend wife or daughter, for defiant talk or for no reason whatever. White women have found incitement to lynching a convenient method of disposing of an unwanted lover and some have even claimed to have been violated by "looking." A Negro who wishes to leave the South under these circumstances would appear to have good reason; less understandable is the desire to return. But there are reasons of the heart. James "Boodle-It" Wiggins was a blues singer from Louisiana who went to Chicago in the twenties seeking work He was a man of prodigious build and strength as even his recorded voice suggests, and he obtained employment. In 1929 he wanted to return to the South and he sang:

240.   "Mister Conductor Man, I wanna talk with you,
        I wanna ride your train, from here to Bogalou'.
        I'm leavin' this mornin', I haven't got my fare,
        I want t' see if I can find my good girl there."

But when he reached Bogalousa he had forgotten the ways of the South and did not step off the pavement when a White woman approached him in a crowded street. She screamed that he was assaulting her and within the hour his body was swinging from a tree, hanged by the neck and with four bullets embedded in his flesh. Wiggins, however, was a man of astounding physique and when his friends secretly cut him down there was still a breath of life in his body. As soon as he was well enough he was carried to Baton Rouge and was still alive though permanently deformed when Big Bill Broonzy saw him recently. He did not record a blues about the incident. . . .

Lynchings and floggings have often been committed on the most slender grounds only for the proof to come too late that there has been no basis for the suspicions. But "suspicion" also constitutes grounds for legal arrest in most states: more than twenty-seven per cent of all arrests on grounds of suspicion have been against Negroes, and amongst Negro "crimes" these vague and unspecified reasons, account for more arrests than any other category. Inevitably, many flagrant injustices can be committed as a result of this, though it does afford a slight measure of preventative action. Lack of visible means of support, begging and vagrancy are all grounds for arrest in many states; many Negroes are punished for having carnal knowledge by spying—a charge open to the most serious abuse; in all but three states adultery is a criminal offence. Whereas the law is not always rigidly applied in these and other "offences" there are many opportunities for misapplication, whilst the variability of the states' laws underlines the anomalies. An unwanted man can easily be victimized by unscrupulous application of the law and grounds of "suspicion" can terminate the freedom of many an innocent person.

241. Got me accused of peepin'—I cain't even see a thing,
       Got me accused of beggin'—I can't even raise my hand.

REFRAIN
Bad luck, bad luck is killin' me,
I just can't stand no more of this third degree.

Got me accused of taxes, I don't have a lousy dime,
Got me accused of children an' nary one of them is
      mine.

Got me accused of murder, I never harmed a man,
Got me accused of forgery, I can't even write my name.

Out of slavery rose the convict lease system, whereby convicted prisoners were leased out to contractors to provide labour in the cotton fields, the sugar plantations or the coal mines. The system also provided a convenient method of adding to the state income by exploitation of the convicts. A man would be fined perhaps thirty dollars and ten dollars costs for a statutory offence making a total of forty dollars which he had to pay off with his own labour. The value of his labour would be assessed at fifty cents per day and he would thus be obliged to work for nearly three months to pay off his fine. The contractor would hire his labour at seventy cents per day and be obliged to provide food and "board." This was cheap enough but the standard of board provided can be imagined; provided the county received the money, it paid no attention to the welfare of its prisoners who were slaves to be disciplined and worked by the contractor at his will. In a period when humane treatment of prisoners and of Negroes was scarcely evident, through the protests against this legal slavery by genuine humanitarians and by labour unions, for somewhat less noble reasons, the convict lease system was outlawed by Congress in 1887. This did not deter the majority of the Southern states, who were anxious not to lose so useful a source of revenue and the ruling was flagrantly ignored. In Alabama the method was pursued with particular ruthlessness and prison officers were paid a fixed sum for making an arrest, one for writing the warrant, another for filing it and so on. It paid to keep the prisons full. Sang Barefoot Bill from Alabama:

232. Say, High Sheriff been here, got my girl and gone,
     (*twice*)
     Got here 'leven in the mornin', get her all alone.

     "Oh Mr. Nelson, what have my baby done? (*twice*)
     I just want to know if she done anybody wrong.

     You took her gun, hit her razor hand, (*twice*)
     And you were wrong, 'cause she ain't never harmed a
     man."

     My baby in jail an' I can't get no news, (*twice*)
     I don't get nothin' but these mean ole High Sheriff
     blues.

In 1928 the last convicts left the Flat Top coal mine of Alabama and this event marked the cessation of convict lease. It had been already superseded elsewhere by the contract system in which the contractors came to the prisons bringing with them the materials for labour and instructions for the manufacture of certain articles, paying the prison according to the output rather than to the number of hours worked by the men. This had the unfortunate result that the men were overworked in order to increase the output, and the evil of one system was scarcely less than that of the other. It was still useful to have prisoners for employment in the work-house and the prison shops, to be engaged in the manufacture of boots, the trimming of tombstones, the making of automobile registration plates and the many other items that contractors required.

243. Thirty days in the workhouse, six long months in jail,
    (*twice*)
Yes, I'm in trouble, no one to go my bail.

Please, Mister Jailer, please unlock this door for me,
    (*twice*)
This jail is full of blues, I know they'll come down on me.

I'm a hard-working prisoner, been judged without a trial, (*twice*)
My heart is almost breakin', must be that last long mile.

Though open to abuse the contract system did employ men usefully and, when they were not overworked, prevented the degeneration of morale that results from being idle. Until the Depression such internal employment worked satisfactorily enough, but when millions of men were without work in the free, outside world, the unions complained that the convicts were being engaged on labour that could be given to unemployed men. Subsequently, businessmen producing goods that were close or identical in kind to the goods made in the prisons complained of the low prices against which they could not compete if they were to pay fair wages. As a result of these attacks the prison-made articles were forced off the market by a succession of legal measures, and many of the prison workshops became redundant. Whilst "sweatshop" methods were now abandoned, the prisons were blighted instead by the disease of idleness, the prisoners degenerating in long years of inactivity. A sentence of thirty days that once seemed insufferable when spent in ceaseless toil in the workhouse, now

seems as interminable and as hard to bear to the man who
spends it with nothing to occupy his mind, his hands or body.

244. Well, I wouldn't mind stayin' in jail but I got to stay
        there so long, (*twice*)
      You know, it seems like all my friends, you know, they
        done shook hands and gone.

      Thirty days in jail with my back turned to the wall,
        (*twice*)
      Yes, yes, you know some of you skinners must be
        kicking in my stall.

      "Hey, Mister Jailer, will you please bring me the key?
        (*twice*)
      I just want you to open the door, sir, 'cause this ain't
        no place for me."

The forms of labour that have persisted in the prison system are those that are classified as under "state use." These
are the means of employment for convicts under which they
are either self-supporting or provide amenities for the state.
In theory the principle seems logical and constructive; its
practical applications are frequently far less praiseworthy.
Their roots lie in the convict lease system for the means and
conditions of employment are often not greatly different,
whilst the methods of punishment have their origins in the
basest iniquities of slavery.

When slavery was abolished the Negroes believed that
shackles and chains were at an end, but paradoxically the
liberation coincided with changes of the penal methods which
were to find new uses for them. The ball and chain shackled
to the ankle of a convict who was set to work in the market-
place had been instituted in Pennsylvania as far back as the
1780's, but the building of the prisons in the ensuing years
put the majority of convicts behind bars. During the nineteenth century the population of the prisons far exceeded the
provisions made for them, and the insanitary holes in which
they were incarcerated caused widespread disease. So appalling had the conditions become that a sentence of ten years
became a sentence of death. The unfortunate prisoners fought
the rats, tossed in fever, and rotted in filth until death released

them. Into prisons with cells as small as seven feet by three feet the convicted men were herded and the overcrowding demanded immediate relief—although one such prison with five hundred cells of this size was still in use in the nineteen-thirties. A solution was found in a scheme simple to implement, lucrative to the state if frequently fatal to the prisoner—the chain gang. By leasing gangs of convicts chained, and under armed guard, and by using them on state projects, the prisons were relieved whilst railroads were built, the gravel quarries worked, swamps drained and roads constructed. In 1902 there were 2,221 convicts employed in the chain gangs of Georgia alone, and of these 2,113 were Negroes—amongst them 103 Negro women. Children of twelve years of age were to be found working in chains with old and embittered men in the very streets of Atlanta, and men and women were shackled together under inhuman conditions. In some states the system was abolished at the beginning of this century. When the camps in Louisiana were cleared in 1901 hundreds of forgotten men were found in conditions of appalling suffering; in one, every man was found to be dying of smallpox. Elsewhere the chain gangs continued, the convicts in the Brazos Bottoms of Texas dying like flies from disease, sun-stroke, beatings and buckshot wounds, and the women were forced to work alongside the men. From the chain gangs the State of Georgia made a profit of $354,853 in 1907—thirty-five years later they were still operating.

245. Says the judge he found me guilty, and the clerk he
    wrote it down, (*twice*)
Says the judge, "Tell everybody that, Lawd, you' chain
    gang boun'."

Says I didn't mean to kill her, but bloody murder was
    my crime, (*twice*)
Now I'm out here on the chain gang, Lawd, jus' servin'
    my time.

Says I got chains round my body, chains all around my
    shoes, (*twice*)
Now that's the reason, Cap'n, hear me singing, Lawd,
    these chain gang blues.

Playing cards on a Texas train, being found in the street without proof of means of support, being under the influence of drink—these were sufficient grounds for committing a man for months to the chain gang to work in a forced-labour logging-camp, to build a road whilst working waist-deep in swamp water, to break rocks under a broiling sun. The convicts rose with the sun and were bedded down with the sun. When they lay down for their rest on the hard earth their ankles were shackled to a long logging chain that ran the length of their miserable quarters. Those that had to travel a considerable distance to the place of work on the county roads were shipped in horse-drawn box cars in which five tiers of hardwood bunks were affixed on either side with but eighteen inches of head-room. The mobile cages that have recently replaced them are little better equipped. When not working, the convicts—men and women—were heavily manacled, but when employed on their tasks their hands had to be free, and except when engaged in work requiring close order—ditch digging for example—it was found expedient to free them from the long chain. Instead, a step-chain, allowing a pace of only eight inches, was used, or a twenty-pound ball chained to the ankle.

246. Many days of sorrow, many nights of woe, (*twice*)
And a ball and chain, everywhere I go.

Chains on my feet, padlocks on my hands, (*twice*)
It's all on account of stealing a woman's man.

It was early this mornin' that I had my trial, (*twice*)
Ninety days on the county road, and the judge didn't even smile.

Boys and girls scarcely in their teens were worked side-by-side for sixteen or more hours a day and slept chained in line in the ditches. In the early part of the century as many as 250 prisoners, many of them first offenders, were shackled together on the "long chain" to work on the railroads, the wheat farms and in the dreaded phosphate mines. When prisoners were punished they were brutalized with clubs and compelled to wear needle-sharp points affixed to their ankles which lacerated their legs as they walked. When Governor Arnall of Georgia instituted an investigation of the prison system in 1943 he discovered that such methods were still in use; that leg irons with the heads of picks welded to them were being worn by luckless prisoners and that some twenty-five men were suffering from the open, festering wounds caused by unbelievably barbarous irons. To escape the horrors of the chain gang sixteen men had severed the tendons of their legs and were lying helpless. Women suffered privations and humiliation scarcely less brutal, being flogged naked before the eyes of men prisoners. The campus of Georgia State College was dug by aged Negro women working under the supervision of armed guards whilst young girls carried their picks to the road camps. Small wonder that a Negro's "heart struck sorrow" when he saw his girl join the long chain for a sentence of "11.29"—a year, which under these conditions would seem an eternity.

247. Now I'm gonna see that judge and talk to him myself, (*twice*)
    Tell him that he sent my gal to the county road and left me by myself.

    Now never felt so sorry till the keeper walked down the lane, (*twice*)
    And my heart struck sorrow when he called my good gal's name.

    Then I heard the jailer say, "Hello! Prisoners all fall in line, (*twice*)
    I'm also talkin' about that long-chain woman that got 11.29."

    I've got the blues so bad that I just can't rest, (*twice*)
    I'm gonna ask that jailer, "Can I do my good gal's time myself?"

The majority of workers in the camps and chain gangs build and maintain the state roads, North Carolina which has nearly ninety road camps having its prison division under the direction of the State Highway and Public Works Commission. More than seven thousand prisoners are employees in its camps. Alabama has only a third as many camps and Virginia's state convict road force employs a third the number of men. Elsewhere in the South convicts are employed outside in the state prison and county farms which cover many thousands of acres and occupy tens of thousands of men and women. Agricultural work on a considerable scale in the production of sugar and cotton, the clearing of timber and the growing of vegetable produce is undertaken, and meat and canning factories are usually associated with the farms.

248. Oh the judge he sentenced me, and the clerk he wrote
it down, (*twice*)
"My man," he says, "I'm sorry for you babe, but you
are county farm bound."

Oh six months on the county farm, work against my
back, (*twice*)
But my baby's gonna be sorry he treated me this way,

Oh six months in jail, seven months on the county farm,
(*twice*)
If my man he had been any good he would have met
my bond.

I'd like to build me a scaffold just to hang myself,
(*twice*)
Because the man I'm lovin' I just don't know where
he is.

Conditions on both the county and the state prison farms are hard, the work is long, the punishments brutal; there has been little change since slavery times. For this reason the prison farms have become storehouses of traditional work songs and group labour songs which may have varied little from those sung before the Civil War. Here are kept the long-term prisoners, some of whom have spent a lifetime within the bounds of the camps, men who have committed serious crimes and whose long confinement would prevent their re-settlement in the outside world. Many of those released from Sugarland, Clements or Darrington State Farms in Texas soon return to face the rest of their days working on the state plantation. It was to Sugarland that the great folk and blues singer, Leadbelly, was sent until he obtained a pardon after singing a plea for his release to Governor-elect Pat Neff. A decade later in 1930 he was sent to the Angola Prison Farm, Louisiana, where he was found by John and Alan Lomax when they were making their celebrated collection of prison songs for the Music Division of the Archives of the Library of Congress. As notorious as these are the Kilby and Atmore Prison Farms of Alabama, the Cumins State Farm in Arkansas, Reid in Boykin, South Carolina and, perhaps best known of all, the Parchman Prison Farm, Mississippi, where Bukka White spent many years of his life:

249. Judge give me life this mornin' down on Parchman Farm, (*twice*)
   I wouldn't hate it so bad, but I left my wife and home.

   Oh, good-bye wife, all you have done done, (*twice*)
   But I hope some day, you will hear my lonesome song.

   Oh listen you men, I don't mean no harm, (*twice*)
   If you won' a-do good, you better settle for Parchman Farm.

   We go to work in the mornin', just at dawn of day, (*twice*)
   Just at the settin' of the sun, that's when the work is done.

   I'm down on old Parchman Farm but I sho' wanna go back home, (*twice*)
   But I hope some day I will overcome.

There is no denying that the prison farms demand extensive measures of reform; the guards are often sadists drawn from the "poor Whites" with an inborn hatred of Negroes, ignorant and incapable of getting employment elsewhere. Inhuman beatings with the "bat"—a fourteen-pound leather strap which can break a brick with a single blow—caused forty convicts in Angola Prison to hamstring themselves in 1951, rather than submit to its torture. More recently still, in 1957 more than a dozen men smashed their legs with sledge-hammers at Kilby because they could no longer cope with the ceaseless slave labour on the rock-pile. Yet Negro prisoners prefer to

be in the state farms than in the jails where the congestion,
the inactivity, the boredom destroys the soul. They can smell
the earth, see the sky, sing and work with their companions:
in the jail they can at best, smell carbolic; the vista is one of
stone walls and steel bars; they hear the sounds of the turnkey
and communication may be restricted to furtive taps in code.
They are left to the monotony of their thoughts and desperate
hopes of commuted sentences.

250. Gettin' tired of sleepin' in this low-down lonesome cell,
Lord, wouldn't a-been here if it had not been for Nell.

Stay 'wake at night and just can't eat a bite,
Used to be my rider, but you just won't treat me right.

Oh, a red-eyed captain, and a squabblin' boss,
Got a mad-dog sergeant, honey, an' he won't knock off.

I ask the Gov'ment to knock some days off my time,
Well, the way I'm treated I'm bound to lose my min'.

I wrote to the Gov'nor, "Please turn me a-loose,"
Just didn't get no answer, no it ain't no use.

The worst sore on the American prison system has been the
conduct and operation of its county jails. Every county has
its jail which is theoretically the responsibility of the county
authorities. In practice its maintenance has been too often
left in the hands of the sheriff who delegates his authority to
a number of guards, some of whom are corrupt, dissolute and
disinterested. In the inadequate cages men of all ages and
classes of crime are thrown together to stagnate in idleness.
Of recent years some improvements have been made in many
districts but there is no system of inspection and there are no
standards to be maintained. In 1930 Federal Authorities visited
a large number of county jails, applying a minimum standard
to which it was agreed they should conform. The Report of
the Director of the Bureau of Federal Prisons showed that of
650 prisons visited, only fifty reached this minimum standard.
Though they deplored the filthy, immoral conditions that they
uncovered, no significant improvements were to be made for
many years. Small wonder that Blind Boy Fuller sang, "Lord,

I never will forget the day they transferred me to the county jail. . . ."

251. And I sent for my friends: "Please spare the rod," (*twice*)
Then my friends sent me word, "Lord this town is too doggone hot."

I got friends 'as got money: "Please tell 'em to go my bail." (*twice*)
And my friends sent me word, "Had no business in the county jail."

And I felt right till the judge turned around and frowned, (*twice*)
Says, "I'm sorry for you buddy, but you're on your last-go-round."

Arrested persons awaiting trial, young first offenders and old habitual criminals are thrown together in the county jails, where some attempts are made to keep the insane and the drug addicts apart from the others but where cramped conditions sometimes make even such a rudimentary measure impossible. At one time it was the practice to charge the prisoner when he entered and to charge him a further sum when he left. With no chance to make any money apart from gambling with newcomers this encouraged corruption amongst the prisoners and the guards alike. In order to obtain his release a prisoner had to bribe someone to "go his bail"—literally to buy him out, unless they came with that specific purpose.

252. Well, here I am, locked up in this county jail, (*twice*)
Well, well, it's on a Sunday, oh well, well, and no one to go my bail.

Run for my mother, tell her the shape I'm in, (*twice*)
Well, I'm locked up in the county jail oh well, well, and I haven't got no friends.

(*Spoken*) Yes, when you locked up in jail an' you ain't got no friends,

Way down here in this county jail . . . everything will
　be all right . . .
Just phone my mother, she'll take care.

When I got the news it was just about four o'clock,
　(*twice*)
When the judge discharge me, oh well, well, my heart
　begin to reel and rock.

Says I'm going back home, won't be bad no mo', (*twice*)
'Cause the county jail, oh well Lord, it ain't no place
　to go.

If he has committed an infraction of the law and is sent
to the county jail, a man who makes his living by share-
cropping is unlikely to have any capital from which his wife
or family might draw to pay his bond. For the man without
family connexions or for whom there is no one prepared to
go bail, the outlook is bleak indeed. Food is generally of the
poorest quality and cigarettes, Coca-Cola and other luxuries
can only be purchased by bribing a guard, unless the jail is
one in which a small trolley of goods is trundled past the cells
so that prisoners may buy items whilst their two or three permitted dollars last. As the prisoner is a drain on the resources
of the county, a system has been rife which closely approxi-
mates that of the outlawed convict lease. A local plantation
owner who requires temporary labour goes bail for the prisoners in the jail who are then indebted to him for this sum
and must pay it in their labour at a rate fixed by himself.
Many Negroes in Mississippi where this has been especially
prevalent have found themselves unwittingly forced into crop-
lien slavery. When insufficient prisoners have been in the jail
county sheriffs have made "blanket arrests" of all vagrants in
order to provide the requisite number and have quietly taken
their "cut."

253. They picked me up, and put me in the county jail,
　　　(*twice*)
　　They wouldn't even let my woman come and go my bail.

　　Now I'm in prison, but I've almost done my time,
　　　(*twice*)
　　They give me six months but I had to work out nine.

Course I know my baby, she's goin' to jump and shout,
(*twice*)
When that train rolls up and I come walkin' out.

So take these stripes from round me, and these chains
from round my legs, (*twice*)
Well these stripes don't hurt me, but these chains they
keep me here.

Far better regulated than the county jails are the state prisons, though they vary widely in the quality of the administration. Some are archaic in the extreme, some excessively severe
on the prisoners, some dangerously lax, some markedly progressive. The likelihood of violent riots is generally present and
in order that this is kept to a minimum the conduct of many
state prisons is very strict. Delinquents in American state prisons are often of a degree of criminality unknown in Great
Britain and their control presents a major problem. There is
only one panoptic prison in the United States, and in general
the cells are banked in tiers about a main hall like a hen bat-
tery. As the prisons cannot cope with the large numbers by
affording each man separate accommodation, two and even
three men may be forced to use the same cell, causing unneces-
sary distress and inciting tyranny, hostility and homosexuality.
The prisoner has his cell watched by the ever vigilant guards,
as Roosevelt Sykes cynically observes when he speaks of the
wolves that scratch on his cabin door. The blues singer's delight in layers of meaning and pertinent metaphor is well
demonstrated in his *.44 Blues* in which the number of his cell
is the number of a "train" whose "whistle" was the shot from
a .44 gun.

254. Lord, I walked all night long with my .44 in ma hand,
(*twice*)
I was lookin' for my woman an' I found her with another
man.

I wore my .44 so long, Lord, it made my shoulder sore,
(*twice*)

After I do what I want to ain't goin' to wear my .44 no
more.

Lord, in ma baby's face she heard that .44 whistle blow,
(*twice*)
Well, it sounds just like ain't gonna blow that whistle no
more.

Lord, I got a little cabin, on my cabin is Number 44,
(*twice*)
When I wake up every morning the wolves scratches on
my door.

For infringements of the rules prisoners may be punished
severely, losing opportunities for their cases to come before the
parole boards, being sent into solitary confinement or to the
ill-ventilated, lightless cells known in almost every prison as
"the hole." In the early part of the century prisoners in San
Quentin would be punished by being forced to spend a day
up to their necks in water; tepid bath punishments are still
widely practised. In the South the punishments were, and in
many instances still are, inhuman. Amongst them the "derrick," a form of bastinado, was used in Texas where beatings
with "red heifer" whips are common still, whilst throughout
Georgia in the twenties and thirties Negro prisoners were
tortured by being tied in a distorted position round a pick,
were racked in medieval fashion, or were committed to the
"sweat-box" and left to fry in the boiling sun. The "sweat-
box" was still in use recently in Florida and the doors of "the
hole" in Jackson Prison still have a second, curved metal door
hinged to them between which recalcitrant prisoners were confined, unable to move. Some prisoners resisted these methods
of subjugation with such spirit that their rebelliousness became
intensified rather than broken. In such suffering their characters became case-hardened; it is the suppression of all individuality, the depersonalization that is the result of the regi-
mentation of three or four thousand men along identical lines
that is the most likely to destroy the spirit and send a man "stir-
crazy." In such circumstances small events assume an exaggerated importance, minor grievances become obsessions, and
the prisoner with time on his hands and on his mind sits and
broods, whilst his courage ebbs and his resistance weakens.

255. All last night I sat in my cell alone, (*twice*)
I was thinking of my baby and my happy home.

Sometimes I wonder, why don't you write to me?
(*twice*)
If I been a bad fellow, I did not intend to be.

Baby, you may never see my smilin' face again,
Whoa-oo, my smilin' face again,
You can always remember, Frank Busby has been your
friend.

The suppression of the individual causes mental numbness in the passage of time which makes a man little suited for his return to the world outside prison. There is little opportunity for self-expression within prison and consequently no preparation for integration within the free community. Rehabilitation programmes of real effectiveness have been instituted in few prisons, though some jails have made notable advances towards penal reform—Sing Sing, for example, where Thomas Osborne during World War I attempted to introduce revolutionary methods designed to give even the most dangerous of prisoners a valuable role in the closed community which would prepare them for the part that they would eventually play outside. Osborne's scheme was viciously attacked and was destroyed by political pressure, but in the thirties the late Warden Lewis E. Lawes applied an enlightened policy that helped considerably in the welfare of the prisoners in his charge. For the inmate it was still prison:

256. On my way to Sing Sing, there was only one thing I
could say, (*twice*)
Stone walls will be my home for five years and a day.

Early one morning, long between nine and ten, (*twice*)
I thought about that woman and wished I could see her
face again.

My mother told me, "Son, you've got to reap just what
you sow," (*twice*)
Now I'm behind these hard stone walls, may never see
the streets no more.

Much of the misery of imprisonment is borne not by those inside but by those that are left behind. Crimes that are committed as an indirect result of the failure of society by persons whose acts are fundamentally a revolt against sub-human conditions of life may have many far-reaching effects upon innocent persons, quite apart from the victim and his dependants. The family of the imprisoned man suffers, and the lower the stratum of society from which the criminal has emerged the more his dependants have to bear. In their confusion of despair their love and their anger may both be directed towards the immediate cause of their misery, the prisoner himself; homes are broken, new lovers taken, and an habitual criminal is born when at last the prisoner obtains his release.

257. I went to the jail-house crying, "Jailer please,
Please Mister Jailer, let me see my used-to-be," (*twice*)

I turned to the cell, looked my daddy in the face,
"I'm sorry, pretty daddy, but I just can't take your place." (*twice*)

The jailer felt sorry, then looked at me and smiled,
Said, "I'm sorry, pretty lady, but your man's done patricide." (*twice*)

Now girls you'd better buy yourself a padlock and key,
'Cause that's the only way you can keep your man from me. (*twice*)

And if the blues was whisky I'd be drunk all the time,
I had to go and leave my daddy behind. (*twice*)

Fear of the disintegration of his home and of the loss of his loved ones is as big an inducement as any for a man to escape from the confines of prison, jail farm or camp. The chances of escape from jail depend largely upon the initiative of the prisoner in taking advantage of an opportunity when one presents itself, and of seeing the possibility in an unusual situation. Under suitable circumstances many a man has literally walked out of jail. More frequently his escape has been facilitated by poor security measures or the corruption of guards who are open to bribery. Such methods of escape are therefore less available to the Negro against whom security measures tend to be more strict and who is seldom in a position to buy his way out of prison. Escape is facilitated at moments of disorder and incendiaries amongst convicts have set fire to prisons and then escaped in the confusion. Nearly three hundred men died in the Ohio State Penitentiary when the building was fired in 1930 in an abortive escape attempt, because the warders refused to open locked cells. But the possibility of a jail-house fire is a very real fear for all concerned and Buddy Boy Hawkins tells sadly of an unsuccessful attempt at effecting his woman's escape by simulating a prison conflagration.

258. (*Spoken*) "Hey, Mister Jailer, jail-house burnin' down!"

"Hey Mister Jailer, do not sleep so soun'."
I said, "Hey, Mister Jailer, I said do not sleep so soun'.
Jailhouse on fi-yah, place is all burnin' down.

"Because the woman I lo-ove, she is in the jail-house now, (*twice*)
So please, Mister Jailer, you gotta get her out' there somehow."

Mmmmmmmmm my woman's in trou-ble now,
I said mmmm-ah—my woman's in trouble now,
I said one o' these cool mawnin's I'm gonna get her outa jail.

When I get my li'l, fair brownskin ou' I'll be country boun',
I said when I get my fair brown, buddy, I'm goin' up the country boun',
And then, Mister Jailer, I hope your jail-house burn down.

There are far greater chances of escape from the county jails where the guard tends to be more relaxed than from the state penitentiaries, and many instances are known of the open connivance of the guards or the wardens in return for a sure reward. Escape is also possible from the road camps and farms but whatever the form of imprisonment the prisoners run the extreme risk of being shot by agitated and nervously excited guards or trusties on whom the blame for his escape may fall, or of being literally hounded to earth. To learn of her man's escape from confinement may cause a woman extreme mental agonies with considerable justification.

259. When you man's in trouble you can't eat or sleep,
     (*twice*)
     Your heart begins quiverin' and yo' flesh begins to creep.

     And you run to the jail-house, cryin', "Sergeant, please,
     (*twice*)
     Let me speak to my man, just to give my poor heart ease."

     I got the greyhound blues and my heart begins to fail,
     (*twice*)
     I know a long-tailed greyhound is on my rider's trail.

     'Cause the sergeant has tol' me he isn't in that jail,
     (*twice*)
     That's the reason why my heart begins to fail.

     I'm going to the railroad, lay my head down on the rail,
     (*twice*)
     Let that 2.19 take me from this lonesome jail.

Stumbling through the brush, struggling waist-deep through swamp water with salty tongue, pounding heart and aching lungs, the prisoner who has broken free is terrorized by the baying of the bloodhounds that track his path. Almost unerring in their ability to run the escapee to the ground, the hounds are so reliable a method of capturing him that Southern warders have been known many times to have let prisoners go free so that the dependability of the animals can be demonstrated to interested visitors.

260. Well, I broke out of my cell when the jailer turned his
     back, (*twice*)
     But now I'm so sorry, bloodhounds is on my track.

     Bloodhounds, bloodhounds, bloodhounds is on my trail,
     (*twice*)

They want to take me back to that cold, cold lonesome
jail.

Well I know I done wrong, but he kicked me and
blacked my—
I done it in a passion, I thought it was the fashion—
I know I done wrong but he kicked me and blacked
my eyes,
But if the bloodhounds ever catch me in the electric
chair I'll die.

Capital punishment, the atavistic vengeance of the community against one of its number, has been abolished in a number of states but there are still many that continue to apply
the most primitive and uncivilized of all punishments. In some
states hanging is still practised and the sentenced men may
wait a year in the condemned cell until the final, irrevocable
punishment is carried out. They hear the gallows being as-
sembled in the yard and are measured for height and weight
by painful ruses that cause acute embarrassment and agony to
all concerned. Then, at the appointed hour—dawn, or sometimes four p.m., the prisoner, who has had a day's notice of
his imminent death, is taken to the place of execution to see
perhaps a morbid group of pressmen and photographers awaiting the spectacle of his ignoble decease.

261. Hangman's rope sho' is something strong, (*twice*)
They gonna hang me because I did something wrong.

I wanna tell you the gallis sure is a fearful thing,
(*twice*)
Hang you there in the mawnin', cut you down at night.

Mean ole hangman, he's waitin' to tighten up that noose,
(*twice*)
Lord, I'm so scared I'm trembling in ma shoes.

Jurymen heard my case and he said my hands was red,
(*twice*)
And the judge sentenced me he's gonna hang me till I'm
dead.

Crowd round the court-house and the time is going fast,
(*twice*)
Well a good-for-nothin' killer is gonna breath his last.

Well I'm almost dyin', gasping for my breath, (*twice*)
And a triflin' woman waiting to celebrate my death.

Hanging has been replaced by the electric chair in the majority of the states where capital punishment is employed. In theory it is the more humane method—if "humane" is the term—but the period of time between the moment when the condemned man leaves his cell and is executed by hanging may only be a matter of seconds, whereas a few minutes elapse whilst the straps, clamps and electrical apparatus are adjusted when a man is committed to the "chair." Often the electric chair is situated only a matter of yards from the Death Row and sometimes even in the same corridor, so that other men awaiting execution over a period of months hear the sounds of the electrical apparatus in operation and see the lights dim as one by one their companions are committed to their deaths. Again, seats are provided for spectators and as a refinement one or two institutions even permit the condemned man to throw the switch that sends the burning charge through his body. Some have "made their peace with God" and received the ministrations of the chaplain, but the minds of others are dulled to all reality but the chair itself.

262. I'm walkin' to the 'lectric chair, with a preacher by my
side, (*twice*)
It got me for cold-blooded murder and the truth can't
be denied.

I wouldn't mind dyin' but I'm dying in such a cruel ol'
way, (*twice*)
Ain't got the heart to send a message, ain't even got the
heart to pray.

Mmmmmmmmmmm—mmmmmmmmmmm,
Mmmmmmmmmmm—Lord, Lord,
Lord, Lordy, Lord, Lordy, Lord.

Lord, Lord, Lord, Lord, all I can do is sit and cry,
(*twice*)

My poor mother's at home, don't know I even goin' to die.

During the nineteen-thirties and forties the number of men executed exceeded 3,100; the number of women, mercifully a bare two dozen. Of the total number of persons legally executed more than half were coloured, a proportion which represents a *per capita* rate ten times that of White persons relative to the respective populations. Even when related to the respective incidences of culpable homicide the execution figures are excessively weighted against the Negro. Over 350 executions were for rape and these were almost exclusively of Negroes; seldom is the White rapist of a Negro girl brought to trial and the Southern Negro knows better than to make any active protest. In spite of popular conceptions to the contrary Negro rapists are few in number; retribution is swift, certain and horrible. Murders where White persons are the victims are punished severely; the South takes a more compromising view of the murder of Negroes by Negroes. In some localities the law is rigidly applied but in others the crime is dealt with leniently and violence within the race condoned. Generalizations on the attitude to Negro crime can be misleading and conclusions are hard to draw, for the application of the law to Negro offences varies widely from state to state.

The prison population figures give no satisfactory impression of the incidence of crime, for Negroes generally receive longer sentences for identical offences than White criminals, especially—and somewhat surprisingly—in the North. Relative to their proportionate populations there are three times as many Negro males in American prisons and four times as many females. Judges are apt to award impossibly long sentences to ensure that no remission can be given from a life sentence, bringing a feeling of utter hopelessness for the men whom they send to jail. The lack of standardized sentences may cause extraordinary anomalies in which a month in jail, a life term or execution may be the range of legal punishment possible for the same offence. The law differs widely from state to state and is administered with a flexibility that indisputably works against the Negro. There are scrupulous judges who exercise the law with impartiality to all who come before them, and some who even "lean over backwards" to ensure fair hearings for Negroes. But when a man was sentenced to fifteen years' imprisonment in Washington for the murder of five persons, one wonders whether he would have received as light a sentence if his skin had not been White and his victims all Negroes. He is a free man to-day. Some Negroes are incorrigible; too deeply involved in crime to be reclaimed, they are proud of their reputations as "ramblers"—inveterate criminals, promiscuous lovers, social misfits.

263. I'm known as the "rambler," I'm known in every man's
    town, (*twice*)
    Even the little birds begin weepin' when that evening
    sun goes down.

    The judges all know me as a man with a smilin' face,
    (*twice*)
    And there's no other one can ever take my place.

    I'm a roaming man and my home is in no one man's
    town, (*twice*)
    The kids all cry, the women scream when that evenin'
    sun goes down.

    I never had a woman that I couldn't have back again,
    (*twice*)
    I can get the best woman that ever was an' I don't have
    to be in my gin.

But the majority of coloured people who find themselves on the wrong side of the law are simple persons, prone to the same faults and defects of character as members of any other social group, but so placed that in Southern Negro rural communities it is often a matter of pride to be able to claim that one has not "done time." Undoubtedly many Negroes would receive more favourable judicial treatment if their cases were pleaded more sympathetically. The Negro lawyer is still unusual in the South and in the small towns non-existent. Even in the bigger cities he may by his very colour prejudice his client, and no White persons in the South will employ a Negro lawyer no matter how good his qualifications may be. Few lay Negroes understand the process of the law and fewer can afford expert legal advice. The lawyers who plead for Negroes are often failures who do not seek Negro clients from choice but rather from necessity. Consequently they are seldom able to put the case in an adequate manner and many Negroes glumly assume that any action to defend their rights will be lost along with their small savings, and do not bother to employ legal advice. A small number of lawyers with liberal, humanitarian outlooks who are desirous of seeing justice for the Negro do operate on their behalf and show, in Sleepy John Estes's metaphor, that it is possible to reverse the stream of adverse opinion on occasion.

264. Now, got offices in town, resident out on Seventy Road,
He got a nice little lake right inside the grove.

REFRAIN
Boys, y'know I like Mister Clark, yes, he really is my friend,
He says if I just stay out of my grave, he'll see that I won't go round the bend.

Now Mis' Clark is a lawyer, his young brother is too,
When you bound to get hot, he'll tell you just what to do.

He lawyers for the rich, he lawyers for the poor,
He don't try to rob nobody, just brings them round to the door.

Now once I got in trouble, you know I was goin' to take a rap,
He didn't let it reach the co't-house, he kept it on the outside.

Now Mis' Clark is a good lawyer, he good as I have seen,
He first man that proved that water runs upstream.

Negroes who do go "up the river," "down in the valley," "round the bend," or "to the well"—as they euphemistically refer to prison—receive equal treatment with White persons only in the progressive penitentiaries They have come to expect the harshest punishments, the foulest cells, the longest terms, and only the Mexicans and Puerto Ricans are likely to receive worse treatment. The problem of penal reform is not racial, however, but a serious one that concerns the whole nation. Improvements of prison facilities, higher standards of recruitment and pay for prison officials, the abolition of methods of torture and the death penalty, psychiatric treatment for the socially maladjusted and practicable methods of rehabilitation that will ensure that a larger proportion of convicted prisoners can become useful members of society: these are advances that must be made. Prison officers and public alike must be better educated in the understanding of the delinquent mind. But fundamentally, the greatest reform must lie in the elimination of those aspects of society that make the criminals, and in this, too, the problem is not solely a racial one; if the Negro figures in the nation's crime in an exaggerated proportion in relation to his percentage of the population, it is because the "mudsill" still exists. Racial prejudice and segregation, inadequate education, poor housing, broken families—these are only some of the factors that collectively lead to the making of criminals wherein reforms must be made, enormous though the task may be.

On the third day of June 1936, by some unexpected arrangement, a Negro prisoner under guard came into the Decca studios to record four blues. Only one record was ever issued, for the man, known only as Jesse James, broke down under the strain whilst he sang and was led back to prison and oblivion. His voice was rough, uncultured and intensely moving, as he sang his only testament. There is no blues more poignant, none that reproaches more directly the indifference of those who hear and do not attempt to comprehend, or see and do not recognize, than this simple and beautiful creation of a Negro convict. But it is the blues of a man with spirit but without hope, who has been so long severed from the outside world that Oklahoma was to him still the "Territory" of the Indian nations; who has been paying a debt to a society that had given him nothing. "You heah me talkin' to ya, buddy, what made ya stop by heah?" he demands of the listener as a certain man might well have done of those who passed by on the other side of the Jericho road.

265. Now the day's been a long, lonesome day,
　　—D'ya heah me talkin' to ya, did ya heah what I
　　　　　　　　　　　　　　　　　　　　　　　say?
　　Lord, the day has been a—long, old, lonesome day,
　　And now 'morrow eeeh, Lord, will be the same old way.

I been to the Nation, 'round the Territo',
  —You heah me talkin' to ya, gotta reap what ya
                                                sow,
I been all round the Nation, and round the Territo',
But I found no heaven on earth, Lord, nowhere I go.

I'm goin' t' the Big House, and I don't even care,
  —Don't ya heah me talkin' to ya, scoldin' to ma
                                              death!
I'm goin' in the mawnin', an' I don't even care,
I might get four or five years, Lord, and I might get the
  chair.

I don't stop an' listen, see what t'morrow bring,
  —You heah me talkin' to ya, start to prayin'!
You better stop n' listen, an' see what t'morrow bring,
It might bring you sunshine, Lawd, an' it may bring rain.

Some got six months, some got a solid year,
  —You heah me talkin' to ya, buddy, what made ya
                                        stop by heah?
Some of them got six months, pardner, and some got a
                                            solid year,
But I believe my pardner, Lawd, got lifetime heah.

Chapter 9

World Black as Midnight

To THE NORTH AMERICAN Indians the great river that divided the Continent was the "Father of the Waters"—the Mississippi. Appropriately enough, the name that they gave it remains to-day, for though the Indian has virtually disappeared from its reaches, the river forever continues to drain the waters of a score of states and to pour them into the Gulf of Mexico. In so doing, it shapes the lives and controls the destinies of millions of people who through generation after generation depend upon the Mississippi and its thousands of miles of tributaries for their livelihoods. The soil of the valley floor is of great fertility, created by the river from the alluvial deposits carried in its flow. These flat alluvial plains which extend from the influx of the Ohio south for some six hundred miles to the Mississippi outlet are of rich black soil and they naturally became the sites for many great plantations. When, in 1811, Fulton's steamboat the *New Orleans* successfully navigated the length of the river—in spite of the New Madrid earthquake which temporarily reversed the current—a new era of river navigation was born and the shipping of produce became more practicable than by the poled "flat-boats" and "broad-horns" that had plied the waters until then. A few years later Henry Shreve's *Washington*, double-decked but shallow-hulled, set the pattern of future Mississippi steamboats on which, following the

Civil War, thousands of free but ignorant Negroes found employment as roustabouts and deck-hands. Large numbers of their fellows were working on the developing plantations and the height of Negro population density shifted from the South East to the Mississippi Valley where, in some states, coloured people outnumbered Whites. So concentrated did the Negro population become that only recently has the percentage of coloured persons in Mississippi dropped below fifty per cent of the total population.

Negro labour made the production of cotton and corn and the speedy handling of the river-boat cargoes possible. To catch the markets in New Orleans speed was imperative and the boats raced to reach the river ports and landing stages and, having loaded, to beat their competitors in arriving at the wharves of the Crescent City. Early steamboats took five and a half days to make the trip from Natchez; it took the *Robert E. Lee* only ten and a half *hours* in 1870, with boilers at full pressure and a Negro sitting on the safety-valve. Such racing was hazardous: boilers exploded and vessels were wrecked—the fate of Shreve's *Washington*. But an additional hazard was a feature of the Mississippi itself: its total unpredictability. Every steamboat captain knew that the river he negotiated on the return trip would be unlike that which he had navigated to the Gulf. For it sprawls and meanders, floods and abates, changes its course, carves channels, creates ox-bows and cut-offs in the broad spread of the valley where the land falls at a rate of only eight inches to the mile. The treachery of the river is the price paid for the rewards of its lands. From the headwaters of the Missouri the river flows 3,872 miles to the outlet, and from Cape Giradeau, north of Cairo, to the Head of the Passes of the Mississippi Delta, the meandering course of 1,125 miles is double the direct distance. Over this length the depth increases and the river curiously narrows from a mean of nearly a mile at Cairo to half that width at the Delta. There the discharge of water varies with the seasons, at times a million cubic feet a second, sometimes but a tenth of that. As the river flows it continues to leave alluvial deposits which make natural levees or banks at its sides which contain the waters between definite limits though they also raise the water level when the river floods. Often the river is higher than the land adjacent to it, which gradually slopes away from these natural levees. When the river begins to flood the levees may be breached causing the inundation of the surrounding country, a danger which was early appreciated by the French who commenced building artificial levees in 1717 and who had a stretch of the river so protected to a height of three feet for some fifty miles in the vicinity of New Orleans by 1735. Plantation owners were legally obliged to maintain and protect the river walls then, but in later years they became sadly remiss in their duty. The Civil War witnessed the destruction of many of the levees which were poorly repaired and a series of disastrous inundations prompted some Government action, though maintenance was still the responsibility of individuals or district levee boards early in the present century. The railroads had largely diminished the importance of the river transport but the danger to the land remained a real one. Negroes supplied the labour to construct the levees when the plantations owners cared to spare them from the fields. The planters' homes were safe on the higher ground, but the Negroes who worked in the River Bottoms and whose shacks were in sight of the water knew the danger if the levee broke.

266. If it keeps on rainin', levee's goin' to break, (*twice*)
    And the water done come and have no place to stay.

    Well, all last night, sung that levee moan, (*twice*)
    Thinkin' bout my baby an' my happy home.

    I works on the levee, mama, both night and day,
    (*twice*)
    I ain't got nobody to keep the water away.

    Oh, crying won't help you, praying won't do no good,
    (*twice*)
    When the levee breaks, mama, you got to move.

    I works on the levee, mama, both night and day,
    (*twice*)
    I work so hard to keep the water away.

There is no stopping the Mississippi floods: they can only be kept under control. In early autumn and early winter the level of the river is at its lowest, for although there is a slight rise in November the freezing of the Northern tributaries reduces the tendency to a larger flood. In January early rains in the Ohio valley regions where the land is still frozen cause a quick flow of the water to the Ohio river and the snows on the mountains begin to melt, adding to the volume of water carried to the Mississippi. By April the Eastern flood waters are ceasing and the Mississippi subsides. The Mississippi Valley regions normally get their heaviest rainfall in May and the resultant rise in the water is augmented by flood waters from the Missouri which enter the Mississippi in June. Seasonal flooding is anticipated but the levees are constructed to control it to some extent. As the height of the water is excessive, however, breaches in the levee walls are deliberately made at certain points to allow particular areas to flood and thus lessen the pressure of water. These are the "backwaters," which occur in the St. Francis Basin to the west of the river between Memphis and Helena, in the great Yazoo-Mississippi delta north of Vicksburg, in the Tensas Basin west of Natchez, and at other selected points. When freak circumstances occur and the overflow periods clash through the delay of the Ohio floods or the early appearance of the Missouri flood water, even the backwaters cannot take all the excess. By extraordinary ill-fortune all these phenomena occurred together between April and June in 1927 causing the worst flood disaster ever recorded on the Mississippi when the millions of tons of water burst through the levees after a period of heavy rainfall and drowned the land.

267. Water in Arkansas, people screamin' in Tennessee,
    Oooh—people screamin' in Tennessee,
    If I don't leave Memphis, backwater been all over po'
      me.

    People say this rainin', it has been for nights and days,
      (*twice*)
    Thousands of people stands on the hill lookin' down
      where they used to stay.

    Children standin' screamin', "Mama, we ain't got no
      home."—

"Ooooh—we ain't got no home."
Papa says to the children, "Backwater left us all alone."

Backwater risin', come in ma windows and doors,
(*twice*)
I leave with a prayer in ma heart, "Backwater won't
rise no more." (*twice*)

No one had anticipated the full horror of the 1927 floods.
Houses were washed away with their terrified occupants still
clinging to the roof-tops; the carcases of cattle and mules
floated in the swirling, deep brown water; isolated figures
whom none could rescue were last seen crying for help as
they hung in the gaunt branches of shattered trees. Dressers
and table-tops, clothes and toys were caught in the driftwood
and floating timbers, to twist madly in a sudden whirlpool,
and then sweep out of sight in the surging, eddying, boiling
waters which extended as far as eyes could see.

Because it is unaffected by breaches in the levees which
lie to the south, the town of Cairo affords a good station for
measuring the extent of the water flow. There, a rise in the
water of more than fifty feet above the minimum recorded
reading indicates that a severe flood is imminent. In 1927
the water had risen to 56.4 feet—nearly two feet above the
previous highest reading. Further to the south at Vicksburg
less than a hundred thousand cubic feet of water per second
passed when the minimum depth of water had been recorded,
but at the height of the 1927 flood an estimated two and a
quarter million cubic feet per second would have passed if
the waters had been confined to the levees, and an actual
reading of 1,806,000 cubic feet per second of passing river
water was attained. The level had risen some sixty-five feet
and with such a tremendous volume of water that the devas-
tation was on an immense scale. Breaches—or "crevasses"—
in the levees were recorded in fifty places and twenty-eight
thousand square miles of land were under water. Whole
townships were engulfed and the frightened people—largely
Negroes—made for the hills at Helena and Vicksburg.

268. I'm standing in this water, wishing that I had a boat,
(*twice*)
The only way I see is—take my clothes and float.

The water is rising, people fleeing for the hills, (*twice*)
Lord, the water will obey, if you only just say, "Be still!"

They sent out alarm for everybody to leave town, (*twice*)
But when I got the news I was high-water bound.

They dynamite the levee—thought it might give us ease, (*twice*)
But some water's still rising, do it as they please.

Drastic measures were taken to try to keep the floods in check: the levees were blown up in some places to bleed off the excess water, causing further inundation but lessening the danger in more thickly populated areas. Severe flooding in New Orleans was only averted by this method when a short route to the Gulf diverting much of the water was hastily cut. But the levees had been poorly maintained, were of insufficient height and inadequate to withstand the immense pressure, and in spite of the methods used to drain off much of the flood water, it still continued to pour over the walls. In all, the disaster lasted for six weeks; six weeks of horror and confusion for those who had hoped that the waters would soon subside, only to see them continue to rise. The homes of 750,000 people were flooded and every possible means of escape was used. Old and forgotten boats were once more pushed out on to the water, and leaking profusely, loaded to the gunwales with people and pathetic personal belongings were rowed and poled to the higher ground. Families were herded into cattle trucks and hundreds evacuated by the trains. Marooned groups of shocked and numbed Negroes stood huddled together on small islands that still rose above the water and waited for the help that sometimes came. Others did all they could to save the homeless and the stranded.

269. The wind hollers and the rain begin to fall, (*twice*)
My woman was born in Mississippi, that was my one and all.

I received a telegram sayin', "Baby, won't you please come here? (*twice*)

Hell broke a-loose on the Delta, and your baby is way
   down here."

I'm comin' to you baby, if through twenty feet of water
   I wade, (*twice*)
Lord, I can't stand to see my baby fill a watery grave.

Knee-deep in water—tree-tops, men and women be too,
   (*twice*)
But I'm back in my baby's arms with those Mississippi
   Flood Blues.

For some there were joyous reunions as families that had
been separated eventually met each other again. Parents who
had sent their children on ahead to safety whilst they waited
for the next relief had no news of them and had to rely on
hearsay and hurried reports. Husbands and wives, lovers, relatives and friends were parted, and for some, when the waters
began to subside and the thick black mud with its pervading
stench of decay was revealed where homes and plantations
once had been, there was no news, no consolation. With
aching hearts and red-rimmed eyes, bereaved persons scanned
the rows of huddled, homeless figures or with ungainly steps
picked their way to the places where they used to live. Only
the mud remained to greet them.

270. I was walking down the levee with my head hung low,
    Looking for my sweet mama, aah, but she ain't here no
     more—

REFRAIN
That's why I'm cryin' Mississippi Heavy Water Blues.

Lord, Lord, Lord, I feel blue, my house got washed
   away
An' I'm cryin', "How long?" for another three days.

I'm sitting here looking at all this mud,
And my gal got washed away in that Mississippi flood.

I'm in Mississippi with mud all in my shoes,
My gal in Louisiana—with that high water blues.

> Listen here you men, one more thing I'd like to say,
> Ain't no women out here, they all got washed away.

Over six hundred thousand people were rendered completely destitute by the effects of the floods, presenting an immense problem for those who were trying to feed, clothe and house them and who were struggling to ward off the imminent danger of cholera, typhoid and outbreaks of other highly contagious diseases. In six weeks the Government spent five million dollars and the Red Cross stated its expenses to be some fourteen millions, figures that must be borne in mind when the record is considered. For without doubt Herbert Hoover's conduct of the relief was discreditable, and the American Red Cross, under whose auspices the operations were conducted, has much to answer for. Negroes were forced to pay in cash for the relief services and food that were officially provided free by the Government. Needless to say the majority was unable to meet these demands: having lost all that they had they were unable to pay. Their debt was assumed by White landlords who had them transported to the plantations as soon as the emergency was over, there to be bonded in share-cropping peonage. Those refugees who had been share-croppers were ear-marked for return to the planters under whom they had worked. Lists of workers were submitted to the Red Cross who guaranteed their transportation. Negroes were therefore herded into segregated concentration camps, surrounded by barbed wire, and prevented from leaving by National Guardsmen. They received the last and the most inferior issues of food and clothing, and when labour was required, Negroes who entered Red Cross food stations were seized and put to forced labour. By this method workers were conscripted for the construction, cleaning and maintenance of White camps and for the use of employers needing men in the vicinity of the disaster. Negro refugees under armed guards did the entire work on the Vicksburg levees and the treatment of the suffering, homeless people was less than human. The conditions were immediately investigated by Walter White and certain independent bodies, and though Hoover denied the charges, the pressure of opinion was so great that he was obliged to set up the Morton Committee to investigate the situation under the direction of Dr. Robert Morton of Tus-

kegee. By this time some of the worst offences had been modified but the report still made distressing reading. The Negro
camps were closed by the end of June and the occupants
not committed to planters were forced to return to homes
still submerged, whilst the White camps continued until late
in August. "We did not create the social conditions in the
South and it is not our function to reform them," was the
official Red Cross reply to the formal accusations. Small
wonder that starving Negroes were reluctant to go to the Red
Cross store as Alabama Sam, and later, Leadbelly were to
put on record:

271. . . . She talked last night, talked for an hour,
     "Go and get a sack of that Red Cross flour."

     I tol' her, "Nooo . . . I don't wanna go,"
     I said, "Y'know I cannot go down to the Red Cross
     sto'."
     . . . "But you know the Government takin' a change,
     Say they gonna treat everybody right,
     They got them two cans of beans and one little can of
     tripe."

     I tol' her, "Noo . . . I don't wanna go,
     I'll wait till I get a job."

     I said, "You know I can't go down to the Red Cross
     sto'."

     You go early in the morning, "Boy, how you feel?"
     You ask 'em for a li'l rice and they give you a bowl
     of meal.

     I tol' 'em "Noo . . .
     An' I ain't goin' down to that Red Cross Sto'."

A final assessment of the damage put the total figure at
more than three hundred and fifty million dollars' worth and
this prompted the Government to implement a plan prepared
by the United States for the protection of the country and
the improvement of the levees, which involved an expenditure
almost as great as the sum lost by the flood damage. Work

commenced on the building of revetments made from vast mattresses of willow branches laid side by side, with transverse lengths lashing them together. Supplemented by concrete slabs and asphalt layers these prevent the destruction of the levees by underwater erosion. The levees themselves were heightened and strengthened and sub-dykes built of sandbags constructed behind them to hold the water that seeped through. Such schemes were conducted on a large scale but at a heavy and uncredited expenditure of Negro lives. Under the direction of White overseers and straw bosses of their own colour, the Negro labourers in the levee camps were worked until they dropped; difficult men were clubbed and beaten and their bodies buried in the levees. They were paid but ten cents an hour and forced to purchase their goods and food at the commissaries which kept them in debt. But by 1935 over two thousand miles of levee walls averaging twenty-four feet in height had been constructed. Above the Ohio the dams, roller gates and locks controlled the flow of the Missouri waters and to the South dredging and the construction of emergency reservoirs afforded better protection in the Basin. When the heavy flood waters of 1937 poured down the Mississippi the floodways were opened and the strengthened levees held. Along the Allegheny and Ohio rivers, however, it was a different story.

272. It's been snowing forty days and nights, rivers and
     lakes begin to freeze, (*twice*)
     Some places it's through my home town, waters up
     above my knees.

     Storm begin rising and the sun begin sinking down,
     (*twice*)
     I says, "Mother and Dad, pack yo' trunk, we ain't safe
     here in this town."

     When it's lightning my mind gets frightened, my nerves
     begin weakening down, (*twice*)
     And the shack where we was living begin moving
     round.

     Women and children was screaming, saying, "Lord
     where must we go? (*twice*)

The flood water has broke the levees and we ain't safe
here no more."

When it begin, clouds dark as midnight, keep raining all
the time,
I say, Oh, I wonder why the sun don't ever shine?
And the way it keeps raining, it's driving me out of my
mind.

Nine hundred people lost their lives in the Ohio floods
which also took a heavy toll of property and, including the
Mississippi regions, rendered a million White and Negro persons homeless. Only the previous year a grant of over
$270,000,000 had been made by the Government for further
flood prevention measures in the Mississippi Basin, and as a
result of the 1937 floods an additional grant of forty millions
to aid the new schemes along the Ohio was awarded. In
consequence of this considerable expenditure the protection
of the land and the control of the rivers were very substantially improved but the heavy flooding in 1943 when four
million acres were under water, and the disasters in the post-
war years are evidence enough that the river is still a source
of danger to extensive areas of land and to large numbers
of people whose homes lie within reach of the flood waters.
In all probability the river may never be held in complete
control though a considerable measure of restraint will have
been effected. Along the tributaries and streams that empty
their waters into the larger rivers, the levee walls, the upkeep
of the banks and the small wharves are still the responsibility
of local landowners and authorities who have not the benefit
of Government grants. There, minor disasters can and do
occur which are tragic enough for those concerned though
they may be purely local in effect. Underwater erosion may
cause the collapse of the levee, rotting piles bring down the
aged structure of the longshore, or excessive weight cause
the collapse of a bridge already strained by flood water.

273. Now I never will forget that floating bridge, (*three
times*)
Tell me: five minutes time in the water I would be in.

Now when I was rollin' down, I would fall on my
hands, (*three times*)
Please take me on dry land.

Now they carried me in the house and they laid me
    'cross the bed, (*three times*)
'Bout a gallon of muddy water I have drunk.

They dried me off and they laid me in the bed, (*three
    times*)
Couldn't hear nothin' but muddy water in ma head.

And people was standing on the bridge—was screamin'
    and cryin', (*three times*)
"Lord have mercy—where we gwine?"

North America is a continent of extremes—not only of
landscape but of climate, where temperatures in one city
may range from many degrees below zero in the height of
winter, to excessive heat well above 100° in the summer. The
North-East Atlantic Seaboard is noted for its severity of climate, but so, too, is the mid-West where the Great Plains
experience vast differences of temperature and climatic conditions. Up the Mississippi Basin, along the Missouri and
into Canada cyclones and whirlwinds are far from uncommon. Some may expend themselves within a distance of two
or three miles, whilst others may travel much greater distances and be of a force that wrecks all but the most firmly
built structures. The shacks that house the greater proportion
of the city-dwelling Negroes and almost all of those who live
in rural districts are small defence against the ferocity of
these freak storms. Such a cyclone of more than usual
severity struck St. Louis in the early twenties.

274. I was sittin' in my kitchen, lookin' across the skies,
    (*twice*)
I thought the world was ending, I started into cry.

The wind was howling, the buildings begin to fall,
    (*twice*)
I see that mean old twister comin' just like a cannon-
    ball.

The world was black as midnight, I never heard such
    a noise before, (*twice*)

Sounds like a million lions they turned loose, they all
roar.

The shack where we was livin', she reeled and rock but
never fell—Lord have mercy! (*twice*)
How the cyclone started, nobody but the Lord can tell.

Characterized by the heavy, black storm clouds which foretell the imminence of the phenomenon, and the revolving
column of dust, earth and cloud which makes contact with
the land, the cyclone presents a fearsome sight. Revolving in
a counter-clockwise manner it travels invariably in an east-
erly to north-easterly direction laying a path of destruction
in its wake. Though people and animals, farm buildings and
implements are sucked up and cast down by the whirling
force of the wind, the destructive power lies primarily in the
sudden drop in the barometric pressure that occurs with the
advent of a cyclone. The air pressure within the buildings
literally blows them apart and the wind takes up and throws
down the pieces. On the "water coast" of Texas the whirlwinds produce dramatic waterspouts which pass rapidly across
the sea, and travelling on over the land wreak havoc as the
soil is drawn up into the spiralling stem. As the "twister"
approaches and the outer perimeter of the storm sends screens
flapping, doors banging, tears away loose fence rails and
whips the loose earth into choking eddies of dust, the blues-
singing Negro in his shack begins to lose his faith in himself,
and in the face of this manifestation of uncontrollable forces
regains, for a while at any rate, the greater faith that he has
lost.

275. Yes, I was staying in my kitchen, I was looking way
out across the bay, (*twice*)
I see that mean old twister, I started in to pray.

I fell down on my knees, these is the words I begin to
say, (*twice*)
I said, "Oh Lord, have mercy and help us in our
weakening ways."

Yeah, you know the wind was blowing, coming in my
windows and doors, (*twice*)

Yeah, you know my house fell down and I can't live there no more.

I said, "Lawd, Lawd what shall we do? (*twice*)
Yes, there ain't no other help I know, oh Lord, but you."

As the Japanese learned to adopt themselves to the havoc caused by earthquakes and made use of light-framed, thin screen structures that would not cause fatalities if they collapsed, so too the inhabitants of the islands of the West Indies and of the Florida coast adapted their building techniques to combat the effects of the hurricanes that sweep the Gulf of Mexico. Some employ heavy battens and beams to secure all loose fittings and doors, if their homes are sufficiently strong to withstand the force of the winds. Others, less fortunately placed, prepare for the possible wreckage that may occur and accept philosophically the hazards of living in a warm but far from equable climate.

276. Some speak about tornadoes—the hurricane is worst of all, (*twice*)
They comes right through Florida, blow down your fourteen foot of wall.

Hurricane is so powerful, blow the house anywhere I live, (*twice*)
It makes the hair rise on your head, give you fever with cold chills.

Winter clothes are not needed, you spend your money rebuilding your home, (*twice*)
When the ocean gets rough you're not in Florida all alone.

I really like Florida, if the wind don't blow me away, (*twice*)
But if that don't never happen, I'll be in Florida the rest of my days.

With the hurricane then is the added danger of flooding from the seas, which the terrifying winds of a hundred-mile-per-hour force whip to a seething cauldron of immense waves that crush the tiny coastal craft and tumble the boat-houses and jetties into the foam. Negro fishermen plying the coastal waters have little chance of survival when caught in such storms, as their frightened womenfolk left alone at home well know. They watch the storms with dread premonitions in their hearts.

277. Captain, tell your men to get aboard,
Hoist your sails, just pull into another shore.

I'm dreary in mind and so worried in heart,
Oh the best of friends sure have got to part.

It's cloudy outdoors, as can be,
Oh it's cloudy as can be,
That's the time I need my good man with me.

It's rainin' and it's stormin' on the sea,
It's rainin', it's stormin' on the sea.
I feel like someone has shipwrecked poor me.

Since the Negro appeared in any appreciable numbers on the West Coast, there have been no earth tremors of any consequence and away from the Pacific volcanic perimeter ring such subterranean movements are not a serious problem in the United States. But though earthquakes do not bother him, the Negro still feels very much at the mercy of the earth; for so many of his fellows their entire lives have depended upon its fertility. The lives of a large proportion of Negroes are closely associated with the fundamental elements of the Ancients: with Earth and Air, Water and Fire.

In the tinder-boxes of the Negro rural "dog-trots" with their draught corridors separating their rooms, and the "shotgun" shacks, wood-framed and with rooms built in line, that blight the outskirts of many a Southern town, there is great danger of fire. Their structure encourages strong draughts that fan the flames, and the dry timbers, the newspaper-covered walls ignite easily and are soon reduced to ashes. There is little that can be done: amongst the blues singers there is a favourite verse:

278. If your house catches on fire and there ain't no water
     'round,
     If your house catches on fire and there ain't no water
     roun',
     Throw your trunk out the window and let that shack
     burn down.

Similarly in the city apartment buildings the stair-wells act
as funnels in a conflagration, increasing the likelihood of
destruction. Negro homes—whether country shanties or tenement homes in the towns—make a poor risk for the insurance companies. Premiums tend to be high and insurance
companies do not solicit the custom of Negroes whose poverty may make it difficult for them to keep up their instal-
ments. So inflammable are the Negro homes and poor the
property that there exists in some fire departments an indifference to the burning of rural shacks that are sufficiently
apart not to be a source of danger to other buildings. Their
indifference gives further justification for the Negro's despairing fatalism as exemplified in the above quoted verse, but it
also adds to the suffering endured by those who lost the little
that they had in the consuming flames.

On the local government of an "incorporated town" falls
the responsibility of providing adequate drainage, main water
supply and an efficient system of fire prevention. When the
United States entered the war in 1941 there were nearly
66,000 homes in Mississippi without a toilet or privy of any
kind; nearly 78,500 in Alabama and 75,000 in North Carolina of which, needless to say, a disproportionately high percentage were tenanted by Negroes. Of these the majority had
no main water supply near—a grim illustration of the perfunctory discharge of duties by local governments and an
indication of the inadequate facilities available for fire control. Many of these homes were in the Negro sectors of
towns and not in rural areas, but even in New Orleans a
single hydrant has to serve the needs of a whole street for
water supply. Similarly, the services offered for the protection and prevention of fire in these districts is frequently
hopelessly inadequate. When the black smoke rises above a
cluster of Negro homes those near can only pray that the
Fire Department will come and that no one will hinder them
on their way.

279. "Now, I'm gonna call the Fire Department for ma
   house is burnin' down," (*twice*)
   You know that musta be li'l Marthy Hardin what lives
   on the north side of town.

   I see the people is runnin' an' I wonder who could it be,
   (*twice*)
   You know that musta be li'l Marthy Hardin, I saw
   them turn down ole Western Street.

   "When you see the Chief, boys, please clear the street,"
   (*twice*)
   'Cause you know he is goin' down to save li'l Marthy
   Hardin's home for me.

   She's a hard-workin' woman, you know her salaries is
   very small, (*twice*)
   Then when she pay up her house-rent, that don't leave
   anythin' for insurance at all.

   Now I wrote li'l Marthy a letter, five days it returned
   back to me. (*twice*)
   "You know li'l Marthy's house done burned down; she
   done move on Bradford Street."

A high degree of moral responsibility rests on the shoulders
of local government officers in the discharge of their duties,
and it is widely known that openings for graft and corruption are many, and that there is little redress for inefficient
work. Consequently the Negro may have little faith in these
persons appointed to supervise fire prevention, or control and
the investigation of likely and actual causes.

280. "My house is burning down, the firemen are taking
   their time, (*twice*)
   Please, Mister Fire Detective, won't you save this old
   cabin of mine?"

   I spend my money looking to be happy some day,
   (*twice*)
   Now my house burned down, I ain't got no place to
   stay.

That fire detective, he don't mean me no good, (*twice*)
Let my house burn to ashes, didn't leave me one stick
of wood.

My house burned down, didn't leave me a doggone
thing, (*twice*)
It worried me to hear that fire-bell ring.

The singer's tragedy is a private one, shared only by the members of his family and friends within his immediate neighbourhood. But the burning down of a public place is a disaster which is shared by many, and the loss of a public personality who has perished in the flames is the unhappy concern of large numbers of people who have no immediate acquaintance with him. Negro dancers, sportsmen, athletes, entertainers and musicians are frequently termed "Race Heroes" or "Race Men" for they have challenged the alleged supremacy of the Whites on their own terms and have been successful in achieving equal esteem in their fields. As public figures their success is more spectacular than that of an academician, or a scientist perhaps, whose achievements, whilst of great importance in the national interest, have not the same popular appeal. Walter Barnes was a Negro band leader of some distinction in jazz and swing music whose death, under especially tragic circumstances, shocked the Negro world. In spite of the lack of a railroad to the town some five hundred people had gathered in Natchez to attend a dance promoted by the Natchez Rhythm Club where Walter Barnes and his Orchestra were providing the music. To prevent curious outsiders from peering into the dance hall, a timber building, the windows were securely battened across and boarded. When the dance was in full swing there was a sudden outbreak of fire. Panic-stricken dancers unable to escape by the windows jammed the doorways, trampling scores to death as the dance hall became a holocaust. Two hundred people perished in the flames, including Walter Barnes and the members of his Orchestra. With the incident still burning in his memory Leonard Caston—Baby Doo— sang:

281. Now I want everyone to listen, listen to my lonesome
song, (*twice*)

Now I want to state what happened to po' old Walter Barnes.

Now it was just about midnight, just about twelve o'clock, (*twice*)
Poor Walter played his theme song, the place all begin to rock.

Now when these peoples all was dancin', enjoyin' their lives so hard, (*twice*)
Just in a short while—the place was full of fire.

Sharing the sorrow of his friends and that of countless other Negroes on that June day in 1940, Gene Gilmore added his own epitaph and tried to offer a little comfort to the bereaved:

282. Lord, I know, I know—how you Natchez people feel to-day, (*twice*)
Some of them thinking of the fire that their children's lives away.

Lord, it was late one Tuesday night, people had come from miles around, (*twice*)
They was enjoyin' their lives when that rhythm club went down.

Lord, it was sad and misery when the high flames began to roll, (*twice*)
There was over two hundred dead and gone, Lord, and they can't come here no more.

I'm gonna tell all you people, to listen to what I have to say, (*twice*)
Don't be uneasy 'bout your children, because they all is at rest to-day.

The Natchez Fire was a tragedy of great significance to Negroes; it was of little more than passing consequence to White persons—including those in Natchez itself, a notorious centre of racial discrimination. But eighteen months after Caston and Gilmore recorded their blues, an event occurred which had more far-reaching effects than those occasioned by any other disaster; a man-made catastrophe that ultimately exceeded any tragedies caused by natural forces; that embraced all colours, all races.

On 7 December 1941, in the midst of peace negotiations, Japanese dive-bombers, in an act of flagrant aggression, made a sudden surprise attack on the major United States Naval Base of Pearl Harbor in the Hawaiian Islands. Important military and naval installations were wrecked and a battleship, three destroyers, a target ship and other craft were sunk. American naval strength in the Pacific was paralysed by the blow which was timed to coincide with attacks on Guam, Midway and Wake Islands and points in the Philippines, all made without declaration of war. The campaigns of the Non-Interventionists were of no avail now for the United States was dramatically drawn into the war. Anger at the attack surged in the heart of the nation, and White and coloured of every race living under the Stars and Stripes shared the fury and the pain.

283. December the seventh, nineteen and forty-one, (*twice*)
The Japanese flew over Pearl Harbor and dropped them
    bombs by the ton.

The Japanese is so ungrateful, just like a stray dog in
    the street, (*twice*)
Well, he bites the hand that feeds him soon as he gets
    enough to eat.

Some says the Japanese is hard fighters but any dummy
    ought to know, (*twice*)
Even a rattlesnake won't bite you in your back, he will
    warn you before he strikes his blow.

I turned to my radio and I heard Mr. Roosevelt say,
    (*twice*)
"We wanted to stay out of Europe and Asia but now
    we all got a debt to pay."

We even sold the Japanese brass and scrap-iron and it
    makes my blood boil in my veins, (*twice*)
'Cause they made bombs and shells out of it and they
    dropped them down on Pearl Harbor just like rain.

In Dr. Clayton's blues there is evidence of racial hatred directed against others than the so-called "White Race" justifiable under the circumstances and in time of war no doubt, though not when the recipients are loyal countrymen. For no reason apart from their colour and their national origins Japanese Americans were sadly treated during the war and put in concentration camps largely for their own protection against fellow Americans who attacked them for their racial characteristics. Race and nationality were being confused in the familiar manner by persons who saw no incongruity in accepting as the Supreme Commander of Allied Forces a man with a German ancestry when they attacked others of their nation for their derivation. Negroes were guilty too of such discrimination but they were spurred on by their frustration and humiliation when they found that this was to be a "White Man's War." Some Negroes were not surprised. They remembered that only ten per cent of the coloured draftees in World War I saw combat service overseas; that the majority of Negro soldiers had been employed as stevedores, in the sanitary and labour corps; that the French had been issued with official "Secret Information Concerning Black American Troops" insisting on segregation; that the fact that Negro troops were the first of any Allied Forces to set foot on enemy soil had been as swiftly forgotten as the gallant record of the 369th Cavalry; that within a year after the war many returning Negro servicemen were lynched. When they received their registration papers, when they were "billed out and bound to go," when they sat and waited in perplexed helplessness for their medical examinations and their aptitude tests, there was a certain understandable lack of enthusiasm on the part of some Negroes to participate in the war. Others took a more objective view.

284. I was sittin' here wonderin' with my number, in that old goldfish bowl, (*twice*)
       An' when I heard my number called, oooh Lord, I couldn't feel happy to save my soul.

       Everywhere I go I see that same ol' one-fifty-eight, (*twice*)
       I knew I was billed up baby, ooh Lord, Uncle Sam say, "Bill don't be late."

All you young men, I mean come and follow me,
(*twice*)
American soldiers went befo'—oooh Lord, well, why
can't we?

There were only two Negro line officers in the regular
United States Army in 1940 and the four Negro regiments—
two infantry, two cavalry, were comanded by White officers.
It was impossible for a Negro to enter the Marines or for
him to enter the Navy in any other capacity than as a mess
attendant. Coloured troops in World War I had been primarily
used for pioneer work with spade and pick even when they
had been sent overseas for combat duties, and the prospect
seemed little better in 1941. It was with some cynicism that
many a coloured draftee faced the prospect of going to war
to die a hero in a segregated army, with the struggle for
survival in his segregated home district still in his mind.

285. I've got my questionairy and they need me in the war,
(*twice*)
Now if I feel like murder, won't have to break the
county law.

All I want is a 32–20, made on a .45 frame, (*twice*)
Yes, and a red, white and blue flag waving in my right
hand.

Now if I go down, with a red, white and blue flag in
ma hand, (*twice*)
Say, you can bet your life poor Crudup sent many a
man. . . .

Mmmmm—"Hero" is all I crave, (*twice*)
Now when I'm dead and gone, cry "Hero" on my grave.

Three million Negroes registered for service and a million
were drafted, of whom half were to see service overseas: a
considerable improvement on the situation in World War I.
Though there were some who were inclined to let "the Whites
fight their own war" the majority of Negroes were eager to
fight and the disappointment of those who were too old for
service or who were not considered fit enough was very real.

Inevitably some vented their feelings on those who were departing or more good-naturedly goaded them as they left. When a singer said he was going to "carry the coal" for the servicemen and "carry his business on" the soldier knew well enough that the reference was to the care of the woman that he had left behind rather than to his neglected home. But he accepted the joke and felt no bitterness.

286. Uncle Sam ain't no woman, but he sure can take your man, (*twice*)
Yes, gonna be many a young wife left back here cold in hand.

Uncle Sam will send you your questionnaire—what in the world are you going to do? (*twice*)
Well you know you gotta go—no need a-feelin' blue.

Well, all you young men looks worried, blues as blue can be, (*twice*)
Well, I've always got a smile on my face, Uncle Sam shall be my friend.

Well, it's when you gone to the camp, no need to think about home, (*twice*)
I'll be back carryin' your coal, and keepin' in, tryin' to carry your business on.

For any departing soldier the separation from his wife, his sweetheart or his family is a sad and strained one. The tension as the time draws near, the fumbling for words that seem so inadequate to express the mixed emotions of those who depart and those who are left behind, have been shared by millions of men and women as they have tried to comfort and reassure their partners. In couples they stand, each knowing that the parting could be a final one and neither wishing to hint at the fact. And on the crowded platform as the whistles blow and the shouts of the porters rise above the shriek of escaping steam, couples try to snatch a few private moments before the train leaves.

287. I was down at the platform with the tears standin' in my eyes, (*twice*)

Lord, my heart was goin' pitter-patter, because I hate
to say good-bye.

The boys was standin' all around me dressed in that
khaki uniform, (*twice*)
Lord, I heard that train whistle blowin' an' I know it
won't be long.

"Baby, will you please be a sweet girl now, baby, whilst
I'm gone away? (*twice*)
Lord, I won't be back to you soon—but I'll be back,
mama, some ole day.

"Lord, I hear that train whistle blowin', must-a be
comin' after me, (*twice*)
Lord, mama, I'm just as unhappy, Lord, as any po' man
can be."

Negro "rookies" were drafted to strictly segregated camps
for training and commenced to prepare for war in earnest.
The first extensions of the coloured section of the Army had
been the addition of a regiment of engineers, one of artillery
and a dozen truck companies, and further increases were
slowly being made. White officers still commanded the regiments, and in fact the advances that had been made by the
end of World War I in the training of over six hundred
Negro officers had actually been lost. Even at the end of
World War II only four Negro officers had graduated from
West Point and none from Annapolis. But though their chances
of promotion were slender, Negro trainees of all types prepared for combat.

288. You may be as strong as a lion, you may be as humble
as a lamb, (*twice*)
Just take your mind off your wife and put it on Uncle
Sam.

I want all of you draftees to put your mind on the
training camp, (*twice*)
So when you meet Hitler, your powder won't be damp.

Just pack your suitcase, get ready to leave your mate,
(*twice*)
You know you got to go and help the United States.

Came the day of embarkation leave. Negro soldiers were full of hope returning to their homes for the last few days before crossing the U-Boat infested waters for Europe, or commencing the hazardous voyage to the American bases in the Pacific. In those few last hours the truth of the situation is faced and the reality of the imminent separation is inescapable. War is brutal and war is bloody; the soldier knows it. His training has prepared him for its severity; he has learned to shoot and bayonet and he knows that his mission is to "kill the enemy." There is no room for sentiment or reflection in battle but in the quiet hours of the embarkation leave he realizes in truth what he is fighting for. He knows the odds now, like an experienced gambler, and he is no longer afraid to face them or to share them with his partner.

289. Please do the best you can, I'll be back some day,
    (*twice*)
I will keep fighting, do my hardest to battle my way.

To keep you from suffering, baby, I don't mind dyin',
Every Jap I kill, that'll be peace for your po' li'l mind.
I know I can't kill them all, but I'll give them a heck
    of a time.

You gotta watch the headlights shinin' jes' as long as yo'
    poor li'l eyes can see, (*twice*)
And you can tell the world that I'm fightin' for what
    really belongs to me.

The United States Navy and the Marines relaxed their restrictions and admitted Negroes into the services but the majority who embarked for the theatres of war were destined for service in the Army. They were fighting fit and prepared for combat in the front line, but when they arrived at their overseas bases many Negro combat units found that they were to be employed as service troops, as stevedores and pioneers—a misuse of their training which had the gravest effects on their morale. Actual armed fighting broke out between coloured and White servicemen at European and North African bases, and serious instances of Jim Crow discrimination occurred in the Pacific theatre of war. When given their opportunity to fight, Negro troops engaged in battle with almost fanatical recklessness, determined to prove their worth. In spite of the effects of much racial trouble the famous 92nd Division which in Italy fought for twelve months against the crack German Panzer Divisions was covered in glory, though a quarter of its men were lost. Many of the men fought in the front line under the most hazardous conditions for five months without relief, and culminating its advance with the liberation of Genoa, the Division gained twelve thousand decorations. Equally outstanding were the Negro troops that acquitted themselves with such distinction and heroism at Anzio, whilst no White soldiers who fought beside them will forget the courage and tenacity of the Negro 761st Battalion in the Battle of the Bulge. In all, some twenty-two Negro combat units saw service in Europe, and earned the highest praise for their contributions. Equally distinguished was the work of the Negro ordnance troops who unloaded over twenty million tons of cargo and, in the course of operating, the famous *Red Ball Express* performed the remarkable feat of moving 19,000 troops to the front line in a single night. But all this time the Red Cross maintained segregated camps and catering facilities, and contrary to every scrap of evidence available to anthropologists, insisted on segregating Negro blood in the blood banks for transfusion: an action all the more ironic because the blood bank of England was then under the charge of a Negro, Dr. Charles Drew of Howard University. There was good reason to wonder at the stupidity of such discrimination.

290. This war is ragin', what're you men goin' to do? (*twice*)
    If Uncle Sam calls you in the war, there's no use to
        feelin' blue.

        Eeeh, when you' fightin', blood runnin' in yo' face,
            (*twice*)
        There's no use to worryin'—this world is a funny old
            place. . . .

In the United States Air Force the position was somewhat better, though General Marshall had declared in 1940 that "there is no such thing as coloured aviation at this time," even after training of Negroes as pilots had been urged by the Senate. Negroes were trained for flying duties when war broke out and the prospect of getting into the cockpit of a fighter was immensely attractive to coloured men wishing to get into action.

291.   Uncle Sam is gonna give me a Thunderbolt, he wants
       me to fly away up above the clouds, (*twice*)
    He wants me to drop a bomb on the Japanese, I really
       got to make my baby proud.

    I want a machine-gun and I want to be hid out in the
       woods, (*twice*)
    I want to show old man Hitler that Sonny Boy don't
       mean him no good.

    I want to drop a bomb, and set the Japanese city on
       fire, (*twice*)
    Now because they are so rotten, I just love to see them
       die.

    I've got the Victory Blues because I know I've got to
       go, (*twice*)
    Now to keep the Japanese from slipping in through my
       baby's back door.

Justly celebrated were the pilots of the Fifteenth Air Force in the all-Negro 99th Pursuit Squadrons under Colonel B. O. Davis, Jnr., which was continually praised by Field-Marshal Montgomery for its protection and support of the Eighth Army. The 99th were known as the "Red Tails" and their heroism in North Africa and in Italy will not be forgotten either by the American and British troops that saw them in action, nor by the Germans who so feared their low-level strafing attacks. In one outstanding raid the Red Tails destroyed eighty-three German aircraft and many installations at an airfield in Rumania; they gave strong support to Allied landings and were warmly praised by Marshal Tito for their work in Yugoslavia.

Came the end of the war. Negroes had proved that they could live and fight and die as bravely, as well and with as much honour, as any of their countrymen. Some will never return to their country, and their remains lie buried in countries far from their homeland. They died for the preservation of liberty in a country that denied them much. Their women waited, and waited in vain. They bewailed the loss of their men as other bereaved women, years after the end of World War I, mourned the deaths of their menfolk who had fought and fallen "for Uncle Sam."

292. Uncle Sammy thought he was so doggone cute, (*twice*)
He took my daddy out of his box-back and put him in a khaki suit.

Gonna sit down and write a letter to my Uncle Sam, (*twice*)
Tell him the war is over, please send me back my man.

Uncle Sam has told me that things are going around, (*twice*)
He took all the booze away and my good brown from town.

Those who had died were spared the pain that was shared by many of those who returned. Bitter anti-racialism was encountered by many Negroes who anticipated that their war service had cleared away the cruelties of segregation. Within the first three post-war years more than forty Negroes were lynched and many more were murdered or silently disappeared. Tragic though these events were, the war was not lost for the Negro. The men both coloured and White who died in the service of their country, died for the freedom of all their countrymen, and the overwhelming majority of those who lived came back to continue to wage the war for the freedom of the individual at home; a war against prejudice and ignorance. In this are engaged men of all races and social groups who have learned how to live happily in an atmosphere of mutual regard and fellowship.

Chapter 10

Going Down Slow

SOME coloured leaders contend that the Negro has never lost a race riot. In view of the tragic loss of life, the beatings and oppression that have characterized these most bestial of forms of human strife this would seem a curious paradox. Negroes have been jailed for incitement to riot when they themselves have been the victims, whilst their aggressors have escaped punishment. But eventually the truth becomes known and the ire of public-spirited people is stirred. In the long run, reforms have followed the riots and each occurrence has led thousands of men of all colours and classes to try to prevent any such happening again. Not always have they succeeded, but as in the case of lynching, the cumulative effect has resulted in social advancement for the Negro. Similarly, the great natural disasters of flood and fire and storm, and the man-made disaster of war, though bringing great misery and suffering for many at the time, have at least resulted in the betterment of conditions revealed by these calamities.

Two sides there are to every argument, and though in their treatment of Negro refugees and soldiers the American Red Cross were sometimes culpable for much wrong, their actions were sometimes motivated by reasons ultimately designed for his benefit that were not apparent to the Negro. Coloured men were put in "concentration camps" and their confinement was real, often occasioning much hardship, but it was sometimes a necessary expedient to prevent the spread of disease. When the Red Cross found that they had hundreds of thousands of Negroes and poor Whites in their immediate care they discovered sickness and disease rampant to an extent that had scarcely been suspected. The Mississippi floods brought thousands of Negroes to the Red Cross camps whose necks and hands bore the hideous red rash of pellagra. On the bodies of many amongst them ulcers that refused to heal indicated that they were close to death. At this time at least seven thousand people in the South died every year from pellagra and within the flood states alone some fifty thousand persons suffering from the malady were believed to be living. Knowing nothing of pellagra, the temporarily appointed Red Cross medical director, William de Kline, approached Dr. Joseph Goldberger of the Public Health Service, appealing to him to help those who were slowly dying.

293. Some people say that I'm dead, but it's all a big mistake, (*twice*)
Some say they were at my funeral, some say they was at my wake.

I'm in a bad condition, and I'm still going down slow, (*twice*)
The place I'm going, there's a thousand others to go.

The doctor he told me I would get well some day, (*twice*)
People, he may be right—then it may be the other way.

Now the time has come, I've got to take it real slow, (*twice*)
I'm in a bad condition, can't do as I did before.

Goldberger, who had devoted years to the study of pellagra, knew why the victims were in "bad condition," why they were "going down slow" and not dying from a sudden attack of a disease. His experiments had revealed that pellagra was not a contagious disease; injecting himself, his wife and assistants with discharges from the sores, with the excreta of pellagrins, he could not produce the symptoms of the illness. It was patently clear to him that pellagra was the disease of a class. Poor people suffered from it; rich persons did not. The difference he believed, and subsequently proved, was one of nutrition. Negroes and poor Whites lived on three staple items: cornbread, fat meat and black molasses. Convict volunteers from Rankin Prison Farm, Mississippi, submitted themselves as subjects for his experiments in return for their freedom. Those that were kept on this limited diet, which was all too prevalent in the prison farms at the time, eventually contracted the illness, as did thousands of other people who were forced by poverty to live on the identical diet. "Eeh now Alek," explained Sonny Terry, "boy, I'm gonna tell ya about this song—now this is a chain gang song. And now the boys on the chain gang, don't eat, they don't feed on nothin' but cornbread, meat an' molasses. The boys there made—one of the boys made up a song: I know what I'm gonna do, I'm gonna make me a song, 'I don't want no cornbread, meat, black molasses.'"

294. I don't want no cornbread, meat, black molasses,
    I don't want no cornbread, meat, black molasses,
    At supper-time, Lord, Lord, supper-time.

    I ain't got no, got no ready-made money,
    I ain't got no, got no ready-made money,
    I can't go home, Lord, Lord, can't go home.

But though the song was common in the chain gangs it was to be found throughout the South, one of the earliest of blues, and noted by Odum and Johnson before blues appeared on record. Goldberger's cure was two cents' worth of yeast a day for every pellagrin and on the doctor's behalf de Kline requested and obtained from the Red Cross twenty-five thousand dollars with which to purchase yeast for the suffering refugees. His measures proved startlingly successful but when the treated persons became cured they were inclined to dispense with the yeast treatment without making any changes in their diet, and slowly succumbed to the disease once more. It became necessary to persuade Southern Negroes to make up their dietary deficiency by growing greenstuffs which would avert the attacks of pellagra. Figures for the reduction of the disease fluctuated for many years, affected by ignorance, prejudice, famine and drought. In turnip greens, a crop was found that strengthened the consumer's resistance to pellagra immeasurably, but whereas a Pink Anderson might sing that he was "crazy 'bout them greasy greens," a Charlie Jackson moaned that "turnip greens, turnip greens: that's somethin' that I don't eat." The Federal State Department of Agriculture and the Red Cross together had to educate the croppers and landowners who were working the land to its ultimate sterility, to grow food that would provide the nourishment that they needed. In the similar fight against scurvy and other diseases resulting from serious vitamin deficiencies, medical practitioners have been constantly frustrated by the mistrust in which the Negro farmers held them. Many a Negro and poor White alike regarded with suspicion the bottles that were tendered for their benefit and it took many years before they could be assured that they were not the victims of a commercial deception.

295. You go down to the warehouse, White folks say it ain't
      no use,
      You go down to the warehouse, White folks say it ain't
      no use,
      Government ain't givin' away nothin' but that canned
      grapefruit juice.

Whereas pellagra is a disease resulting from a dietary deficiency, and is not contagious, other diseases are transmitted by carriers, by rodents, by food and above all by insanitary conditions of living. In the South the lack of window screens in Negro homes means that there is no prevention against the admission of malaria-carrying mosquitoes and disease-transmitting flies. Typhus and other diseases arising from poor storage facilities for water reserves rage unchecked, and the total lack of sanitation in many homes is the cause of untold illnesses and unnumbered deaths. Amongst the most virulent diseases is tuberculosis which attacks young and old, eating its way through the lungs of its victims. Generally it lies undetected until the sufferer has reached far too advanced a stage in the disease for a cure to be effected. By that time the members of his family and his associates have probably become infected and the coughing consumptive sprays the seeds of death over all whom he meets. "Everybody spit in your face ain't friend to you," sang Jim Jackson, but his words had a deeper, more tragic significance. In the later stages the dread disease becomes apparent to all who see the sufferer and their elementary knowledge of the killing germs warns them to keep away. For the consumptive this is an even harder thing to bear.

296. T.B.'s all right to have if your friends don't treat you
　　　so low-down, (*twice*)
　　Don't you ask them for no favours—they even stop
　　　hangin' aroun'.

　　Oooh—oooh, T.B.'s killing me, (*twice*)
　　I'm like a prisoner, always wishin' I was free.

　　When I was on my feet I could not walk down the
　　　street,
　　For you women lookin' at me from my head to my
　　　feet. . . .
　　But ooooh now, the T.B.'s killing me,
　　I want my body buried in the deep, blue sea.

　　Ooooh—ooooh,
　　I got tuberculosis, consumption's killing me.

For the relatives of the consumptive who in all probability have already breathed in the infection and are themselves in the early stages of the disease, it is acutely distressing to see their loved ones in the terrible throes of tuberculosis. Appalling ignorance through the lack of even elementary education amongst Negroes in the South results in many instances in the failure to take the most fundamental precautions in the care of the invalid. Medical facilities are often pitifully inadequate, Jim Crow hospitals refuse to take Negro patients and the few Negro hospitals have no spare beds to cope with additional cases. Negro doctors have no hope of treating White patients and White doctors will often refuse to treat Negroes. Consequently Negro doctors are overworked by sick members of their own race and have to serve families that are unable to meet their bills. The medical profession for Negroes holds little attraction in the South and the people turn instead to the "White Magic" voodoo doctors, the conjures and the itinerant pill-vendors for aid, or they depend on traditional "cures." Some of the latter undoubtedly have substance but others are pure superstition. Watching his woman slowly dying through the foul complaint, emotionally confused by the conflicting pressures of wishing to care for her himself and the desire to seek assistance, the Negro husband can only plead helplessly for recovery.

297. I tol' her, "Don't you go, baby, cause you sho' is worryin' me,"
I tol' her, "Don't you go, baby, cause you really is worryin' po' me,
I leave in the mornin' now, sweet mama, I goin' back to Jackson, Tennessee."

She said, "Don't go, baby! Ah baby, I believe to my soul I'm dyin', (*twice*)
If I ain't dyin' now, black man, I believe to my soul I'm lyin'."

"Oh, don't go down, baby, cause I ain't gonna tell you no lie,
Don't go down, baby, I ain't ever goin' to tell you no lie,
Say you quit me now, little woman, and oh, that's the day you gonna die.

"Wouldn't mind dyin' now, baby, but I gotta go by myself, (*twice*)
I don't mind dyin' now, little woman, I'm gwina carry me with someone else."

"Mmmmm, well now dyin' is hard to me,"
She say "Well, baby, dyin' sho is hard to me."
"My baby—told you no lies, baby, well you sho's gonna have the doggone T.B."

In the Northern cities where overcrowding has added so much suffering tuberculosis is rife. In Harlem the death rate from consumption is still four times higher than the rate for New York City in its entirety and in the early thirties a single block in Harlem where four thousand Negroes were crammed together had a tubercular death rate which was twice that of the whole of Manhattan. It was known grimly as the "lung block." But at least the Negroes in the North responded to campaigns designed to reduce consumption. When Detroit commenced its fight against the disease in 1936 under a panel lead by Henry Vaughan, the Health Commissioner, Bruce Douglas, tuberculosis-controller, and other determined scientists and doctors, Negro response was encouraging. The plague centres were systematically examined and in nine months three thousand unsuspected cases were under treatment. Before the visits commenced only two per cent of Negroes in these seriously depressed areas voluntarily presented themselves for examination even though dramatic warnings were being publicized and broadcast. Even so the rate was eight times higher than the presentation amongst Whites. The visiting of health officers brought a remarkable response. Nearly half the Negroes in Detroit's plague centres had gone to the city's physicians as a result of the drive, though less than twenty per cent of White persons from these areas had submitted themselves for examination and care. Instead of the bare thirteen per cent of "minimals"—persons in preliminary stages of tuberculosis—amongst those who were diagnosed and treated for the disease before the campaign, it was now possible to anticipate the ravages of the disease in nearly half the cases diagnosed, bringing cure in less than nine months. For the remainder their disease was too far advanced and cure could only be effected for a proportion of those in hospital, whilst the others in the sanatoria succumbed to the "white death."

298. Here I lay a-cryin', something is on my mind,
It's midnight, wonder where the nurse can be?

I feel down, not a friend in this town, I'm blue and all alone,
Sisters are gone, brothers are too, no one to call my own.

I can't keep from cryin', left alone while I'm dyin',
Yes, this man has made me for to feed on my knee,
But if the law is different, he means to break the T.B.
—oh Lord.

Yes, he railroaded me to the sanit-orium,
It's too late, too late, but I have finished my run,
This is the way all the women are done when they got
the dirty T.B.

Yes, I run around for months and months,
From gin-mill to gin-mill to honkey-tonk,
Now it's too late, just look what I've done done,
Now I've got the dirty T.B.

Even more devastating within the Negro race and more
tragic in its effects is syphilis. The social diseases of syphilis
and gonorrhœa destroy the lives of innocent and guilty alike,
blight the health of new-born children and debilitate the race.
Conditions of living in Negro districts both rural and urban
promote promiscuous relationships that cause the rapid
spread of venereal diseases. Many Negroes are totally unaware of the dangers of the disease and how readily it may
be transmitted. The high prevalence of prostitution in Negro
areas, for reasons already outlined, has further promoted the
appalling incidence of these diseases, whilst the break-up of
homes and families both causes and at times is caused by fast
living. The blues is realistic enough to accept the situation
with terse regret but without self-pity.

299. Tell all my good friends, 'cause I know I can't last
    long, (twice)
    "Please don't you wait, for I'll be dead and gone."

    Yes, I'm sinking, sinking, sinking down below my
    grave, (twice)
    Done had a good time but, Lord, how I done paid.

At the end of the nineteen-twenties the mortality rate
amongst Negroes from deaths caused by syphilis was more
than eight times higher than that amongst White persons, and
the lack of proper treatment, of elementary precautions and
education aggravated the problem. In buildings where a
single unhygienic and leaking toilet fixture was shared by a
dozen families the spread of syphilitic infection was all too
possible. Innocent persons thus suffered with the guilty, for
syphilis is highly contagious, and if it is engendered initially

by immoral behaviour, it blights the lives of countless thousands who have led blameless lives. Here the sins of the fathers are visited upon the children and the syphilitic spawn is passed on to the offspring of infected parents who may themselves be unaware of the ravages of the disease. The high incidence of blindness amongst Negroes is largely due to this, some being born without vision, others blind through accident, but many others lose their sight as the effects of the disease spread through the system. At the railroad depots, on the street pavements and in the gutters blind men beg for help from those little better off than themselves. Playing their guitars and shaking their tin cups to attract attention, many sing the blues. In a society where there is insufficient work to keep all employed the blind man has little hope for other employment. So he sings about the life he once knew, of the fortunes of his listeners and only occasionally do his thoughts run to his plight.

300. There was a time that I went blind, (*twice*)
It was the darkest day that I ever saw,
It was the day that I went blind.

Nobody cares for me, (*twice*)
'Cause I lost my sight and I have to be led,
Nobody cares for me.

It's so hard to have to be blind, Lord, (*twice*)
I'm away in the dark and got to feel my way,
It's so hard to have to be blind.

I moaned the day I went blind, (*twice*)
Oh Lord, tell me how long. Am I to be blind always?

The blues singer seldom seeks the sympathy of his listeners and his songs are usually vigorous statements of fact rather than complaints as to his condition. Many a blind blues singer gives no hint of his perpetual darkness in his blues, whilst others only betray the fact by a passing but meaningful reference.

301. I can tell my dog, every time I hear him bark,
I can tell my rider when I feel her in the dark.

You can call, "Bloody murder!" when you wants me
out yo' way.
Say, that's all right, mama, you gwine-a need my help
some day.

In many districts the number of blind Negroes is as much
as five times as great as the respective proportion amongst
the White population and this terrible suffering, whilst often
due to the hazardous nature of the work that Negroes undertake, is primarily the result of syphilitic infection. Though
some attempts to check the spread of the disease were made
during the nineteen-thirties the full extent was not appreciated until the commencement in 1940 of the Draft Board
reports. Of the first hundred thousand White men drafted, it
was found that 18.5 per thousand were suffering from syphilis in some stage of the disease, but of the first hundred thousand Negroes, the appalling figure of 241.2 syphilitics in
every thousand men drafted was revealed. For the first time
the ghastly truth was realized that a quarter of the nation's
Negro men were suffering from some form of the disease in
their blood, though in the majority of instances through no
fault of their own. A vigorous campaign to test and treat
Negro sufferers was instituted and to entice the populace to
submit themselves to Wassermann tests, free ice-cream and
drinks were given to every Negro who offered himself for
examination, mobile units visiting the outlying districts where
infection was rife and unchecked. As a result many thousands of persons were saved, the dreadful parasitic blight that
was sapping their energy and health brought to an end. But
with others the disease had advanced too far and no measures to end its effects were possible. This they knew and
grimly accepted.

302. Well, I've had my fun, well if I never get well no more,
    (*twice*)
    Yes, my health is failing me and I'm going down slow.

    Please write my mother, tell my mother, say for me,
    Oh won't somebody please tell my mother, "Pray for
    me."
    Yes, and tell my mother, "Pray for me, please forgive
    me all my sins."

Oh mother, please don't send for no doctors, doctors
    can't do me no good,
Well, please don't you send for no doctors, well doc-
    tors can't do me no good,
Yes, it's all my fault, I didn't do the things I should.

That venereal diseases flourish in depressed areas is substantiated by a great deal of evidence which indicates that
not only the prevalence of prostitution, but the insanitary and
unhygienic standards of living are prime causes of infection.
Often it is economically impossible for the persons concerned
to better themselves materially and thus avoid the danger of
disease, and the Negro is often more openly exposed to illnesses of many forms because he is insufficiently equipped
to oppose them. Migrant Negroes, homeless men, those that
are obliged to sleep over the gratings of basement kitchens,
on the marble shelves above the station radiators, or on the
park benches, cannot withstand the rigours of a mid-West
winter. Shuffling through the streets with feet wrapped in
sacking and with tattered clothes offering little protection
against rain and snow, they are prone to sickness. Those that
have a share in an apartment may be out of the weather, but
they too are not always able to meet the cost of keeping
warm.

303. My wet clothes in your wash-tub and your washboard
      on your shelf, (*twice*)
   If I change this morning I will have to dry my clothes
    by myself.

   Well, it's dark and cloudy, "Say, can I dry them by
    your fire?" (*twice*)
   She said, "I wouldn't mind but my gas bill runs so
    high."

   (*Spoken*) Well, babe, that's all right, you won't have
    to wash my clothes any more. I'm gonna change; got
    my own way to dry them: just won't wash them
    that's all.

   Have to leave you here with my wet clothes in ma
    hand, (*twice*)
   I didn't hurt your feelin's but I left you raisin' sand.

When my load gets heavy have to get down on my
knees, (*twice*)
Wet clothes in ma hand, rain fallin' down on me.

Suffering from the effects of exposure the folk Negro is
still likely to turn to the conjure doctors and the vendors of
patent medicines for aid. The fees that they charge for their
dubious services are much less, and the sick man is reassured
by the foul-tasting purgative. Sings Bumble Bee Slim between
his choking coughs:

304. Doctor, please give me something just to ease these
awful pains, (*twice*)
I done caught my death of cold and it's settling on my
brain.

I cain't hardly breathe, I got a wheezing in my chest,
(*twice*)
Well, I'm having bronchitis, doctor—you should know
the rest.

(*Spoken*) Give me Oil of Ninety-Nine, Three-Six—
anything!
I done caught my death of cold—Lord have mercy.

I done caught my death of cold, well, my friends cannot be found, (*twice*)
Well, I been wading in deep water an' I been sleeping
on the ground.

Diseases of the chest and lungs account for a high proportion of Negro deaths and these are largely caused by exposure and insufficient protection against the weather both in
housing and clothing, and inadequate attention when the illness has taken a hold on the life of the man. During the late
nineteen-twenties, in the peak years of the pellagra outbreaks,
seven times as many Negroes died from pneumonia as from
pellagra, and the deaths were proportionately three and a
half times as many as the rate for White persons. The resistance of the Southern Negro recently arrived in the North,
ill-clad and ill-housed, and unaccustomed to the bitter climate, was insufficient to withstand the onslaught of the dis-

ease and a trivial occurrence that would normally lead to little more than a severe cold became a fatal illness.

305. I'm achin' all over, baby, I got the pneumonia this time, (*twice*)
An' it's all on account of that low-down gal of mine.

Sneaking round the corners, running up alleys too, (*twice*)
Watching my woman, trying to see what she going to do.

Sitting down in the streets one cold, dark, stormy night, (*twice*)
Trying to see if my good gal going to make it home all right.

Well, baby, in the winter, prowling round in the rain, (*twice*)
Well, baby, give me this pneumonia pain.

A large number of hospitals will not accept Negro patients under any circumstances—in some cases even when a serious accident has occurred—and thousands of coloured people die for want of proper attention. That the celebrated blues singer, Bessie Smith, died from loss of blood after she was involved in a fatal automobile accident because she was not accepted at a Jim Crow hospital, may have been subtle race propaganda. Her arm was nearly severed from her body and careful investigation has revealed that she died on the way to hospital and was not turned away as the legend states. But there is no doubt that Miss Juliette Desmond, the distinguished Dean of Fisk University, and her companion, Miss Edna Johnson, were refused admittance to the hospital at Dalton, Georgia, after they had been involved in a similar accident, and they died as a result. There are only 110 Negro hospitals in the United States and of these less than a quarter are registered. The Julius Rosenwald Fund spent more than a million and a half dollars in fifteen years on Negro health facilities but at the end of World War II there were still only ten thousand hospital beds available in the entire United States for thirteen million Negroes. As the average over the nation is ten beds available for a thousand of the population, the ratio for White persons must be appreciably higher— especially when it is learned that in some Negro depressed areas only seventy-five beds are available for a million persons. That the figures should never have been drawn in terms of colour is obvious—but necessary when discrimination by colour plays so important a part of the medical service. So the sick Negro lies in his fever upon his own bed or pallet— not only by choice but by necessity. He knows what his chances of survival may be for he is well acquainted with sickness and death. With a sardonic humour that does not wince at the truth of his situation, he may still express in sickness and closeness to death a philosophy to which he adheres in health and life.

306. Bring me flowers whilst I'm living, please don't bring them when I'm dead, (*twice*)
And bring them back to my bedside, ooh well, to cool my achin' head.

When a man is sick in bed, please come to my rescue, (*twice*)
When a man is dead and gone, honey, oh well, won't even know what you do.

Bring me water to my bed, a drink will keep me cool, (*twice*)
And just say that I have gone—ooh well, I shall try to help that fool.

I'll stay here long as I can, sleep when I cain't help myself, (*twice*)
We has all got to die, ooh well, well an' I ain't no better than no one else.

Don't bring me flowers after I'm dead, a dead man sure can't smell, (*twice*)
And if I don't go to heaven, I sure won't need no flowers in hell.

Unable to give the sick man the proper attention that he needs as he lies with the shadow of death already falling across him, his kin depend on folk remedies to aid him. Potions are mixed from roots and herbs, a poultice is made from cow-dung and hog-lard to off-set pneumonia. Old superstitions are recalled: a bush is hung over the head of the bed which will ensure that death is kept at bay whilst the thorns remain sharp; no broom will sweep beneath the bed; and the tables—so reminiscent of the mortuary "cooling-board"—are treated with respect. Living and dying alike await in dread the heralds of death: the warning of the hoot owl, the tapping of the woodpecker on the door, the cry of the whippoor-will. These are omens more emphatic, more inexorable to the folk Negro than the onslaught of fever.

307. It was midnight on a Sunday, the clock struck thirteen
        times, (*twice*)
    I was scared and I was frightened 'cause I sure believe
        this sign.

    Lord, I heard the owl a-hootin', I knowed somebody
        was bound to die, (*twice*)
    Put my head beneath the pillow, started in to moan
        and cry.

    Then early in the morning the picture on the wall fell
        down, (*twice*)
    And it ain't no use in talkin', somebody is graveyard
        boun'.

    Hound dog started howlin', somebody's sure to leave
        this land, (*twice*)
    Take who you want, Lordy, but please don't take my
        man.

    Lord, I knows I'm black and ugly, but he's so good and
        kind, (*twice*)
    Lord, take most anybody but please don't take this
        man of mine.

In her distraught state the woman who is watching her husband slowly dying does not draw any distinction between superstition and religion. She is only aware that she is at the mercy of supernatural powers beyond her understanding. So she cries to her God to save her dying man, whilst he, in his delirium, believes that he hears the death bells tolling. The proximity of death may bring him closer to the beliefs of his elders and of the church. Though he may feel it is too late to seek remission for his past way of life, the blues singer who seldom concerns himself with the spiritual world may re-affirm his belief in God and become aware once more of the content of long-forgotten teachings of the ministers. Then the singer becomes humbled with the imminence of death, though the "sweet chariot" now swings low on rubber tyres.

308. Sounds like I can hear this mornin', baby, them bells
     ringin' all in my ears, (*twice*)
    Yes I know I'm gonna leave on a chariot; wonder what
    line it gonna carry me away from here?

    You know every living creeper man was born to die,
    (*twice*)
    Yes, when that chariot comes for you, they gonna
    bring runnin' a trolley here.

    You know my mother tol' me, my papa tol' me too:
    (*twice*)
    "Some day that chariot gonna comin' after you."

    Well I been wonderin' what kind of chariot, Lord, goin'
    to carry me from here? (*twice*)
    Yes, you know the life I been livin', oh Lord, for great
    many years.

For all the portents that the Negro may see death often comes suddenly and unannounced: death from illness and disease; death in childbirth, death through accidents and disputes. Separated by war or by the search for employment, many a family has suffered bereavement when its members were apart. The mail man brings the stark, tragic news and the man who has travelled North to find work, has planned to bring his wife and family to him as soon as he has found a home and sufficient money to support them, has his plans shattered in the single, terrible moment that he unfolds the "letter edged in black."

309. An' I went off in that far distant land,
I wasn't there long before I got a telegram—what did it
say?

Sayin', "Man, won't you please come home?"
Sayin', "Man, won't you please come home?"

Then I went back home and I looked upon the bed,
And that best ole friend I had was dead.

REFRAIN
Lord an' I ain't got no lovin' baby now,
Lord an' I ain't got no lover now.

Lord, I'm sorry, sorry, sorry to my heart,
But that best ole friend some day must part.

Now sure as the birds fly in the sky above,
Life ain't worth livin' if you ain't with the one you
love.

If I'd a know'd she didn't love me and didn't want me
to,
Lord I'd've taken morphine and die.

And in the share-cropper's cabin, the Catfish Row shanty,
the Bronzeville apartment, the women await in fear of the
news of the collapse of an aged field-hand in the turnrow; the
discovery of a ragged tramp frozen to death on the pavement; the fall of the "top" in the mine; or the accident on the
production line. A crumpled body is brought home; a man
lies upon his death bed and his wife moistens the waxen
features with her weeping.

310. Daddy, oh daddy, won't you answer me please?
(*twice*)
All day I stood by your coffin trying to give my poor
heart ease.

I rubbed my hands over your head and whispered in
your ear, (*twice*)
And I wonder if you know that your mama is near.

You told me that you loved me and I believed what
you said, (*twice*)
And I wished that I could fall here across your coffin
dead.

When I left the undertaker's I couldn't help but cry,
(*twice*)
And it hurt me so bad to tell the man I love, "Good-
bye."

It is hard for the bereaved to keep back the tears, and during the wake which sometimes lasts for two or three days
and nights, the women moan the blues through the long
hours much as the Jewish women cried at Jerusalem's Wailing Wall and the Irish sing the "keen." Fatalistically, the sick
man faces death and, trying to spare the suffering of those
that he leaves behind, asks only that he be remembered with
love and not with tears when he is laid in the cold ground.

311. Just remember me, baby, when I'm in six feet of cold,
cold ground, (*twice*)
Always think of me, mama, just say, "There's a good
man gone down."

Don't cry, baby, baby, after I'm gone,
Don't cry, baby, don't cry after I'm gone,
I'd let a good man love you, and I ain't done nothing
wrong.

After a life of hard toil with little at the end of it to show
for all the years of manual labour, of sweat and tears, death
comes as a welcome release for many of the poorest Negroes.
"It's a bad wind that never changes," they say fatalistically,
and look forward to an after-life that is a rest from suffering.
For years they may cherish the prospect of a splendid funeral
which they believe will give them an appropriate send-off to
a world more rewarding than the one that they leave. So for
years they contribute to burial societies, select their casket,
plush-lined and glass-topped, paying for it on installment
plans with hard-earned cash, and plan the details of a funeral
in which every sign of affluence and expense is evident, and
in which the hearse is drawn by "white horses standing in
line," and the coffin is lowered on a chain of gold.

312. It's a long lane that's got no end, (*three times*)
It's a bad wind that never change.

Lord, it's two white horses in a line, (*three times*)
Will take me to my burying ground.

Oh, dig me my grave with a silver spade, (*three times*)
You may lead me down with a golden chain.

Have you ever heard a church bell tone? (*three times*)
Did you know that a poor boy's dead and gone?

Burial practices in Negro society vary greatly from the rich and sumptuous funerals afforded by the Negro societies and Masonic Lodges to the sad, humble interment in a "shallow grave just six by three," on which a crude wooden cross is the only marker and a bunch of wild flowers the only wreath. Many a Negro, conscious of his simple station in life, would rather be buried in the surroundings in which he has lived and in accordance with the folk traditions of his fathers, than with all the splendour of a Harlem or New Orleans funeral parade. The women turn the pictures to the wall, hang *crêpe* on the doors and affix it to their sleeves. Then they "re-rag in red"—don their bright red mourning gowns and their leather slippers, and follow the coffin to the burying ground.

313. I went down in Death Valley, nothin' but the tombstones and dry bones, (*twice*)
That's where a poor man be, Lord, when I'm dead and
gone.

Now if I die—if I should die before my time, (*twice*)
I want you to bury my body down by the Frisco Line.

Aah, bye-bye, baby, I said, "Good-bye," (*twice*)
Death Valley is my home, mama, when I die.

Tell all the women, please come dressed in red, (*twice*)
They goin' on 61 Highway, that's where the poor boy
fell dead.

Wear a pair of leather slippers, put on your mourning
gown, (*twice*)
You gonna follow a po' critter to his buryin' ground.

Some Negroes derive little pleasure from the preparations for a brave funeral that they as the principal characters will not see. With aggressive irreligiousness even in death they implore their companions to "raise hell as we march along" and ask for six whores to be their pall-bearers. These are the tough, embittered characters who die as hard as they have lived, who do not care where their bodies are to be interred and who have no faith. The blues is still primarily the song of those who have turned their backs upon religion, and though some singers may be brought nearer to their God with the closeness of death, the singer who has "rambled"—who has led a sinful life in the eyes of the Church—is more than likely to maintain in his last hours the attitude that he has borne in the past without compromise or eleventh-hour repentance. To the church member, the blues are "devil songs" and the singer who walks hand-in-hand with the devil in life sardonically greets him as a friend.

314. Early this mornin' when you knocked upon my door,
     (*twice*)
     And I said, "Hello Satan, I b'lieve it's time to go."

     Me and the devil was walkin' side by side, (*twice*)
     An' I'm goin' to beat my woman until I get satisfied.

     You may bury my body down by the highway side—
     . . . Hey, I don't care where you bury my body when
        I'm dead and gone,
     You may bury my body, ooh, down by the highway
        side,
     So my ole evil spirit can get a Greyhound bus and ride.

Amongst those who have lost relatives and friends that are close to them will be some whose disregard for death is as great and as unrepentant. The heaven and hell of his parents' belief means nothing to him and the "rounder" cynically observes that he is unlikely to meet them in the after-life unless he changes his way of living, and this he has little intention of doing. He exploits the folk Negro's fear of the graveyard, using the cemetery as a place in which to sleep at night, safe in the knowledge that no one would dream of robbing a man who sleeps with the dead. Ignoring the superstitions he declares that death came to the members of his family because their time had come.

315. Dear mother's dead and gone to glory, my old dad
    done gone straight away, (*twice*)
    Only way to meet my mother, I will have to change my
    low-down ways.

    Nobody knows my trouble, but myself and the Good
    Lord, (*twice*)
    I used to have a sweet woman to love me, now she
    treats me like a low-down dog.

    She stalks my pillow, graveyard gonna be ma bed,
    (*twice*)
    Blue skies gonna be my blanket, and 'e pale moon
    gonna be my frien'.

    Black cats calls me out at midnight, night mares ride
    to the break of day, (*twice*)
    What's the use of loving some woman, some man done
    stole your love away.

    Stop your crying, do away with all your tears, (*twice*)
    If you can't stay with me, mother, it must've been your
    time to leave from here.

Such hard-boiled cynicism and lack of sympathy and feeling is common only to a few though some assume a superficial hardness of mind to hide the misery in their hearts. With gruesome imagery Billy Bird sings that he cannot love the body of a woman on whom rigor mortis has even touched her hair. But he cannot sustain his mask of callousness and the beauty of the woman that he has lost is still before his eyes as he makes promises, too late, to give her almost everything he has.

316. I went to the cemetery, look down in ma baby's face,
    (*twice*)
    Said I love you baby, but I sure cain't take yo' place.

    I'm gwine away, baby, wear you off my mind, (*twice*)
    Says if I stay roun' here be crazy all the time.

I don't want me no woman with hair like drops of
rain, (*twice*)
Every time she combs her hair you can hear them hard
nails ring.

My woman's got teeth like a lighthouse on the sea,
(*twice*)
Every time she smiles she throws them lights on me.

Mmmmmm—mmmmmmmm,
Speak to me, mama, mama, speak with me.
I'm gonna make me a hundred, gonna give you ninety-
nine.

Most recently bereaved persons meet the great tragedy in
their lives with unsuspected resources of courage and forti-
tude. Their sorrow is deep and their sense of helplessness at
times may seem almost unbearable, but the very suffering itself summons unknown reserves of strength. At first the enor-
mity of the personal loss weighs heavily on the thoughts of
the bereaved. Every object, every scrap of clothing has associations; a chance, casual, thoughtless word brings back
memories. The favourite chair that now seems empty; the
unplayed guitar with its slackening strings; the unused cos-
metics; the photographs that echo an unreal past; the thousand personal and intimate effects that are encountered and
disturbed as every drawer is pulled and cupboard door
opened: every aspect of a once-shared home overflows with
meaning that the heart is too full to bear. The one desire is
to get away: to think and yet to have no time to think; to
remember and yet to be spared the memories; to forget and
yet to recall with tenderness; to try to understand what has
happened. And so at last a calm acceptance of the inevitability of death eventually eases the pain and settles the dis-
quieted mind.

317. Shine on risin' sun, shine on, (*twice*)
Now just keep on shinin' 'cos the one I love is gone.

I'm goin' down to the station, get me a ticket for one
way, (*twice*)
Now I'm goin' keep on ridin', I know I'll feel better
some day.

I love that woman, why did death make her part?
    (*twice*)
Now she is gone, an' she left me with a broken heart.

The good Lord give it and the good Lord take it away,
    (*twice*)
Yes it's sad, but we all gotta pay that debt some day.

Bereavement is a lonely state and the tears of the lover are seldom shared by any but the closest friends and relatives. Mourning a well-loved person does at least bring the comfort and condolences of those who also share the bitter sorrow of his loss. In the Negro world there are perhaps only a few persons who are known and loved outside a small and close community, but the death of a great blues singer is a grievous occurrence which probably touches more Negroes personally than that of almost any other member of Afro-American society. Admittedly the direct effect upon their lives of the activities of a militant race leader in achieving, for example, the relaxations of segregational practices may be greater, but the feeling of personal association with such people is far less. A closer bond is felt with the coloured sportsman or entertainer whose achievements, family lives, homes and opinions are featured in detail in the race periodicals and are followed avidly by the Negro masses. But the blues singer enters their own homes; his voice is known to all, his experiences are their own and his blues are the mirror to their own lives. Whether it is Blind Lemon Jefferson in the twenties, Bessie Smith in the thirties, Blind Boy Fuller in the forties or Johnny Ace in the fifties, the death of a blues singer has been a tragedy recorded in grief by his closest friends and shared by a multitude. No singer was more loved than Leroy Carr and none was more deeply mourned when he died under mysterious circumstances at Indianapolis in 1935. Only thirty years of age when he died, he was sadly missed by his friends and many posthumous blues were composed in his honour. Sang his friend Bumble Bee Slim in a blues dedicated to his memory:

318. Now people, I'm gonna tell you, as long as I can,
    (*twice*)
    'Bout the death of Leroy Carr, well, he was my closest friend.

On one Sunday morning, just about nine o'clock, (*twice*)
Death came an' struck him, an' he began to reel and rock.

He said, "Lawd have mercy, I'm in so much misery, (*twice*)
He's my friend, you all got to do (what) you can for me."

So on Monday mornin' just about the break of day, (*twice*)
He began cryin' and he was passin' away.

I then called the doctor on the telephone, (*twice*)
When the doctor came Leroy was dead and gone.

The death of a blues singer is a tragedy within the Negro race and its repercussions are little felt by other Americans. Similarly the loss of a national figure is seldom recorded in the blues, for though the Negro desires nothing more dearly than that he should be accepted without distinction or reserve in American society, he has yet to obtain that state, and because of the consciousness of his separation he does not always feel sufficiently a part of the nation to share in its joys and sorrows. But the death of Franklin D. Roosevelt left a more profound impression. The instigator of the New Deal and the signator of Executive Order 8802 had seemed to the ordinary Negro man to be a saviour on whom they could depend and to whom they could appeal for help. It was Roosevelt in person who provided relief funds for the workless, as Red Nelson implied in his *Relief Blues*:

319. Gonna call up Headquarters, I'm gonna write to Roosevelt,
Gonna call up Headquarters, I'm gonna write to Roosevelt,
Tell him my women's done got evil—please don't send me nothin' else.

When Roosevelt died at the commencement of his fourth term, thousands of Negroes felt that they had lost a true friend, a credit to the race—the human race.

320. I sure feel bad with tears runnin' down my face,
    (*twice*)
    I lost a good friend, was a credit to our race.

    F.D.R. was everybody's friend, (*twice*)
    Well, he helped everybody, right up to the end.

    They called to Heaven, "Have mercy on his soul,
    (*twice*)
    And tell the angels, well, well, take him right into the
    fold."

    I know I can see, with my friends got sad news,
    (*twice*)
    'Cause he run away and left me and I got the F.D.R.
    blues.

That Rossevelt had good intentions and that he did much
to improve the lot of the Negro is undeniable, but it is also
sadly true that he was often evasive, equivocal and apathetic,
and that many of the principal measures that he took to improve race relations were the result of the painstaking diplo-
macy and firm pressure of honourable if often little-known
race leaders. To Roosevelt went all the credit but they believed
it right that it should be so, for it was essential that such
moves should emanate from the head of the State. So the
race leaders sat quietly back and the common Negro man
often felt far from them. When Walter White, the secretary
of the National Association for the Advancement of Coloured People, died in 1957 after a lifetime of service to the
members of his race whose colour strangely he did not even
share, no one sang a blues to his memory.

Occasionally therefore the death of someone outside the
immediate circle of relatives and friends is the concern of
many, but soon even they forget the departed in the trials of
living and the wreaths, the bunches of flowers and the grave
markers are forgotten by all save the husband, the wife, the
lover, the parent or the child.

321. People, I had a woman, she was nice and loving, kind
    to me in every way, (*twice*)

Lawd, but she die and left me, Lord, so I have the
blues on every Decoration Day.

Lord, I was standin' round her bed, these is the last
words my baby had to say: (*twice*)
She says, "Sonny Boy, I want you to bring me some
flowers on every Decoration Day."

So sorry, Sadie Lee, I just hate to see my Lord take her
away, (*twice*)
Now that's the reason why you hear me sing the blues,
I sing them on every Decoration Day.

And we have no good times now, just like the flowers
that come in May, (*twice*)
Now, but I always remember, I never will forget Decoration Day.

Cemeteries are fearsome places to superstitious people,
where "haints" and "pool doos"—disembodied, troubled
spirits—may be encountered. Often the blues singer arro-
gantly laughs at the superstitions, and calls the cemetery the
"bone-yard," the "ape-yard," the "bone orchard." He does
not wish to be reminded of death and he does not go there.
But the day comes when he has lost all that he has cherished
and the only thing left to him is the memory of the love that
once was given to him. So he finds himself, a stranger, by
an unmarked grave.

322. I'm a stranger at this place and I lookin' for my
mother's grave, (*twice*)
Well, it seems like to me, ooh well, some of us goin' to
wail.

I was at mother's grave, when they put my mother
away, (*twice*)
An' I can't find no one to take her place.

After my mother's put away, I thought my wife would
take her place, (*twice*)
I'm sure you remember my wife, ooh well, my wife
done throw me away.

I wished I could find someone to take my mother's place, (*twice*)
An' if I can't find no one you'll find me at her grave.

I'm standin' on my mother's grave and I wished I could seen her face, (*twice*)
I'll be glad when that day comes, ooh well, when it be to carry me away.

Negroes have a low suicide rate for, though the conditions under which many still live may seem to offer little hope of happiness, they have engendered a certain philosophical detachment which helps them to wait to "see what to-morrow bring." The despairing intention of the singer to "lay his head on some lonesome railroad line" to let the passing train "pacify his mind," is often sublimated in singing the blues. For some life is indeed hard and death is not unwelcome, but for every man who sings:

323. Now when I'm dead, baby, don't you cry over me,
        I'm trying to get back to my used-to-be,
            Because this world's a hard place to live before you go,
            When you ain't got nobody that you can call your own.

    Yes, I'm going up to Heaven, gonna talk to the good Lord above,
    If I can't get me no angel, give me back the one I love,
    Because this world's a hard place to live before you go,
    When you ain't got nobody that you can call your own.

there is another who sings:

324. Between midnight and dawn, baby, we may ever have to part, (*twice*)
        But there's one thing about it, baby, please remember I've always been your heart.

    So let us say good night don't let it fill our heart with pain, (*twice*)
    And may God bless you till we be let down with a golden chain.

Chapter 11

Blues Like Showers of Rain

AN APPRECIATION of the part that the Negro plays in the society of the United States and the aspects that are denied him is of major assistance in understanding the meaning of the blues. But there are barriers to appreciation presented by the manner of delivery, of speech and of form, and when these are overcome the full significance of the blues to the Negro still remains elusive. One has yet to learn why the Negro has the blues, why he sings the blues and listens to the blues. For those unaccustomed to blues singing the words are frequently incomprehensible, presenting difficulties which are seldom a problem to the Negro audience for whom the recordings are primarily intended. To the European ear and even to that of the New Englander the soft burr of Southern speech, whether White or Negro, is as difficult to understand as is the "Geordie" of the Tynesider to the Londoner. Even amongst Negroes the characteristics of local dialects cause some perplexity and amusement, the speech of the rural Southern coloured men being mimicked and ridiculed by their fellows in the North— most frequently by those who desire to forget their own Southern origins.

There are a few examples on record of blues singers, from the Deep South, who employ such distinct and localized dialects as Gullah—or Geechee—the speech of the Georgia Coast and the Sea Islands. Words such as "juke" and "buckra" which stem from Gullah have entered the speech of the blues singer. In the omission of the article of the noun and the employment of the present tense alone some blues singers show that vestiges of "Flat Talk"—the primitive compromise between African and European by which the slaves learned to speak English—still remain. Within recent years a number of recordings have been made employing "Gumbo"—the Louisiana dialect which is an admixture of Negro and French idiom, incorrectly but not infrequently confused with the Louisiana Acadian speech "Cajun." These have primarily been made in the jazz field and the blues is seldom if ever represented.

Singers who have been tied by economic circumstances to one country or urban district, or who have chosen to remain there, naturally retain the characteristic speech patterns of their milieu, and the blues is subject to many dialectual variations which have not been entirely eliminated by the redistribution of the Negro population. Some singers have voices so thick and accented that their speech is quite alien to European ears, whilst others, especially those living in areas where the density of the coloured population is not great, have a diction closely related to that of their White neighbours. The voices of Lulu Jackson, for example, and even the Tennessee-born Leroy Carr are clearly understandable and almost indistinguishable from those of White persons from the same territories, whilst at the opposite extreme the strong, megaphonic voice of Perry Dixon or the half-uttered end syllables and rough intonation of Son Bonds reach a maximum of obscuration. There is evidence to confirm the suggestion that the physiological structure of the mouth of the Negro coming from nearly pure African stock causes him to favour certain dental and labial consonant forms and to speak in a fashion that was all too recently a sad source of humour on the variety halls. But this is easily modified by training or by changes of environment and the fact that Southern "poor Whites" speak in similar manner suggests that these characteristics are largely accultural.

Much of the obscuration of meaning in the blues arises through the peculiarities of phrasing, the imposed rhythms, the qualities of timing and enunciation in which lie a great deal of the unique beauty and fascination of the music but which do not assist in the clarification of the content. Enjambments, elisions and glottal stops are features common in the blues which add greatly to the dramatic intensity of the verses though they sometimes cloud the meaning. Blues singers use their voices instrumentally, introducing extended syllables that follow through successions of rising and falling notes, permitting their vocal lines to ululate in order to heighten the expressiveness of their singing. For the true blues singer this is only partially a conscious process; rather it is one governed and even necessitated by the purpose of his improvised song. He declaims and hollers his words in anger or protest, he moans them soft and low in sadness and sorrow. Sometimes his words assume their shape as they emerge from seemingly formless murmurings; sometimes they are nailed home with vocal hammer-blows half-shouted, half-sung to the beat of the music. There are times when words are dispensed with altogether: when they are supplanted by long-drawn groans and hummed phrases or by the utterance of joyous if unrecognizable syllables—"scat vocals" that are redolent with abstract meaning. Now the singer's words are brutally stabbed home; now they are punctuated with shrill falsetto cries; now they are uttered softly and scarcely audibly. Within the blues are to be heard the compelling rhythms of work song and spiritual that embrace the listener and draw him into inevitable participation, much as the exhortations of the gang-leader or the preacher exert their influence on workers or congregation. Here too are the overtones of meaning and expressive content that are to be found in the hollers of the "yard and field Negro," the calls of the section-hand and the joyous exclamations of the member of the camp-meeting. The spontaneous utterances, the unexpected asides, the canonical overlapping of lines and phrases, whether made instrumentally or vocally by his companions or created by himself on his instrument, link the blues singer to his musical heritage. When he plays his guitar he makes it "talk" and "sing"; he exhorts his piano to "tell 'em ivories"; he causes his harmonica to wail and cry as a complementary voice, speaking for and with him. He makes of his instrument a second voice, though he does not try to make it a human voice. Imitative passages traceable to vocal origins occur in almost all instrumental blues but they amplify and extend the vocal, expressing what the voice is unable to say. This is the part played by the guitar or the piano of the

blues singer and it is the part played by his accompanying instrumentalists, be they jug band, Fletcher Henderson group,
Chicago washboard band or rhythm and blues combination.

Their comparative isolation has caused many Southern Negroes to devise their own idiomatic phrases and to invent their
own terms, many of which have been illustrated in the foregoing pages, and without a knowledge of the more common of
these the listener cannot be expected to understand the content
of the blues. In many instances such phrases are traditional,
their origins forgotten by their users and often lost to the
etymologist. Some undoubtedly arose through misapplication
or misunderstanding of the meaning of White words. Fondness
for alliteration, pleasure in the creation of rhyming phrases
and delight in the coining of neologisms account for the in-
vention of many such terms.

Many Negro terms have arisen through the deliberate intention of their creators to conceal the meaning of their conversation. In the South the Negro may resort to "Pig Latin"
(he calls it "Dog Latin" in the North), in which a type of
backslang is employed. Here the syllables are reversed and the
vowels are sounded first followed by the consonants with the
addition of the vowel sound "Ay." A slang form as useful
when referring to persons outside the social or racial group
as it is when employed for the declarations of love, its effect is
to scramble the sentence so completely that only the practised
can comprehend the meaning.

325. Oomanway, oomanway, oomanway; ouway urshay eesay
    oodgay ooshay eemay, (twice)
  Eemay oingay ooshay akeshay ooway ackbay, ooshay
    Ennessee esstay.

  (Woman, woman, woman; you sure is good to me,
    (twice)
  I'm goin' to take you back, right back to Tennessee.)

  Ouway ontday alkshay oosay ainplay, outbay ouway
    urshay ancay aemay amenay, (twice)
  Eemay oosay adglay, oosay adglay atshay aemay ouryay
    eetsway, eetsway anmay

  (You don't talk so plain, but you sure can call my
    name, (twice)

I'm so glad, so glad that I'm your sweet, sweet man.)

Innocuous words are often given secondary meanings which are closed to all but the initiated and by their use the Negro can be more outspoken in the blues than might otherwise be prudent. Some of these have become traditional terms recognized and used the states over by Negroes, for whom the coloured man is the "monkey," the White man the "baboon." With comparative immunity they can sing:

326. Monkey and the baboon playing Seven-Up,
    Monkey win the money, scared to pick it up.

    The monkey stumbled, the baboon fell,
    Monkey grabbed the money an' he run like hell!

But the monkey is also a traditional character in Negro folk tales, the "monkey man" can be a homosexual and he can also be a "bumbole," a West Indian Negro. For reasons that are readily apparent the Negro has delighted in such mixed terminology since early slavery, and as he places layer upon layer of meaning on a phrase he protects himself with a cloak of obscurities.

Although the Harlem Negro will look contemptuously on the country idioms of his Southern cousins, his own speech is liberally interlarded with phrases and words whose meanings are singularly elusive. He "shoots the jive," using slick, witty, racy terms that enjoy a brief vogue before they are misplaced by others as ephemeral and as picturesque. "Jive talk" is a part of Negro culture; the telling, cruel metaphors and spontaneous slang being the creation of a poetic form of language of the most uncompromising kind. With its use goes hand-in-hand the utterance of long, rolling words that give cynical recognition to the advantages of education rather than a false impression that the user has been well educated.

327. Mama meant me twist it to the slammer and let me cut
        my throat, (*twice*)
    I been throwed in the hole, black baby, ain't been able
        to dig no gold.

    Baby, I'm beat to my socks, do you dig just what I
        mean? (*twice*)

I've got a terrible financial embarrassment and I'm stick-
ing with Jim Clean.

I'm gonna dig me some jive and try to knock myself out,
    (*twice*)
Then everything will be foxy, I won't know what it's all
    about.

I'm gonna buy me a show and get on the old riverside
    dive, (*twice*)
I've got to sell from this bin, everybody's getting hip to
    the jive.

Much jive is invented on the spur of the moment by Negroes gifted in the art and versed in its use, but the process of
creation is also a conscious one. Negro magazines and periodicals encourage their writers to use such phraseology and invite their readers to take part in the creation of new words in
this ever-growing and perplexing language. Fundamentally the
reasons for its creation are still those that cause the Southern
Negro to invent his own country expressions; there is genuine
pleasure in being "hip to the jive"—in being well-informed
in the use of "sharp" terms, and there is a feeling of protection
and security within the racial group afforded by their application. The illusion of racial solidarity that the Negro so often
desires and so often fails to obtain is created by the use of
these "in-group" expressions, and hidden by the screen which
they afford he can give expression to his feelings of protest
and frustration. Though all blues that are sung in jive are by
no means on protest themes they do demonstrate a form of
passive revolt: an assertion on the part of the Negro of his
identity. But in the withdrawal into himself that the use of such
terminology implies they demonstrate also the unfortunate result of his exclusion from society. He is drawing attention to
himself and indirectly to his predicament, but he is also voluntarily forcing still wider the schism between himself and
White America.

Blues sung in jive and Pig Latin are blues sung to a certain
extent in a spirit of protest: protest that finds in this form
of expression a means both of defence and arrogance. It has
been stated frequently that the whole of blues is created in
the spirit of protest. The inference is that the blues is a form of

expression against racial discrimination, though there are whole categories of blues in which this belief is demonstrably insupportable. In a very general sense, however, the argument may be loosely upheld, for the blues is usually sung as an unburdening of the heart, and it is therefore giving voice to protest against the circumstances that have brought about such a condition of mind. Often, the circumstances of segregation and colour discrimination are the root causes of these troubles, but in many instances the singer is the victim of the foibles and frailties of human nature irrespective of class or colour. There are blues that are sung in the spirit of remorse, or in the warmth of affection and in these the measure of protest is negligible.

When an exhaustive examination is made of recorded blues it becomes apparent that the number of items that are directly concerned with protest themes is exceedingly small. It is scarcely conceivable that the singers, commenting broadly on the multitudinous facets of Negro life, would deliberately ignore or reject those that are the result of racial prejudice and intolerance. The segregated waiting-rooms, the Jim Crow cars, the forbidden beaches, bathing pools, theatres . . . the short measure, the cropper's "share," the stale goods . . . the Race Riot, the hooded Klansmen, the lynch mob, the hit-and-run killer—the countless manifestations of ignorance, brutality, race hatred and violence, of discriminatory practices and segregation by colour must have been the raw material for innumerable blues created by a legion of singers both recorded and unknown. That many of these sad and ugly scars upon the ageing face of the nation are now slowly healing does not entirely hide the fact that during the near two-score years of recorded blues many of them have been sore and open wounds. But the periods when they were most rife and when they would have been uppermost in the minds of the singers that recorded would also have been the times when reference to them on disc would have been the most inadvisable. Amongst other Negroes their effect might well have been inflammatory with results that would have been disastrous, whilst those White persons that came across them in troubled areas would have been similarly incensed. At periods when inter-racial disturbances were at a minimum the blues singer would tend to ignore the subject, for his concern is with the present. Further, the personal character of the blues would require the singer to experience the effects of prejudice himself to inspire him to sing on the theme, and a man who had so suffered would be rather less likely to bring further attention and trouble to himself. Amongst the record companies precautions were generally taken to ensure that material likely to cause embarrassment and possible distress was rejected: a practice of censorship that may be criticized with some justice but which is readily understandable.

A number of blues have been recorded on themes of protest, however, in spite of the foregoing restrictions. Some of these have been the work of socially conscious singers who have intentionally sought and found an outlet for just such material and have deliberately composed "protest blues," whilst others have been incited by small recording companies motivated by humanitarian or ideological principles. When the incitement or the sublimation of the social or racial sentiments of others is deliberate, the blues usually becomes self-conscious. It is seldom that the blues becomes an electioneer's soap-box, a politician's stand from which declamations are made and the sentiments of the listeners aroused. When the blues is used for this purpose, it is almost always a deliberate gesture on the part of a socially conscious singer who is removed from the folk but who uses the idiom as a vehicle for steering the people along a path of his own making. Their calculated intentions have invalidated the resultant recordings as examples of genuine spontaneous and unsolicited blues improvisations based on aspects of living. In contrast with these is a small percentage of examples that have slipped through the net by virtue of the use of interracial terminology or oblique references whose obscurity has permitted their inclusion in the record lists.

That the number of protest blues is small is in part the result of the Negro's acceptance of the stereotypes that have been cut for him. In rural areas where education is meagre and the coloured people have known no better environment, there is little with which to compare their mode of life. They are primarily concerned with the business of living from day to day, of "getting along" with the Whites, of conforming and making the best of their circumstances. As surely as the Southern White intends them to "keep their place" the majority of Negroes are prepared to accept it. They know that they cannot change the world but that they have to live in it. An apathy develops which the racial leaders find exasperatingly hard to break, and even when aggravation reaches the point where the spirit of revolt against the system arises, this is often soon dissolved in minor personal disruptions and eventual disregard. Sings Bill Gaither:

328.   Looks like everybody gives me a hard way to go, (*twice*)
        I'm gonna get me a hard shootin' pistol, I don't intend to be walked over no more.

        People tell me life is what you make it, but the whole thing seems jazz to me, (*twice*)
        If my woman says she loves me, well I just wait and see.

        It seems like old bad luck follows me each and everywhere, (*twice*)
        Now I'm at the place I don't even care.

In this manner the blues acts as an emotional safety-valve, canalizing the feelings of anger and resentment. The music is enriched whilst the disappointment and frustration that have been experienced are diverted from more dangerous and possibly violent forms of expression. There are militant blues though; blues that are uncompromisingly aggressive in their outlook, though in a familiar psychological transference the aggression may be directed through bitterness and disillusion against the singer's own kind rather than against a hostile system. According to the altering circumstances under which the singer lives, his blues may change, for his song is a direct expression of his immediate experience. From this his listener takes heart for he shares his predicaments and his fortunes and is reassured by his statements of reactions to living that are common to them both.

Here then is one of the functions of the blues. Though they may lie deeply hidden there are functional purposes for every form of folk song: they are seldom if ever created whimsically, though in the course of time their original meaning and function may be lost, leaving "fractured" verses and seemingly irrelevant nonsense choruses. For the simple community— Scottish, rural English, Scandinavian, Balkan, African, Polynesian—folk song has its functions which may vary in kind according to the nature of other aspects of the culture. Song is a vehicle for speaking with God; for placating the gods. Song plays a major part in tribal custom, in ritual, in witchcraft, in the understanding of mysteries, and in the preparation of initiates to secret societies. Through folk song the elders teach the uneducated, pass on the traditions of the social group, record its history. It provides a vehicle for courting and disownership alike; for evoking some emotions and suppressing other; for declaring passions and for easing pain. Speculations on the after-life, comments on the present social scene figure prominently in folk song; it is a means for enticement, for amusement, for incitement and appeasement. These and many others in varying degree are its functions the world over; they were the functions of the spirituals, the ballads and the work songs of the American Negro and, with important differences of emphasis again, they are the functions of the blues.

Work songs had a profound formative influence on blues both in structure and in mode of expression, but they were the creations of men engaged in work. Blues on the other hand may be said to be primarily the creation of men at leisure. Such an arbitrary distinction does not take into account that a working man may pass his time singing the blues to himself, nor that singing the blues for some men is itself a form of work, but it does indicate the fundamental difference between the immediate pre-blues form of the field holler and the blues as a definite category of folk song. As the blues crystallized as an extemporized song performed with improvised instrumental accompaniment, its practical function as an aid to work virtually ceased. On commercial records the blues is not sung in the process of work, and labour figures in the blues in retrospect, the singer reflecting upon employment and still more on the lack of it. Blues serves as a projection of the sufferings, the aspirations, the thoughts of the singer and in this respect the ballad is closer to the blues, putting similar emotional and mental states into symbolic form. Many ballads are concerned with the exploits of folk heroes, of characters larger than life whose abilities were prodigious and whose feats were those which could not be challenged by ordinary men. They defeat the machinery of their overlords and of the state, they cunningly avoid or overcome their enemies, they outwit prison guards, murder ruthlessly but give generously and die nobly against incalculable odds.

In an era of social advancement there would seem to be

excellent opportunities for this symbolic ballad conception within the blues, the "Race Man" and "Race Hero" being admirable material. Amongst the most admired of all Negroes of his day, Joe Louis was the idol of the coloured masses who saw a symbol of the New Negro in his invincibility within the ring, and a number of blues were composed about him.

329. I came all the way from Chicago to see Joe Louis and
      Max Schmelling fight, (*twice*)
Schmelling went down like the *Titanic* when Joe gave
      him just one hard right.

Well, you've heard of the King of Swing, well Joe
      Louis is the King of Gloves, (*twice*)
Now he's the World Heavyweight Champion, a man
      that the whole world loves.

It was only two minutes and four seconds poor Schmel-
      ling was down on his knees, (*twice*)
He looked like he was praying to the Good Lord for
      "Mercy on me, please!"

If I'd had a million dollars I'd've had every one on Joe,
      (*twice*)
I'd've been a rich man this very day and I wouldn't have
      had to worry no more.

More than any other character, Joe Louis approached the stature of a folk hero whose exploits were celebrated in the blues as they might have been in the ballads of an earlier era. But even so the singer, whilst admiring him, speaks of him as one seen rather than as one worshipped, and by the end of the blues has turned from Louis the hero to his own personal predicament. He is concerned more with the material gain that he might have made than with adulation. A ballad symbolizes the desires of the suppressed Negro singer when he can see no way of overcoming his oppression. It is a vocal dream of wish-fulfilment. In the indomitable boll-weevil he sees himself as small, crushable but unsuppressed: the unbeatable "Stewball" runs a race for the race. The maturity of the blues came with the dawning realization that an equal place on earth was the Negro's right and perhaps within the bounds of possibility. Whilst the ballad singer projected on his heroes the successes that he could not believe could be his own, the blues singer considers his own ability to achieve them. The ballad hero of noble proportions has little relevance to modern life but the blues is realistic enough for the singer to declare his successes and failures with equal impartiality. Far from extolling the virtues of the folk hero, the blues singer is so brutally determined to deny them as to be markedly ungenerous towards the achievements of others even of his own race. He does not identify himself with others; the members of his race are more inclined to identify themselves with him. The blues singer is himself the race hero, and in this lies his popularity and the phenomenal success of the blues as a musical form.

Blues is above all the expression of the individual Negro. Declaring his loves, his hates, his disappointments, his experiences, the blues singer speaks for himself alone. The highly personal nature of the content of his songs makes them appear exceedingly remote from the world of the European listener, though the sentiments expressed in them may be fundamentally universal ones. A blues singer seldom considers his themes apart from himself, seldom narrates incidents in which he has not actively participated. He does not view his subject as an objective outsider but rather from within. Statements and reported accounts that are concerned solely with the lives and experiences of others with whom he has no direct contact are, therefore, rare, for the blues singer does not comment on a world as seen through a window but as a member circulating within it. It is a peculiar feature of the blues that this highly subjective approach does not manifest itself in over-Romanticism. Unable to sing with completely dispassionate objectivity, he sings with uncontrolled emotion. Above all he is a realist, intimately concerned with his subjects but having no illusions about them: neither carried away with transports of sentiment nor totally insensible and devoid of feeling; he is not repulsed by the uglier side of the world in which he lives but accepts the bad with the good.

In the sharply defined images of life that the blues reflects are mirrored the minutiæ of experience of the ordinary Negro man. The words that the blues singer utters, the thoughts, passions and reactions to which he has given voice are those that are shared by countless thousands of his fellows. An unem-

ployed labourer finds comfort in the blues of a man who has
suffered the despair of the penniless, the "cold-in-hand"; the
forsaken lover shares the bitterness of one who has been "mistreated" and the would-be philanderer swaggers along the pavement with the pathetic bragging blues of the "high-brown
sheik." When the blues singer tells of his escape from disaster,
when he addresses the absent woman that he loves, when he
sings of the train that may take him to a happier district, he
sings to himself, but he is aware that others whom he does
not know would sing the blues in like circumstances.

330. Did you ever wake up lonesome—all by yourself? (*twice*)
    And the one you love was loving someone else?

    I wrote these blues, I'm gonna sing them as I please,
    (*twice*)
    I'm the only one liking the way I'm singing them, I'll
    swear to goodness there's no one else t'please.

    I tell you people, I don't know your name, (*twice*)
    But takin' other men's women—I'll swear to God you'd
    do the same.

His blues is echoed in the hearts of his unknown listeners.
The appeal of the blues and the love and warmth of affection
in which the blues singers are held by so many of their fellow
Afro-Americans lies in this feeling of kinship. It is not that
the singers are racial spokesmen from the militant gestures of
whom the blues singer often feels far removed; it is simply
that in singing for himself the blues artist sings also for them.

In singing about himself and for himself the blues singer
may be considered egocentric, selfish and self-pitying, but
though there are examples of such attitudes the blues has a
wider significance. The blues singer like the poet turns his
eyes on the inner soul within and records his impressions and
reactions to the world without. His art is introverted and only
when the blues becomes a part of entertainment and of jazz
does it become extrovert. As if aware of the dangers implicit
in these declarations of his inner self, the blues singer is as
brutally self-examining as the true philosopher, recounting his
desires, acknowledging his faults, stating his thoughts with almost frightening honesty. His hard realism, his lack of sen-

timentality, his harsh reporting make grim and painful listening to the outsider and for those who seek comfortable escapism and the glamour of the commercial popular singer the blues has no appeal. But for the Negro there is assurance in these forthright and unequivocal statements made by a person from within his own group. When setbacks and disappointments threaten to shake his confidence and destroy his morale he turns for support to the blues singer—or sings the blues himself.

Because the blues is self-orientated the singer is seldom interested in things exterior to him, and unless they have a direct impact upon his life he is not concerned with them. Even the simplest, the most obvious features of natural beauty have little importance for the blues singer. There are no blues that tell of the beauties of a landscape, of the splendour of magnificent scenery or of a glorious sunset—experiences which seldom fail to move even the most sterile mind and cause even the mediocre thinker to wish that he had a paint-brush with which to express the scene, if not the gift of poetry. The artist tends to eschew such subject-matter because the appreciation of the beauties of the arc of a rainbow, the colours of a butterfly wing or of a flower in a hedgerow is too commonplace though it ennobles the spirit. But it is not for this reason that the blues singer ignores such themes: it is not these that give him the blues. That he is aware of such beauties and is moved by them is evident in many passing references, but the singer employs them for the metaphoric or comparative value and does not use them as themes.

331. The sun begin sinkin' down behind the Western horiz-
        zone, (*twice*)
     The evenin' dew begin to fall and I'm here all alone.

     I would go out and sit down under the old oak tree,
        (*twice*)
     But I ain't got nobody to talk baby-talk to me.

Though it can be said with truth that the themes of the blues are to a large extent universal ones which have stimulated artists in all fields to create, it cannot be denied that many of the higher virtues and emotions that have inspired great art are absent. There are shortcomings to the blues. The spiritual values that are to be found in the gospel songs are seldom to be found in the "devil songs" of those who have turned away from the Church. Blues is a worldly form of song and its values tend to be worldly also. The Church promises a life after death and the spirituals looked forward to "crossing Jordan" into the Hereafter, the "Promised Land." Blues offers no such reward, though half-hearted references stemming from the singer's background frequently appear. Yet the blues is much concerned with death and is little concerned with birth. This could be an emphasis that has lasted over from the spirituals. But it may also be symbolic of a hopelessness that sees little future for the coloured child. Childbirth itself would never seem to be the theme of the blues and the women blues singers on record do not sing of the pains of labour or the joys of parenthood. There are few blues that take pleasure in children or even express concern for them, but when they do enter the blues it is often as victims of circumstances:

332. Heard a baby crying, what do his mama mean? (*twice*)
    He's crying 'bout his sweet milk, and she won't feed him just the cream.

    Well, he crawled from the fireplace, stopped in the middle of the floor, (*twice*)
    Says, "Mama, ain't that your second daddy standing back there in the door?"

    Well, she grabbed my baby, spanked him, and I tried to make her leave him alone, (*twice*)
    I tried my best to stop her an' she said, "The babe ain't none of mine."

    Some women rocks the cradle, I declare she rules the home, (*twice*)
    Married man rocks some other man's babe, fool thinks he's rockin' his own.

Looking back on his past life the blues singer brushes quickly over his childhood with but a passing, perfunctory reference to where he was born and raised. He neither yearns for the idle days of his childhood with the sentimental nostalgia of a fictitious Stephen Foster plantation Negro, nor does he reminisce with self-pity on childhood unhappiness. The acquisition of education and knowledge except by experience is also generally absent from the blues, though the singer may sometimes dwell upon his own illiteracy as a cause of his present plight. In his development as an adult personality the blues singer apparently shows little inclination to build a home and little pleasure in home-making—but these are eloquent omissions. When he sings of prosperity and comfort it is usually with wry humour; a racial joke rather than an outright cynicism.

333. I could just phone, anywhere in town, (*twice*)
 Mr. Livingood wanted it o—ooh well, well, and they
  rush it on down.

 On big parties, I throw money on the floor, (*twice*)
 And leave it for the sweeper, and walk on out the door.

 I buy my baby a silk dress every day, (*twice*)
 She wear it one time, ooh well, well, then she throw it
  away.

As a rule he is not jealous of those who live in "Striver's Row," the successful Negroes who reside in the exclusive Sugar Hill district of Harlem. They are the members of his race who have competed with White persons and have succeeded in meeting them on equal terms, and it is only those who have stepped on the shoulders of other Negroes who merit his reproaches. As for the professional Negro men and the economically successful, they neither wish nor need to sing the blues, a fact which imposes further limitations on its content. There are no blues by Negro teachers and professors; no blues that speak for the Negro lawyer, the Negro attorney, the coloured doctor, dentist, news editor. . . . But there are blues that are sung by the recipients—and, in some instances, the victims—of their services, for they have reason to sing them. And it is in this that the explanation lies of the vexed problem of the supposed current Negro rejection of the blues.

To the "New Negro" and most of all to the Negro recently arrived from the South who is earnestly seeking to acquire the worldly Northerner's veneer of sophistication, there are overtones of the "Uncle Tom" element in the blues. Southern blues, folk music and talk, jive speech and other creative forms that reinforce the morale of the under-privileged Negro signify for him an acceptance of segregation and may even appear as devices that give it support. By being essentially "Negro" arts they stress the division between coloured and White. Many Negro intellectuals look upon the blues as retrograde and as a sort of corollary; they even resent the increased interest in Negro "Primitive" arts, which they consider condescending, at a time when the Negro's status is improving. Though it would seem undeniable that the Negro in his own culture has developed great gifts in music, dance, the stage and in other arts where poetry, rhythm and grace of movement are outstanding virtues, undue emphasis upon them may provoke anger. To speak of the Negro as a "born entertainer" is to invoke associations of black-faced minstrel shows, plantation and "jungle" cabaret scenes. In the recesses of the racial memory still fall the shadows of slavery, and the arts that arose as a means of escape from the miseries of that era still bear for the hyper-sensitive Negro mind the traces of lick-spittle servility. Thus the unsophisticated arts of the uneducated Negro classes offend the cultivated coloured persons who are striving for complete integration in which essentially racial qualities are absorbed into the culture of the nation as a whole. In contrast with this attitude there exists that section of the coloured intelligentzia which is primarily drawn from the literati rather than from the members of the while-collar professions that takes exceptional pride in the cultural contribution of the folk Negro. The Negro poet, writer, actor recognizes the beauty of such a blues metaphor as:

334. Mama, I love to look in your face, I like the way you
          spread your wings,
       Mama, I love to look in your face, I like the way you
          spread your wings,
       I'm crazy 'bout your way of lovin', mama, I love to hear
          you call my name.

—the evocativeness of a blues simile:

335. If you use my key, well, you bound to love me some,
       Throw your arms around me like a circle around the
          sun.

—or the poetic imagery of such a blues stanza as:

336. In the wee midnight hours, long 'fore the break of day,
　　　In the wee midnight hours, long before the break of day,
　　　When the blues creep upon you and carry your mind
　　　　　away . . .

He does not look upon such blues verses as trends of thought and modes of speech that let down the race and help to add further stones to the barriers that obstruct its progress; he is proud of this especial Negro song form that as a part of the whole field of Afro-American music may well be considered the one indigenous gift of the modern Americas to the world's art. This pride has at times stimulated attempts to create a new Negro poetry in the blues idiom but the blues curiously defies imitation, however sincere the desire to use its form. It is essentially a folk form of expression, at its best when least self-conscious, when least sophisticated: an art created by the Negro lower classes.

In spite of the advances made during the past decade, Negroes are still predominately employed in unskilled or semi-skilled labour and the educated intelligentzia represents a very small minority. For the latter the blues may have little significance, but for the great majority of coloured Americans the blues as an art form is still a vital part of their lives, for the blues is still all around them.

337. Well, it's blues in my house, from the roof to the
　　　　　ground, (twice)
　　　And it's blues everywhere since my good man left town.

　　　Blues in my mail-box, cause I cain't get no mail, (twice)
　　　Says blues in my bread-box, 'cause my bread got stale.

　　　Blues in my meal-barrel and there's blues upon my
　　　　　shelf, (twice)
　　　And there's blues in my bed, 'cause I'm sleepin' by my-
　　　　　self.

For those who have the blues, for those who live the blues, for those who live with the blues, the blues has meaning. But for those who live outside the blues the meaning of the blues is elusive. For the blues is more than a form of folk song, and though its meaning becomes clearer with an understanding of the content of the verses, the reason why the Negro sings the blues and listens to the blues is still not wholly explained. But though the blues may frequently be associated with a state of depression, of lethargy or despair, it is not solely a physical or a mental state. It is not solely the endurance of suffering or a declaration of hopelessness; nor is it solely a means of ridding oneself of a mood. It is all of these and it is more: it is a part of the Negro's being, living with him and within him.

Implicit in the term is the whole tragedy of the Negro race since Black Anthony Johnson, the first of the "twenty and odd Negers" to set foot on American soil, landed from a Dutch "man of warre" at Jamestown in 1619. At that time to "looke blue" had been current for well over half a century as a phrase to describe low spirits, and by the end of the eighteenth century "the blue devils" was a familiar condition of mind. As early as 1807 Washington Irving referred to "a fit of the blues" and colloquial use of the phrase is not uncommon after that date. At some indeterminate time the Negro embraced the term into his own vocabulary and invested it with a meaning of far deeper significance.

For the folk Negro the blues is an Immanence whose existence is never held in question; it is an abstract presence which brings with it the "blues" as a state of mind. The blues is Mister Blues—Mister Blues who comes before daybreak and who is never busier than when others are in need. The Negro knows the blues and recognizes the blues.

338. Did you ever wake up with the blues and didn't have
     no place to go, (*twice*)
    An' you couldn't do nothin' but just walk from door to
     door?

    Good Morning, Mister Blues, Mister Blues, I come to
     talk with you, (*twice*)
    Mister Blues, I ain't doin' nothin' an' I would like to
     get a job from you.

The blues is seldom far away, though it may be lying dormant, half-forgotten like an inactive cancer. When times are good the blues disappears, but when trouble comes the blues comes too, and the Negro realizes that it has never been far away. He recognizes the blues and the blues is the cause of his misfortune.

339. Howdy, Mister Blues, where have you been so long?
     (*twice*)
   I've been telling everybody that you were long gone.

   Tell me, Mister Blues, how long did you come to stay?
     (*twice*)
   Please go right now, you gonna drive my baby away.

   Oh Mister Blues, as soon as you got in town, (*twice*)
   My baby told me she would leave, she was Texas
     bound.

   Now look here, Mister Blues, I want you to leave my
     door, (*twice*)
   And when you go this time, I don't want you back no
     more.

The blues comes unexpected, unheralded, trapping the unwary, disillusioning those who have built up false hopes:

340. Now the blues got up on last Sunday morning they
       trip me, t'rowed me down.
     The blues grabbed my leg this morning' they trip me,
       t'rowed me down,
     Lord, I wouldn't hate it so bad, but the news done got
       all over town.

   I had the blues 'bout that baby on one Sunday morn,
     (*twice*)
   Well, I hate to hear my baby when she gone.

Now the blues takes possession of his whole being:

341. Got the blues so bad, I can hardly sleep at night,
       (*twice*)
     Tried to eat my meal, my teeth refuse to bite.

   Did you ever feel lonesome, just to hear your good
     man's name? (*twice*)

If the jinx is upon you, the blues fall like showers of
rain.

And still the blues continues to fall. . . .

160. My blues fell this morning and my love come falling
     down,
     Says my blues fell this morning and my love come
     falling down,
     Says I'll be your low-down dog, mama, but please don't
     dog me aroun'.

There is no escape. . . .

342. I got to keep movinnnn', I got to keep movinnnn',
     Blues fallin' down like hail, blues fallin' down like hail,
     Mmmmm-mm-mm-mm, blues fallin' down like hail,
     blues fallin' down like hail,
     And the days keep on worryin' me, for a hell-hound
     on my trail,
     Hell-hound on my trail, hell-hound on my trail.

The invincibility of the blues is seldom held in question:

343. I hate to leave you, mama, God knows I sure hate
     to go, (twice)
     Had the blues so long it made my poor heart so'.

     The blues jumped the devil, run the devil a solid mile,
     (twice)
     Well, the devil sat down an' he cried like a new born
     chile.

For some it is easier to surrender to the blues:

344. I'm going to the river, take me a rocking chair,
     I'm going to the river, take me a rocking chair,
     Let the blues overtake me, and rock me away from here.

Others try to make of the blues an ally:

345. Blues, Blues, what makes you worry me so? (twice)
     You worried me last night, and all last night you come.

Blues, Blues, I don't need you nohow, (*twice*)
But I feel much better sleepin' in my baby's arms.

Blues, Blues, give me your sympathy, (*twice*)
Go and find my woman and bring her back to me.

Blues, Blues, say, can't you understand? (*twice*)
You can be my enemy, or you can be my friend.

A man may compromise with the blues whilst making of the blues a scapegoat for his own defects. He reasons with the blues, talks with the blues: "Now look here, Blues, I want to have a little talk with you, you been making me drink and gamble and stay out the whole night too. Now you got me to the place I don't care what I do; yeah, now, Blues, I wanna have a little talk with you. Now I believe you been drinkin' moonshine, Blues, cause you don't care what you do."

346. Yeah now, Blues, why don't you give poor Bill a break?
Yeah now, Blues, why don't you give poor Bill a break?
Now why don't you help me to live instead of tryin' to break my neck?

But the blues remains enigmatic and does not explain why it comes:

347. Early this morning, the blues came walking in my room, (*twice*)
I said, "Blues, please tell me what you are doing making me feel so blue?"

They looked at me and smiled but, yes, they refused to say, (*twice*)
I seen them again and they turned and walked away.

"Blues oh, Blues, you know you've been here before. (*twice*)
The last time you were here you made me cry and walk the floor."

The blues is not trouble or hardship, it is not loneliness or misery, but it is friend to them all:

348. My blues and trouble both running hand-in-hand, (*twice*)
Even when my baby running from man to man.

My heart's in trouble, mind's in misery, (*twice*)
Got the blues so bad, I really can't hardly see.

Though he may know that for some there is a life without the company of the blues, many a coloured man sees little prospect of freedom in his own lifetime from his unwanted companion.

349. Now the stars really are shinin'—clouds look awful grey,
Now the stars really are shinin'—clouds look awful grey,
I believe to my soul my blues and trouble are goin' to carry me to my grave.

When lives are upset, families broken, love is lost, the blues comes falling down. The blues dogs the footsteps of the migrant, walks in the shadow of the destitute, sits at table with the hungry, shares the bed of the forsaken. It is the comrade-in-arms of those whose work is strenuous, monotonous and ill-paid; it is the partner of the share-cropper, the section-hand and the road-sweeper.

An argument might be advanced that the belief in the blues as an entity which influences the lives of men is a survival of African totemism. It could be reasoned that it is a substitute for a godhead made by those who have no faith in the Church; that "devil songs" is an accurate enough term. Justification could be found for considering the blues to be a symbol of White domination: it seems likely that the belief has grown from the persistent condition of repression that the Negro in the United States has endured for long centuries. It is not possible to comprehend the reasons why the Negro sings the blues unless this dual conception of the nature of blues as an ever-present power and as a condition of mind is appreciated, for it is in this that the key to understanding lies. In the blues as folk song the Negro gives form to the blues of his experience. The blues are the utterances of his innermost feelings, the outpourings of his heart. When he sings the blues he sings to drive away the blues and to relieve his mind of the blues.

350. People, if you hear me humming on this song both
         night and day,
      People, if you hear me humming on this song both
         night and day,
      I'm just a poor boy in trouble, trying to drive the blues
         away.

There are signs that the blues as a truly creative folk song may be on the wane, for the tragic themes of suffering and misery that have arisen from poverty and destitution, from disease and disaster, violence and brutality, from bad living conditions and aimless migration, are less frequently heard to-day than in former years. The improved status of the Negro during the past decade, the gradual but definite moves towards integration, the slow but perceptible advances towards equality of opportunity may thus be reflected in the blues on record, for the blues is now primarily concerned with personal relationships of love and desertion. On these subjects the blues as all forms of song has been more than eloquent and probably has little new to add. But if the more vital, if more disturbing, themes are disappearing in the passing shades of an old and ignominious era, and if the blues as a virile form of folk song passes with them, the loss is a small enough price to pay. The true and complete integration of the Negro into American society may mean the death of a folk art form of great simplicity, beauty and meaning.

But the blues still fell this morning.

Discography of Quoted Blues

All blues quoted in the preceding chapters have been transcribed from gramophone recordings, a Discography of which follows, the items being listed in the order in which they occur in the book. Beside each quotation a number is to be found and this is entered in the left-hand column. Record details are given as fully as possible and the matrix number allocated by the issuing company, where known, is noted in the second column and followed by the title of the blues. Next is given the name of the singer or pseudonym where this applies, together with any instrument played by the artist on the record. Pseudonyms are identified where possible in the following section: Index of Quoted Blues Singers. Where supporting instrumentalists appear on the disc, their names and the instruments played are listed where known, but instruments alone are entered when the identities of the musicians have not been ascertained (see Abbreviations: Instrumental below). The issuing company (see Abbreviations: Labels below) and the serial number allocated to the record is given in the fifth column. Except where otherwise indicated, this is understood to be the original American issue, but for the convenience of readers the number of any currently available British reissue of the American disc is noted in brackets below, though in one or two instances this may be from a different "master." Recording dates in the order day/month/year are supplied in full, if available; otherwise according to information at hand. Where known the recording venue is noted below. In the final column the source from which the record has been obtained is listed (see Abbreviations: Collections below).

ABBREVIATIONS: INSTRUMENTAL

alt sax	alto saxophone	gtr	guitar	tmb	trombone
bjo	banjo	hca	harmonica (harp)	ten sax	tenor saxophone
bs	bass (string)	im bs	imitation string bass	tpt	trumpet
bs sax	bass saxophone	jug	jug	tu	tuba or brass bass
clt	clarinet	pno	piano	vln	violin
cnt	cornet	sax	saxophone	vo	blues vocal
dms	drums	sop sax	soprano saxophone	wbd	washboard
el gtr	electric guitar	stp	stovepipe		

ABBREVIATIONS: LABELS

Ald	Aladdin	J.O.B.	J.O.B.
AM	American Music	KJ	King Jazz
Ap	Apollo	Lon	London (Origins of Jazz)
ARC	American Record Company	Mlt	Melotone
Arct	Aristocrat	Modern	Modern
Bb	Bluebird	Mus	Musicraft
Br	Brunswick	OK	Okeh
BrE	British Brunswick	PaE	Parlophone (British)
Cap	Capitol	Pm	Paramount
CapE	British Capitol	Ph	Philips
Chess	Chess	Riv	Riverside
Co	Columbia	Sav	Savoy
CoE	British Columbia	Stin	Stinson
Cq	Conqueror	Van	Vanguard
De	Decca	VanE	British Vanguard
DeE	British Decca	Vg	Vogue (British)
Domino	Domino	Vic	Victor
Fkwy	Folkways	Vo	Vocalion
GS	Gold Star	VoE	British Vocalion
HMV	His Master's Voice (British)	Vrs	Varsity
J.Dvs	Joe Davis		

ABBREVIATIONS: COLLECTIONS

BB	Beryl Bryden	JDe	Jacques Demetre
BD	Brian Davis	JJ	John Jack
BR	Brian Rust	JL	John Langmead
DC	Derek Coller	MV	Max Vreede
DJP	Jack Parsons	NJ	Norman Jenkinson
DSB	Derrick Stewart-Baxter	PHO	Paul Oliver
ET	Eric Townley	SB	Sam Benjamin
GG	Gerald Grounsell	VS	Vic Schuler
JRD	James R. Davis		

ITEM	MATRIX	TITLE	ARTIST AND ACCOMPANIMENT	CAT. NO.	DATE LOCATION	COLL.
1	S-7275-E	That Thing Called Love	Mamie Smith (vo) acc. Rega Orchestra: Ed Cox (tpt); Dope Andrews (tmb); Ernest Elliott (clt; ten); Leroy Parker (vin); Willie Smith (pno)	OK 4113	14/2/20	PHO
2	21020-4	Poor Boy Blues	Ramblin' Thomas (vo, gtr)	Pm 12722	–/–/29 Chicago	PHO
3	93008	Tell Me How About It	Sleepy John Estes (vo, gtr) acc. Noah Lewis (hca); wbd	De 7766B	4/6/40 Chicago	PHO
4	C 3904	Going Back to My Plow	Big Bill Broonzy (vo, gtr)	OK 6484	17/7/41 Chicago	DSB
5		Bo Weavil Blues	acc. Washboard Sam (wbd); pno; bs Kokomo Arnold (vo, gtr)	De 7191	–/–/36 Chicago	PHO
6		I'm Gonna Take It Easy	Gabriel Brown (vo, gtr)	JD 5015	–/–/45 N.Y.C.	PHO
7	DAL 378	I'm a Steady Rollin' Man	Robert Johnson (vo, gtr)	Vo 03723	19/6/37 Dallas	DSB
8		Lazy Mule Blues	Florida Kid (vo, pno)	Bb 8625	–/–/40	SB
9	91531	Bleeding Heart Blues	Jimmy Gordon and his Vip Vop Band (vo) acc. pno; gtr; dms	De 7536	18/10/38	PHO
10	BS 40520	Cotton Farm Blues	Walter Davis (vo, pno)	Bb B-8393	21/7/58	MV
11	149105	On Our Turpentine Farm	Pigmeat Pete and Catjuice Charlie (vo duet, gtr)	Co 14485-D	–/7/29 N.Y.C.	PHO
12	15666	Mosquito Moan	Blind Lemon Jefferson (vo, gtr)	Pm 12899	–/10/29 Richmond, Ind.	PHO
13	16685	Honey, I'm All Out and Down	Huddie Ledbetter (vo, gtr)	Mlt 13326	23/1/35 N.Y.C.	PHO

ITEM	MATRIX	TITLE	ARTIST AND ACCOMPANIMENT	CAT. NO.	DATE LOCATION	COLL.
14		*Red-River*	Sonny Terry (vo, hca) acc. Alec Stewart (gtr)	Vg L.D.E.137	–/–/53 N.Y.C.	PHO
15	145366	Gravel Camp Blues	Lewis Black (vo, gtr)	Co 14291	–/–/27 Atlanta	JJ
16	401488B	Spike Driver Blues	Mississippi John Hurt (vo, gtr)	OK 8692	28/12/28 Memphis	PHO
17	K.J.-1	Saw Mill Man Blues	Pleasant Joe (vo) acc. Sidney Bechet (sop sax); Hot Lips Page (tpt); Sam Price (pno); Pops Foster (bs); Danny Barker (gtr); Sid Catlett (dms); Mezz Mezzrow (clt)	KJ 144	30/7/45	PHO
18	399:3054-2	Sawmill Blues	Elzadie Robinson (vo) acc. Will Ezell (pno)	Pm 12417	c./11/26	PHO
19	C 4678	Harvest Moon Blues	Charles 'Speck' Pertrum (vo, pno)	Br 7146	1/11/29 Chicago	DSB
20	C 91520	Big Leg Woman	Johnny Temple (vo) acc. Odell Rand (clt); Joshua Altheimer? (pno)	De 48002	17/10/38 Chicago	DJP
21	67483	Chicago Mill Blues	Peetie Wheatstraw (vo) acc. Lil Armstrong (pno); Sid Catlett (dms); Jonah Jones (tpt)	De 7788	4/4/40 N.Y.C.	DC
22	20567-2	Detroit Bound Blues	Blind Blake (vo, gtr)	Pm 12657	c./3/28	MV
23	C 15503	Starvation Farm Blues	Bob Campbell (vo, gtr)	Vo 02798	c./–/34	GG
24	62480	Poor Man's Friend (T. Model)	Sleepy John Estes (vo, gtr) acc. Noah Lewis (hca): Hammie Nix (gtr)	De 7442	3/8/37 N.Y.C.	DSB
25		*Warehouse Blues*	Frank Tannehill (vo) acc. gtr; pno; tps	Bb B-7945	c./–/37 Chicago	BD

ITEM	MATRIX	TITLE	ARTIST AND ACCOMPANIMENT	CAT. NO.	DATE LOCATION	COLL.
26	148237	Rolling Mill Blues	Peg Leg Howell (vo, gtr) acc. vln	Co 14438-D	10/4/29 Atlanta	PHO
27	21198-1	Tin Cup Blues	Blind Lemon Jefferson (vo, gtr)	Pm 12756 (Lon AL 3564)	–/4/29 Chicago	PHO
28	403305-B	Broke Man Blues	Sylvester Palmer (vo, pno)	Co 14524-D	c.–/–/29 N.Y.C.	BR
29	147307	Cold Wave Blues	Barbecue Bob (vo, gtr)	Co 147307	26/10/28	DSB
30		My Friends Don't Know Me	Walter Davis (vo, pno) acc. dms	Vic 20-2156	–/–/45	DJP
31	C 91340	Hard Times Ain't Gone Nowhere	Lonnie Johnson (vo, gtr)	De 7388	8/11/37 Chicago	PHO
32	BS 044244	Cotton Patch Blues	Tommy McClennan (vo, gtr) acc. bs cano	Bb B-8408-B	22/11/39 Chicago	NJ
33	C 90917	Don't Take Away My P.W.A.	Jimmy Gordon (vo) acc. pno; gtr; bs	De 7230	–/10/36 Chicago	PHO
34	C 91164	Working on the Project	Peetie Wheatstraw (vo) acc. gtr, Kokomo Arnold; pno, possibly Peetie Wheatstraw	De 7311	30/3/37 Chicago	DC
35	C 91766	Lazy Woman's Blues	Little Bill Gaither (vo) acc. pno; bs	De 7668	13/9/39 Chicago	PHO
36	C 1976	Got a Man in the 'Bama Mine	Merline Johnson (vo) acc. Blind John Davis (pno); dms; gtr	Cq 8924	22/6/37 Chicago	PHO

ITEM	MATRIX	TITLE	ARTIST AND ACCOMPANIMENT	CAT. NO.	DATE LOCATION	COLL.
37	BS 074168	On the Killing Floor	Doctor Clayton (vo) acc. Blind John Davis (pno); Alfred Elkins (im bs); Ransom Knowling (tu)	Bb 34-0702	27/3/42	BB
38	D8-VB-3267	Southern Blues	Roosevelt Sykes (vo, pno) and his Original Honeydrippers	Vic 22-0056	30/12/48 N.Y.C.	VS
39	D 386	Defense Blues	Huddie Ledbetter (vo, gtr) acc. Willie Smith (pno); Brownie McGhee (gtr); Pops Foster (bs); Sonny Terry (hca)	Disc 5085	–/6/46 N.Y.C.	PHO
40	25632	L.A. Blues	Charles Waterford (vo) acc. pno; ten; gtr; dms	Cap 40132	c./–/45-6	PHO
41	U-62	Somewhere, Before Long	Jimmy and Walter (vo, gtr) acc. traps.	Sun 180	–/–/40's Memphis	BB
42	93588	The Good Lawd's Children	Peetie Wheatstraw (vo) acc. pno; hca	De 7879	Chicago	DJP
43	403360	Thirty Day Blues	Texas Alexander (vo) acc. Lonnie Johnson (gtr)	OK 8785	27/11/29 Chicago	PHO
44	51-V-4105	Make My Getaway	Big Bill Broonzy (vo, gtr)	VgE V2078	20/9/51 Paris	PHO
45	45A-4085-3	Jim Crow Blues	Cow Cow Davenport (vo, pno) acc. B. T. Wingfield (cnt)	Pm 12439	–/–/29	PHO
46	63753	Bad Luck Blues	Kokomo Arnold (vo, gtr) acc. pno?	De 7540	11/5/38 N.Y.C.	PHO
47	20766	Worn Out Daddy Blues	Ida Cox (vo) acc. Her Five Blue Spells: Joe Smith (cnt); Charlie Green (tu); Buster Bailey (clt); Fletcher Henderson (pno); Charlie Dixon (bjo)	Pm 12704 (Lon AL 3517)	–/–/27	PHO

ITEM	MATRIX	TITLE	ARTIST AND ACCOMPANIMENT	CAT. NO.	DATE LOCATION	COLL.
48		Leaving Blues	Huddie Ledbetter (vo, gtr)	Fkwy FP4	–/–/40's	PHO
49	985	Fattening Frogs	Mobile Strugglers; acc. Lee Warren (vo); bull fiddle; two vlns; gtr; bjo	AM 104	–/–/40's Mobile	Bill Colyer
50	D5-AB-316-1	Kid Man Blues	Big Maceo (vo, pno) acc. Tampa Red (gtr); Melvin Draper (dms)	Vic 20-2687-B	26/2/45 Chicago	PHO
51	C 90960	Mother's Day	St. Louis Jimmy (vo)	Ap 420	c./–/50	JDe
52	C 90960	Mother Blues	Jimmy Gordon (vo)	De 7250	28/10/36	JDe
53	JAX 202	So Cold in China	Mississippi Moaner (Isaiah Nettles [vo, gtr]) acc. pno; gtr; bs	Vo 03166	–/10/35 Chicago	JRD
54	C 3764-1	In My Girlsh Days	Memphis Minnie (vo, gtr, bs)	OK 06410	–/5/41 Jacksonville	DJP
55	BS-070378	I've Been Treated Wrong	Washboard Sam (vo, wbd); acc. Big Bill Broonzy (gtr); Memphis Slim (pno); Alfred Elkins (im bs)	Bb B-9007	4/11/41 Chicago	BB
56	63540-B	Road Tramp Blues	Peetie Wheatstraw (vo, pno); acc. bs; gtr; Lonnie Johnson	De 7589	1/4/38 N.Y.C.	JRD
57	C 97008	Bad Luck Child	Bill Gaither (vo)	De 7202	4/5/36 Chicago	BB
58	C 4413	Broken Down Man	acc. Honey Hill (pno); gtr; Buster Bennett (vo); acc. trio	Co 37560	24/2/45 Chicago	BB
59	074069	Lonesome Road	Lonnie Johnson (vo, gtr); acc. Blind John Davis (pno); bs	Bb 34-0714	13/2/42 N.Y.C.	PHO
60	65272	Jeff Davis Highway	Lee Brown (vo); acc. Sam Price (pno); and his Fly Cats (bs, dms)	De 7587	24/3/39 N.Y.C.	PHO
61	BS-044-986	Highway 51	Tommy McClennan (vo, gtr); acc. bs	Bb B-8499	10/5/40 Chicago	PHO

ITEM	MATRIX	TITLE	ARTIST AND ACCOMPANIMENT	CAT. NO.	DATE LOCATION	COLL.
62	20107-2	Hard Road Blues	Blind Blake (vo, gtr)	Pm 12583	late/27 Chicago	MV
63	C 6891	C. & A. Blues	Peetie Wheatstraw (vo, pno) acc. gtr, Charlie Jordan	Vo 04592	17/3/31	DJP
64	C 90814A	Standing By a Lamp Post	David Alexander (vo, pno)	De 7211	1/7/36 Chicago	MV
65	C 1780	If I Make It Over	Bumble Bee Slim (vo) acc. Eurreal 'Little Brother' Montgomery (pno); gtr	Vo 04042	27/1/37 Chicago	PHO
66	L-1254-2	The Gone Dead Train	King Solomon Hill (vo, gtr)	Pm 13129 (Lon AL 3535)	–/–/31 Grafton, Wis.	PHO
67	6248A	Hobo Jungle Blues	Sleepy John Estes (vo, gtr) acc. Noah Lewis (hca)	De 7354	3/8/37	PHO
68	63661	Old Bachelor Blues	Son Bonds (vo, gtr) acc. 2nd gtr, probably Hammie Nix	De 7558	–/4/38 N.Y.C.	PHO
69		Lake Front Blues	Little Brother Montgomery (vo, pno)	Bb Test	c.–/–/35	ET
70	BVE-70676	M. & O. Blues	Walter Davis (vo, pno)	Bb B-5129	–/–/32	BD
71	20111-1	I.C. Moan	Tampa Red (vo, gtr) acc. Georgia Tom Dorsey (pno)	Mlt 7-03-73	–/6/30	GG
72	BS-064480	Flying Crow Blues	Washboard Sam (vo, wbd) acc. Big Bill Broonzy (gtr); Memphis Slim (pno); William Mitchell (im bs)	Bb 8844	26/6/41 Chicago	PHO
73	65208B	If I Could Holler	Johnny Temple (vo) acc. Sam Price (pno); Teddy Bunn (gtr); bs	De 7599	6/3/39 N.Y.C.	JDe
74	85498	Big Four Blues	Leroy Carr (vo, pno) acc. Scrapper Blackwell (gtr)	Bb 5916	25/2/35 Chicago	PHO
75	140607	Dixie Flyer Blues	Bessie Smith (vo) acc. pno; clt; tmb	Co 14079-D	15/5/25 N.Y.C.	JRD

ITEM	MATRIX	TITLE	ARTIST AND ACCOMPANIMENT	CAT. NO.	DATE LOCATION	COLL.
76	67577	Panama Limited	Georgia White (vo) acc. Fess Williams (clt); Jonah Jones (tpt)	De 7783	18/4/40 N.Y.C.	NJ
77		Shorty George	Huddie Ledbetter (vo, gtr)	Fkwy FP 14A	–/–/40	PHO
78	85517	Southern Blues	Big Bill Broonzy (vo, gtr) acc. pno	Bb 5998	26/2/35 Chicago	PHO
79	9547A	Special Delivery Blues	Sippie Wallace (vo) acc. Louis Armstrong (cnt); Hersal Thomas (pno)	OK 8328	–/–/26	BR
80	67464	Ups and Downs Blues	Roosevelt Sykes (vo, pno) acc. Sidney Catlett (dms)	De 7747	3/4/40 Chicago	JDP
81	305A	Mean Tight Mama	Sara Martin (vo) acc. Clarence Williams and his Orchestra: possibly King Oliver (tpt); Charlie Green (tmb); Clarence Williams (pno); Cyrus St. Clair (tu)	QRS R7043 (Lon AL 3510)	c./12/28	PHO
82	GM 501	De Kalb Blues	Leadbelly (vo, gtr)	Mus 226	1/4/39 N.Y.C.	BD
83	BS-070147	My Black Name Blues	Sonny Boy Williamson (vo, hca) acc. Blind John Davis (pno); Charlie McCoy (gtr); Washboard Sam (wbd); Alfred Elkins (im bs)	Bb 8992	11/12/41 Chicago	JRD
84	146054	Chocolate to the Bone	Barbecue Bob (vo, gtr)	Co 14331-D	13/4/28	JJ
85	145315	Brownskin Blues	Lillian Glinn (vo) acc. Willie Tyson (pno); Octave Gaspard (tu)	Co 14275-D	2/12/27 New Orleans	PHO
86	81242	Evil Woman Blues	Texas Alexander (vo, gtr) acc. Clarence Williams (pno)	OK 8688	17/8/27 N.Y.C.	JJ

ITEM	MATRIX	TITLE	ARTIST AND ACCOMPANIMENT	CAT. NO.	DATE LOCATION	COLL.
87	26562	Ashley Street Blues	Leola B. Wilson (vo) acc. Blind Blake (gtr)	Pm 12392	–/9/26 Chicago	MV
88	144279	Brownskin Woman	Barbecue Bob (vo, gtr)	Co 14257-D	15/6/27	PHO
89		Short Haired Woman	Lightnin' Hopkins (vo, gtr)	G.S. 3131	–/–/46 Houston	PHO
90	BS 074060	River Hip Woman	Washboard Sam (vo, wbd) acc. Frank Owen (alt sax); Big Bill Broonzy (gtr); Roosevelt Sykes (pno)	Bb 9039	10/2/42 Chicago	PHO
91	BVE40309	Stole Rider Blues	Blind Willie McTell (vo, gtr)	Vic 21124A	18/10/27	GG
92	W142025	Willie Jackson's Blues	Willie Jackson (vo) acc. Steve Lewis (pno)	Co 14136	14/4/26 New Orleans	PHO
93	459:3060	Blake's Worried Blues	Blind Blake (vo, gtr)	Pm 12442A	–/–/46	PHO
94		Copper Coloured Mama	Doctor Clayton (vo) acc. Blind John Davis (pno); Willie Lacey (gtr)	Vic 20-2323		PHO
95	C 4303	When You Love Me	Memphis Minnie (vo, gtr) acc. Little Son Joe (gtr); dms	OK 6733	19/12/44 Chicago	DJP
96	149534-1	Heart Wrecked	Whistling Alex Moore (vo, gtr) acc. pno	Co 14518-D	5/12/29 Dallas	JRD
97	C 1228	You Got to Live and Let Live	Bumble Bee Slim (vo) acc. pno; bs; dms	Vo 03929	6/2/36 Chicago	DJP
98	BVE-69417-1	What Made You Love Me So?	Walter Davis (vo, pno)	Vic 23282	10/6/31 Louisville, Ky.	MV
99	C 3961	Don't Leave Me Baby	Curtis Jones (vo) acc. pno; bs	OK 06428	18/8/41 Chicago	DJP

ITEM	MATRIX	TITLE	ARTIST AND ACCOMPANIMENT	CAT. NO.	DATE LOCATION	COLL.
100	63796	Little Pigmeat	Ollie Shepard (vo) acc. and his Kentucky Boys: tpt; ten clt; pno; dms	De 7508	c./6/38 N.Y.C.	PHO
101	BS 064491	Million Years Blues	Sonny Boy Williamson (vo, hca) acc. Blind John Davis (pno); Ransom Knowling (bs)	Bb B-8866-B	2/7/41 Chicago	PHO
102	BS 044990	It's Hard to be Lonesome	Tommy McClennan (vo, gtr) acc. bs cano	Bb B-8669	–/–/40 Chicago	ET
103		Cotton Picking Blues	Robert Petway (vo, gtr)	Bb 9036B	–/–/41	DJP
104	20558	Leavin' Gal Blues	Bertha Henderson (vo) acc. Blind Blake (gtr)	Pm 12697	–/–/28	BB
105	402768	T.P. Window Blues	Jack Ranger (vo, gtr)	OK 8795	–/8/29	PHO
106	20106-2	Brownskin Mama Blues	Blind Blake (vo, gtr)	Pm 12606	–/–/26	PHO
107	15635	Cruel Woman Blues	Leroy Carr (vo, pno) acc. Scrapper Blackwell (gtr)	Vo 02893	15/8/34	MV
108	80749-1	Court Street Blues	Stovepipe No. 1 (vo, stp) and David Crockett (gtr)	OK 8514	–/3/27	PHO
109		I Get Evil When My Love Comes Down	Gabriel Brown (vo, gtr)	J.Dvs 5003	c.–/46	PHO
110	2064-2	Pleading Misery Blues	Elzadie Robinson (vo) acc. possibly Will Ezell (pno)	Pm 12676	28/8/28 Chicago	BD
111	9029	Strange Lovin' Blues	Sara Martin (vo) acc. possibly Sylvester Weaver (gtr); Charles Washington (bjo); vln	OK 8214	c.–/25 St. Louis	PHO
112	145154	Backdoor Blues	Emery Glen (vo, gtr)	Co 14472-D	–/–/27 Atlanta	PHO

ITEM	MATRIX	TITLE	ARTIST AND ACCOMPANIMENT	CAT. NO.	DATE LOCATION	COLL.
113	63519A	I Ain't Gonna Be Your Fool	Lonnie Johnson (vo, gtr) acc. possibly Roosevelt Sykes (pno); bs; dms	De 7509A	31/3/38 N.Y.C.	PHO
114	402305B	Hambone Willie's Dreamy-Eyed Woman's Blues	Hambone Willie Newbern (vo, gtr)	OK 8693	-/4/29	MV
115		Automobile	Lightnin' Hopkins (vo, gtr)	GS 666	-/-/46 Houston	BD
116	MEM 103	Baby, Quit Your Low Down Ways	Blind Boy Fuller (vo, gtr)	OK 05083	12/7/39 Memphis	PHO
117	DAL 377	Stones In My Passway	Robert Johnson (vo, gtr)	Vo 03723	19/6/37 Dallas	DSB
118	C 91855	Triflin' Woman Blues	Leroy's Buddy (vo) acc. Honey Hill (pno); gtr; bs	De 7826	22/10/39 Chicago	DJP
119	20667	Victim of the Blues	'Ma' Rainey (vo) acc. Tub, Jug, Washboard Band. Unknown tub, jug, wbd, kazoos, bjo	Pm 12687	-/-/29	GG
120	142608	Black Snake Blues	Martha Copeland (vo) acc. Cliff Jackson (pno)	Co 14161-D	14/9/26	PHO
121	62368	Trembling Bed Springs	Rich Trice (vo, gtr)	De 7701B	13/7/37 N.Y.C.	PHO
122	80805	A Worried Woman's Blues	Helen Humes (vo) acc. pno	OK 8467	30/4/27	DSB
123	16997	Man Stealer Blues	Bessie Jackson (vo) acc. Walter Roland (pno); gtr	ARC 350913B	6/3/35 N.Y.C.	VS
124	60346	Can't Read, Can't Write	Georgia White (vo, pno); gtr	De 7166	16/1/36 N.Y.C.	MV

ITEM	MATRIX	TITLE	ARTIST AND ACCOMPANIMENT	CAT. NO.	DATE LOCATION	COLL.
125	64328	*Mailman Blues*	Tiny Mayberry (vo) acc. possibly Sam Price (pno); clt; dms; Jonah Jones (tpt)	De 7593	20/7/38 N.Y.C.	PHO
126	42344	*People Are Meddlin' In Our Affairs*	J. B. Lenoir (vo, gtr) acc. Sunnyland Slim (pno)	J.O.B. 112	c. –/–53 Chicago	PHO
127	145133	*My Mistake Blues*	Barbecue Bob (vo, gtr)	Co 14350	5/11/27 Atlanta	ET
128	AC-3655	*Money Blues*	Lazy Slim Jim (vo, gtr) acc. gtr	Sav 854	–/–/52 N.Y.C.	PHO
129	CAP 459-2	*Sweet Mary Blues*	Leadbelly (vo, gtr)	Cap 40038 (Cap E:LC 6597)	27/10/44	PHO
130	149345	*Freeze to Me Mama*	Barbecue Bob (vo, gtr)	Co 14507-D	3/11/29	PHO
131	562	*Freakish Blues*	George Hannah (vo) acc. Meade Lux Lewis (pno)	Pm 13024 (Lon AL 3544)	–/–/30	PHO
132	8483	*Peach Tree Blues*	Guilford 'Peach Tree' Payne (vo) acc. Ed Heywood (pno)	OK 8103	–/–/23 Atlanta?	JRD
133	2628	*Sissy Blues*	Gertrude 'Ma' Rainey (vo) acc. tpt; tbn; sop sax; pno; bjo; dms; swanee whistle	Pm 12384 (AL 3558)	–/9/26 Chicago	PHO
134	16991	*B.D. Woman's Blues*	Bessie Jackson (vo) acc. Walter Roland (pno)	ARC 5-12-58	7/3/35 Chicago	ET
135		*Pullet and Hen Blues*	Bob White (The Woogie Man) (vo, pno)	Bb B-8595	–/–/40 Chicago	DSB
136	C 91855	*Sweet Woman Blues*	Leroy's Buddy (vo) acc. Honey Hill (pno); bs	De 7826	22/10/39 Chicago	JDP
137	2112	*Black Girl Blues*	Roosevelt Scott (vo, pno)	Vo 05206	13/9/39 Chicago	PHO

ITEM	MATRIX	TITLE	ARTIST AND ACCOMPANIMENT	CAT. NO.	DATE LOCATION	COLL.
138	148109	You Can't Sleep In My Bed	Mary Dixon (vo) acc. cnt, Louis Metcalfe; pno, J. C. Johnson	Co 14415-D	–/3/29 N.Y.C.	PHO
139	402642	Water Bound Blues	Texas Alexander (vo, gtr) acc. gtr	OK 8785	15/6/29 Chicago	GG
140	22691	I'm a Good Stem Winder	Blind Boy Fuller (vo, gtr)	Vo 04137	6/4/38 N.Y.C.	JRD
141		Tush Hog Blues	Bo Carter (vo, gtr)	Bb 8514	–/–/40	PHO
142	D.A-3-6	Black Wolf	Champion Jack Dupree (vo, pno)	J.Dvs 5104B	–/–/46 N.Y.C.	PHO
143		Rootin' Ground Hog Blues	Big Joe (vo, gtr) and His Rhythm	Bb 7065	–/–/36	DJP
144	61794	Lowing Heifer	Black Ace (vo, gtr) acc. unknown gtr	De 7387	15/2/37 N.Y.C.	PHO
145	68137	My Pony	Johnny Temple (vo) acc. Buster Bailey (clt); tpt; pno; dms	De 7817	23/9/40 N.Y.C.	JDe
146	WC 3765	Me and My Chauffeur Blues	Memphis Minnie (vo, gtr) acc. Little Son Joe (gtr); bs	OK 06288	–/5/41 Chicago	PHO
147	C 2485	Easy Towing Mama	The Yas Yas Girl (vo) acc. Blind John Davis (pno); gtr; dms	Vo 04830	10/2/39 Chicago	BD
148	DAL 302	Coal Woman Blues	Black Boy Shine (vo, pno)	Vo 03757	–/6/37 Dallas	PHO
149	143941-1	New Jelly Roll Blues	Peg Leg Howell (vo, gtr) acc. Eddie Anthony (vln)	Co 14210	8/4/27 Atlanta	PHO
150		Morning Blues	Lightnin' Hopkins (vo, gtr)	Ald 3035A	25/2/48	PHO
151	81223	Cornbread Blues	Texas Alexander (vo) acc. Lonnie Johnson (gtr)	OK 8511	12/8/27	PHO

ITEM	MATRIX	TITLE	ARTIST AND ACCOMPANIMENT	CAT. NO.	DATE LOCATION	COLL.
152	140860	Kitchen Mechanic Blues	Clara Smith (vo) acc. Her Jazz Band: Bob Fuller (alt sax); Stanley Miller (pno); Buddy Christian (bjo)	Co 14097-D	20/8/25 N.Y.C.	PHO
153	145785	Empty Bed Blues Pt. 1	Bessie Smith (vo) acc. Porter Grainger (pno)	Co 14312	20/3/28 N.Y.C.	PHO
154	3028	Pigmeat Blues	Ardella Bragg (vo) acc. Tiny Parham (pno); gtr	Pm 12398	–/–/26	JRD
155		Peach Tree Blues	Yank Rachell (vo, gtr) acc. Sonny Boy Williamson (hca); Washboard Sam (wbd)	Bb 9033-A	11/12/41	PHO
156	M 187	The Dirty Dozen	Speckled Red (vo, pno)	Br 7116	14/9/29 Memphis	PHO
157	C 5584½	Dirty Dozen No. 2	Speckled Red (vo, pno)	Br 7151	8/4/30 Chicago	PHO
158	C 954	Feather Bed Blues	Bumble Bee Slim (vo) acc. Cripple Clarence Lofton (pno); Big Bill Broonzy (gtr)	Vo 03446	4/4/35 Chicago	PHO
159	(19201) 404938	Ants In My Pants	Bo Carter (vo, gtr)	Vo 03259	–/9/31 N.Y.C.	PHO
160	C 9428	Milk Cow Blues	Kokomo Arnold (vo, gtr)	De 7026	2/3/35 Chicago	PHO
161	20661-1	Black Cat, Hoot Owl Blues	Ma Rainey (vo) acc. Tub Jug Washboard Band	Pm 12687-A	–/–/27	GG
162	20712-2	Fogyism	Ida Cox (vo) acc. Dave Nelson (cnt); Arthur Campbell (pno); bjo	Pm 12690 AL 3510	–/–/27	PHO
163	BVE-36098	Going to Have Bad Luck for Seven Years	Elizabeth Smith (vo) acc. unknown cnt; clt; pno	Vic 20297	6/9/26 N.Y.C.	JL

ITEM	MATRIX	TITLE	ARTIST AND ACCOMPANIMENT	CAT. NO.	DATE LOCATION	COLL.
164	50-0032B	Hoodoo Lady Blues	Arthur 'Big Boy' Crudup (vo, gtr) acc. bs; dms	Vic 22-0048-B	7/10/48-9	JDe
165	D7/BB/1062 W73821A	Gypsy Blues	Joshua Johnson (vo, pno)	De 48027	21/3/47 N.Y.C.	JDP
166	509	Big Fat Mama Blues	Charlie Spand (vo, pno)	Pm 13005	–/12/30	PHO
167	462-1	Broke and Hungry Blues	Blind Lemon Jefferson (vo, gtr)	Pm 12443	–/–/26	PHO
168	VEP 47	Louisiana Blues	Muddy Waters (vo, gtr) acc. Little Walter Jacobs (hca)	Vg:EPV 1046	c. –/–/50	PHO
169	W145105-3	Mojo Blues	Charlie Lincoln (vo, gtr)	Co 14475D	4/11/27 Atlanta	JJ
170	62654A	Hoodoo Woman	Johnny Temple (vo) acc. Harlem Hamfats: Odell Rand (clt); Horace Malcolm (pno); Joe McCoy (gtr); Chas. McCoy (gtr); John Lindsay (bs); Fred Flynn (dms)	De 7385	6/9/37 N.Y.C.	JDe
171	14637	Tallahasee Blues	Tallahassee Tight (vo, gtr)	Mlt M-13073	18/1/34	JJ
172	D7-VB-1056	Handreader Blues	William Jazz Gillum (vo, hca) acc. Robert Call (pno); Willie Lacey (gtr); Ransom Knowling (bs); Judge Lawrence Riley (dms)	Vic 20-2964	2/10/47 Chicago	PHO
173		Root Doctor Blues	Doctor Clayton (vo) acc. Blind John Davis (pno); Alfred Elkins (bs); Willie Lacey (gtr) ?	Vic 20-2323	–/–/42-3	BB
174	65658	Voodoo Blues	Fats Hayden (vo) acc. Sam Price (pno); Teddy Bunn (gtr); bs	De 7614B	26/5/39 N.Y.C.	JDe
175	5023-B	The Jinx Is On Me	Gabriel Brown (vo, gtr)	J.Dvs DA-5-6	c. –/–/46	PHO
176	B 8013	Playing the Races	John Lee Hooker (vo, gtr)	Modern 20-730	c. –/–/46	PHO

ITEM	MATRIX	TITLE	ARTIST AND ACCOMPANIMENT	CAT. NO.	DATE LOCATION	COLL.
177	65421A	The Numbers Blues	Ollie Shepard (vo) acc. and his Kentucky Boys: Sam Price (pno)	De 7585	18/4/39 N.Y.C.	JDe
178	C 91532	Number Runner's Blues	Jimmy Gordon (vo) acc. and his Vip Vop Band: pno; gtr; dms	De 7536B	18/10/38 Chicago	PHO
179	15248A	Poker Woman Blues	Blind Blake (vo, gtr) acc. Taylor (pno)	Pm 12810	–/7/29 Richmond, Ind.	MV
180	90857	Gambling Man	Red Nelson (vo) acc. pno, probably Charles Avery; gtr; bs	De 7256	–/9/35 Chicago	JJ
181	C 4677	Gambler's Blues	Charles 'Speck' Pertum (vo) acc. pno	Br 7146	1/11/29	DSB
182	60512A	Coon Can Shorty	Peetie Wheatstraw (vo) acc. Kokomo Arnold (gtr); Roosevelt Sykes (pno)	De 7159B	18/2/36 N.Y.C.	DJP
183	W145185-2	Skin Game Blues	Peg Leg Howell (vo, gtr)	Co 14473D	9/11/27 Atlanta	JJ
184	9548A	Jack o' Diamonds	Sippie Wallace (vo) acc. Louis Armstrong (cnt); Hersal Thomas (pno)	OK 8328	–/–/26	BR
185		Jack o' Diamonds	Brother John Sellers (vo) acc. Sonny Terry (hca); Johnny Johns (gtr)	VAN VRS 7022 (VanE PPT12017)	10/3/54	PHO
186	15483-1	Dice's Blues	Bob Campbell (vo) acc. gtr	Vo 02830	30/7/34	GG
187	WC2644	Money Green	Alfred Fields (vo) acc. pno; gtr; wbd	OK 06129	–/7/39	DJP
188	91207	Monte Carlo Blues	Roosevelt Sykes (vo, pno)	De 7352	29/3/37 Chicago	DJP

ITEM	MATRIX	TITLE	ARTIST AND ACCOMPANIMENT	CAT. NO.	DATE LOCATION	COLL.
189	90176A	Drop Down Mama	Sleepy John Estes (vo, gtr) acc. Noah Lewis (hca); wbd	BrE 03562	–/–/35 Chicago	PHO
190	401348	St. Louis Fair Blues	Texas Alexander (vo) acc. Eddie Lang (gtr)	OK 8688	20/11/28 N.Y.C.	JJ
191	20728	Low Down Mississippi Bottom Man	Mr. Freddie Spruell (vo, gtr) acc. gtr	Pm 12665	c./–/29	GG
192		Big Night Blues	Blind Lemon Jefferson (vo, gtr)	Pm 12801 (Lon AL 3546)	–/3/29	PHO
193		Slow Boogie	Champion Jack Dupree (vo, pno)	Fkwy FP53	–/–/43	PHO
194	C 4300	Head Rag Hop	Romeo Nelson (vo, pno) acc. female vo	VoE V1011	5/9/29 Chicago	PHO
195	L178	Barrell House Flat Blues	Mary Johnson (vo) acc. Ike Rodgers (tbn); pno	Pm 122996 (Lon AL 3512)	–/–/29	PHO
196	W140191-2	Good Time Flat Blues	Maggie Jones (vo) acc. Louis Armstrong (cnt); Fletcher Henderson (pno)	Co 14055D	17/12/24 N.Y.C.	PHO
197	404149	Bootlegger's Blues	Mississippi Sheiks (vo) acc. Bo Carter (gtr); vln; bjo; bs; Walter Jacobs (gtr)	OK 8820	c./6/30	PHO
198	C 2292	Alley Bound Blues	Curtis Jones (vo) acc. pno; gtr; bs	Vo 04249	23/6/38 Chicago	JRD
199	C 91212	Bootleggin' Ain't Good No More	Blind Blues Darby (vo) acc. Roosevelt Sykes (pno)?; bs	De 7816	30/4/37 Chicago	PHO
200	91775	Beer Tavern	Peetie Wheatstraw (vo) acc. pno; Lonnie Johnson (gtr); hca	De 7657B	14/9/39 Chicago	PHO

ITEM	MATRIX	TITLE	ARTIST AND ACCOMPANIMENT	CAT. NO.	DATE LOCATION	COLL.
201	C 91232	Grandpa Got Drunk	Kokomo Arnold (vo, gtr)	De 7319	7/4/37 Chicago	PHO
202	149541	Riverside Blues	Nick Nicholls (vo, gtr) acc. gtr; pno	Co 14512D	5/12/29 Dallas	DSB
203	D4-AB-321-1	One More Break Blues	St. Louis Jimmy (vo) acc. Ted Summitt (gtr); Roosevelt Sykes (pno); Armond Jackson (dms)	Bb 34-0727	14/12/44	DJP
204	2166	You've Been Drunk	Jack Dupree (vo, pno)	J.Dvs 5106A	–/–/46	PHO
205		I Staggered in My Sleep	Clara Morris (vo) acc. pno; gtr	Bb 8700	–/–/40	DSB
206	030829	Cuttin' off My Days	Walter Davis (vo, pno) acc. gtr	Bb 7978	19/12/38	BD
207	BVE 40311	Mr. McTell Got the Blues	Blind Willie McTell (vo, gtr)	Vic 21124B	18/10/27	GG
208	C 3592	Junker Blues	Champion Jack Dupree (vo, pno) acc. Wilson Swain (bs)	OK 06152	28/1/41 Chicago	PHO
209		I Gotta Find My Baby	St. Louis Jimmy (vo)	Bb		SB
210	C 4081	Creole Queen	Little Bill Gaither (vo) acc. Horace Malcomb (pno); Big Bill Broonzy (gtr)	OK 06561	2/12/41 Chicago	PHO
211	21018-4	Hard Dallas	Rambling Thomas (vo, gtr)	Pm 12708	–/–/28 Chicago	PHO
212		East Chicago Blues	Pinetop and Lindberg (vo, pno)	Bb B-10177 from Vic 23330		ET
213	142027	Old New Orleans Blues	Willie Jackson (vo) acc. Steve Lewis (pno)	Co 14136-D	14/4/26 New Orleans	PHO

ITEM	MATRIX	TITLE	ARTIST AND ACCOMPANIMENT	CAT. NO.	DATE LOCATION	COLL.
214	37975	Haven't Got a Dollar to Pay Your House Rent	Genevieve Davis (vo) acc. Louis Dumaine's Eight: Louis Dumaine (cnt); Earl Humphrey (tbn); Wally Joseph (clt); Louis James (ten sax); Morris Rouse (pno); Leonard Mitchell (bjo); Joe Howard (bs); James Willigan (dms)	Vic 20648	5/3/27 New Orleans	BR
215	GM 504	Bourgeois Blues	Huddie Ledbetter (vo, gtr)	Mus 227	1/4/39 N.Y.C.	PHO
216		Down South Blues	Jazz Gillum (vo, hca) acc. pno; gtr	Bb B-9004-B	24/7/41 Chicago	DJP
217	142137	Jelly Bean Blues	Clara Smith (vo) acc. Tom Edwards (tmb); Clarence Adams (clt); Stanley Miller (pno)	Co 14294-D	1/5/26	JD
218	BB2	Country Gal	Smokey Hogg (vo, gtr)	Modern 20-532		PHO
219	059205	Crowing Rooster Blues	Lonnie Johnson (vo, gtr) acc. Lil Armstrong (pno); Andrew Harris (bs)	Bb B8804	7/2/41 Chicago	JDe
220	2288	Maxwell Street Blues	Charlie Jackson (vo, bjo or gtr)	Pm 12320	–/–/25	BD
221	W 76712	Owl Stew	Cecil Gant (vo, pno) acc. bs; dms	De 48231	7/7/50	DJP
222	149538	Elm Street Blues	Texas Bill Day (vo) acc. Billiken Johnson (duet vo); pno; gtr	Co 14514	5/12/29 Dallas	DSB
223	9929A	Mighty Tight Woman	Sippie Wallace (vo) acc. Dave Nelson (cnt); Hersal Thomas (pno)	OK 8439	–/–/25	BR
224	146176	Jacksonville Blues	Nellie Florence (vo) acc. Barbecue Bob (gtr)?	Co 14342	21/4/28 Atlanta	JD

ITEM	MATRIX	TITLE	ARTIST AND ACCOMPANIMENT	CAT. NO.	DATE LOCATION	COLL.
225	65206	The Sun Goes Down in Blood	Johnny Temple (vo) acc. Sam Price (pno); Teddy Bunn (gtr); bs	De 7632	6/3/39 N.Y.C.	PHO
226	C 1346	Fast Life Blues	Bumble Bee Slim (vo) acc. pno; gtr	Vo 03446	2/4/36 Chicago	PHO
227	65316	Easy Way Blues	Peetie Wheatstraw (vo) acc. pno, Sam Price; Teddy Bunn (gtr); O'Neil Spencer (dms)	De 7641B	30/3/39 Chicago	DJP
228	C 3885	Two By Four Blues	Merline Johnson (vo) acc. pno; bs	OK 06446	19/6/41 Chicago	PHO
229	15559	Good Chib Blues	Edith Johnson (vo) acc. Baby Jay (cnt); Ike Rodgers (tbn); Roosevelt Sykes (pno)	Pm 12864 Lon AL 3512	7/9/29 N.Y.C.	PHO
230	BVE-45448-1	Got Cut All to Pieces	Bessie Tucker (vo) acc. K. D. Johnson (pno)	HMV7EG8085	30/8/28 Memphis	PHO
231	149535-1	Ice Pick Blues	Whistlin' Alex Moore (vo, gtr) acc. pno	Co 14518-D	5/12/29 Dallas	JRD
232	BVE-70677	Hi-Jack Blues	Walter Davis (vo, pno)	Vic 23343	–/–/31-2	MV
233	1273	Guter Man Blues	George Hannah (vo) acc. pno; gtr; dms	Pm 12788-A	c., /–/29	JRD
234	6822	Gangster Blues	Peetie Wheatstraw (vo) acc. Jonah Jones (tpt); Lil Armstrong (pno); Sidney Catlett	De 7815	–/7/40 N.Y.C.	PHO
235		Mad Mama's Blues	Violet Mills (vo)	Domino		JRD
236	BVE-45424-1	Furry's Blues	Furry Lewis (vo, gtr)	Vic V-38519	28/8/28 Memphis	MV
237	C 738	Cold Blooded Murder	Bumble Bee Slim (vo) acc. pno; gtr	Vo 02865	20/10/34 Chicago	PHO

ITEM	MATRIX	TITLE	ARTIST AND ACCOMPANIMENT	CAT. NO.	DATE LOCATION	COLL.
238	93571	Lookin' for the Blues	Jimmy Gordon (vo) acc. pno	De 7865	–/3/41 Chicago	PHO
239	D5-AB-350	Maceo's 32–20	Big Maceo (vo, pno)	Vic 20-2028	5/7/45	PHO
240	N 18392	Evil Woman Blues	acc. Tampa Red (gtr); Tyrrell Dixon (dms) James Wiggins (vo) acc. Dobby Bragg (pno)	AL 3544	–/–/28 Chicago	PHO
241	BMI 1541	Third Degree	Eddie Boyd (vo, pno)	Chess U-4374	c./–/50	JDe
242	149356-2	Big Rock Jail	Barefoot Bill (vo, gtr)	Co 14481-D	4/11/29 Atlanta	MV
243	C 2694	Prison Bound	Leroy Carr (vo, pno) acc. Scrapper Blackwell (gtr)	Vo 1241	1/2/29 Chicago	DSB
244		Jail House Blues	Lightnin' Hopkins (vo, gtr)	GS 662A	c.,/–/46	JDe
245	9792A	Chain Gang Blues	Kokomo Arnold (vo, gtr)	De 7069	–/–/35 Chicago	PHO
246	2372	Chain Gang Blues	Ma Rainey (vo) acc. Joe Smith (tpt); Charlie Green (tbn); Buster Bailey (clt); Fletcher Henderson (pno); Charlie Dixon (gtr); Kaiser Marshall (dms); Coleman Hawkins (bs sax)	Pm 12338	–/1/26	PHO
247	16429	Eleven Twenty-Nine Blues	Leroy Carr (vo, pno) acc. Scrapper Blackwell (gtr)	Vo 03157	14/12/34 Chicago	MV
248	15449	Prison Blues	Alice Moore (vo) acc. Ike Rodgers (tbn); Henry Brown (pno)	Pm 12868 Lon AL 3512	–/–/29	PHO
249	WC 2981A1	Parchman Farm Blues	Bukka White (vo, gtr) acc. wbd	OK 05683	–/5/40 Chicago	MV
250	20388-2	Prison Cell Blues	Blind Lemon Jefferson (vo, gtr)	Pm 12622B	–/2/28	PHO

ITEM	MATRIX	TITLE	ARTIST AND ACCOMPANIMENT	CAT. NO.	DATE LOCATION	COLL.
251	SC 25	Big House Bound	Blind Boy Fuller (vo, gtr) acc. Sonny Terry (hca)	Vo 04897	29/10/38 South Carolina	PHO
252	J.S.559	County Jail Special	Champion Jack Dupree (vo, pno)	J.D.5103	–/–/46	PHO
253	BS-064192	County Jail Blues	Big Maceo (vo, pno) acc. Tampa Red (gtr)	Bb B8798	24/6/41	PHO
254	65408	'44 Blues	Roosevelt Sykes (vo, pno) acc. traps	De 7586	13/4/39 N.Y.C.	DJP
255	91195A	Prisoner Bound	Frank Busby (vo) acc. Honey Hill (pno); gtr; bs	De 7295	6/4/37 Chicago	MV
256	91764	Sing Sing Blues	Bill Gaither (vo) acc. pno; bs	De 7784A	13/9/39 Chicago	PHO
257	S-71-981-A	I've Got To Go and Leave My Daddy Behind	Sara Martin (vo) acc. Sylvester Weaver (gtr)	OK 8104	–/–/23	PHO
258	657-4419-2	Jailhouse Fire Blues	Buddy Boy Hawkins (vo) acc. gtr	Pm 12489 Lon AL 3535	–/–/27	PHO
259	826A:4651-2	Greyhound Blues	Alice Pearson (vo) acc. F. Coates (pno)	Pm 12523	–/5/27	GG
260	56732	Bloodhound Blues	Victoria Spivey (vo) acc. Luis Russell's Orchestra; Henry Allen (tpt); J. C. Higginbotham (tmb); Charles Holmes (alt sax); Will Johnson (gtr); Pops Foster (bs); Luis Russell (pno)	Vic 38570 HMV 7E98190	1/10/29	PHO
261	20751	Hangman's Blues	Blind Lemon Jefferson (vo, gtr)	Pm 12679B		PHO
262	G15514	Electric Chair	Blue Boy (vo) acc. pno; clt	Vrs 6059	–/–/29	PHO

ITEM	MATRIX	TITLE	ARTIST AND ACCOMPANIMENT	CAT. NO.	DATE LOCATION	COLL.
263	074068	Rambler's Blues	Lonnie Johnson (vo, gtr) acc. Blind John Davis (pno); Andrew Harris (bs)	Bb 34-0708	13/2/42 Chicago	PHO
264		Lawyer Clark Blues	Sleepy John Estes (vo, gtr) acc. Son Bonds? (gtr)	Bb 8871	–/–/41	DSB
265	C 90762	Lone Lonesome Day Blues	Jesse James (vo, pno)	De 7213 VoE V1037	3/6/36	PHO
266	148708	When the Levee Breaks	Kansas Joe and Memphis Minnie Joe McCoy (vo, gtr), Minnie McCoy (vo)	Co 14439D	18/6/29	JJ
267	4491-5	Rish' High Water Blues	Blind Lemon Jefferson (vo, gtr) acc. George Perkins (pno)	Pm 12487	–/–/27	PHO
268	80840B	The Flood Blues	Sippie Wallace (vo) acc. Louis Armstrong (cnt); Artie Starks (clt); Lil Hardin (pno); Bud Scott (gtr)	OK 8470	6/5/27	BR
269	87753	The Mississippi Flood Blues	Joe Pullum (vo) acc. Rob Cooper (pno)	Bb B-5844	29/1/35 San Antonio	MV
270	144277	Mississippi Heavy Water Blues	Barbecue Bob (vo, gtr)	Co 14222D	15/6/27	JRD
271		Red Cross Blues	Alabama Sam (vo) acc. Walter Roland (pno)	Mlt 12753	–/–/33	JL
272	91341	Flood Water	Lonnie Johnson (vo, gtr)	De 7397	8/11/37 Chicago	JDe
273	62465	Floating Bridge	Sleepy John Estes (vo, gtr) acc. Noah Lewis (hca); Hammie Nix (gtr)	De 7442	2/8/37	DSB
274	20192	St. Louis Cyclone Blues	Elzadie Robinson (vo) acc. Bob Call (pno)	Pm 12573	–/–/27	PHO
275	91946 58-1	That Mean Old Twister	Lightnin' Hopkins (vo, gtr) acc. Wilson Thunder Smith (pno)	Ald 167	9/11/46	JDe

ITEM	MATRIX	TITLE	ARTIST AND ACCOMPANIMENT	CAT. NO.	DATE LOCATION	COLL.
276	V-9290	Florida Hurricane	St. Louis Jimmy (vo) acc. Muddy Waters and his Blues Combo: Waters (gtr); Sunnyland Slim (pno); ten; bs	Arct 7001	–/–/50 Chicago	DC
277	151597	Shipwreck Blues	Bessie Smith (vo) acc. Louis Bacon (tpt); Charlie Green (tmb); Clarence Williams (pno); Floyd Casey (dms)	Ph BBL 7049	11/6/31 N.Y.C.	PHO
278	1612	Southern Blues	Gertrude 'Ma' Rainey (vo) acc. Lovie Austin and her Blues Serenaders: Tommy Ladnier (cnt); Jimmy O'Bryant (cit); Lovie Austin (pno); Jasper Taylor (dms) or Kaiser Marshall	Pm 12083	–/–/23	PHO
279	63650	Fire Department Blues	Sleepy John Estes (vo, gtr) acc. Hammie Nix (gtr)	De 7571	27/4/38	PHO
280	15557	Fire Detective Blues	Dobby Bragg (vo, pno)	Pm 12827	–/–/29-30	PHO
281	C 93003	The Death of Walter Barnes	Baby Doo (vo) acc. Walter Davis (pno); Lee McCoy (hca)	De 7763	4/6/40 Chicago	PHO
282	C 93001	The Natchez Fire	Gene Gilmore (vo) acc. Walter Davis (pno); Lee McCoy (hca)	De 7763	4/6/40 Chicago	PHO
283		Pearl Harbor Blues	Doctor Clayton (vo) acc. Blind John Davis (pno); Alfred Elkins (im bs)	Bb 9003	27/3/42	JDe
284	C 3510	That Old Number of Mine (Number 158)	Big Bill Broonzy (vo, gtr) acc. Memphis Slim (pno); Ransom Knowling (bs)	OK 06080	17/12/40 Chicago	BD
285		Give Me a 32–20	Arthur 'Big Boy' Crudup (vo, gtr) acc. dms	Bb B-9019A	–/–/41:2	PHO

ITEM	MATRIX	TITLE	ARTIST AND ACCOMPANIMENT	CAT. NO.	DATE LOCATION	COLL.
286	C 3791	Million Lonesome Women	Brownie McGhee (vo, gtr) acc. Jordan Webb (hca); George Washington (wbd)	OK 06329	23/5/41 Chicago	PHO
287		I Hate to Say Goodbye	Walter Davis (vo, pno)	Bb B-8694	–/–/41	DJP
288	C 4057	Training Camp Blues	Roosevelt Sykes (vo, pno) acc. bs	OK 6709	21/11/41 Chicago	DJP
289	BS 074071	Baby Remember Me	Lonnie Johnson (vo, gtr) acc. Blind John Davis (pno); Andrew Harris (bs)	Bb 34-0714-B	13/2/42	BB
290	WC 3144	When You Are Gone	Blind Boy Fuller (vo, gtr)	OK 05756	19/6/40 Chicago	PHO
291	D4-AB-326	Win the War Blues	Sonny Boy Williamson (vo, hca) acc. Blind John Davis (pno); Ted Summitt (gtr); Armand Jackson (dms)	Bb 34-0722-A	14/12/44 Chicago	PHO
292	81253	Uncle Sam Blues	Clara Smith (vo) acc. Fletcher Henderson (pno)	Co 12-D	1/10/23	PHO
293	D4-AB-323-1	Bad Condition	St. Louis Jimmy (vo) acc. Roosevelt Sykes (pno); Ted Summitt (el gtr); Armand Jackson (dms)	Vic 20-2650	14/12/44	DJP
294		Cornbread, Meat and Molasses	Sonny Terry (vo, hca) acc. Woody Guthrie, Alec Stewart (gtrs)	Stin SLP 7	c.,/–/53	PHO
295	WC3110	Warehouse Man Blues	Champion Jack Dupree (vo, pno) acc. bs	OK 05656	13/6/40 Chicago	PHO
296	145561	T.B. Blues	Willie Jackson (vo) acc. pno; gtr	Co 14284-D	21/1/28 New Orleans	PHO

ITEM	MATRIX	TITLE	ARTIST AND ACCOMPANIMENT	CAT. NO.	DATE LOCATION	COLL.
297		Don't Go Down Baby	Robert Petway (vo, gtr)	Bb 8756	c.,-/40	DJP
298	56733	Dirty T.B. Blues	Victoria Spivey (vo) acc. Luis Russell's Orchestra: Henry Allen (tpt); J. C. Higginbotham (tmb); Charlie Holmes (alt sax); Will Johnson (gtr); Pops Foster (bs); Luis Russell (pno)	Vic V38570 HMV 7EG8190	1/10/29 N.Y.C.	PHO
299	C 1450	I Can't Last Long	Jane Lucas (vo) acc. pno	Vo 03314	20/8/36	PHO
300		There Was a Time That I Went Blind	Reverend Gary Davis (vo, gtr)	Riv RLP 12-611	29/1/56 N.Y.C.	PHO
301	22674	Pistol Slapper Blues	Blind Boy Fuller (vo, gtr)	Vo 04106	5/3/38	JRD
302	SBW-4255	Goin' Down Slow	Billy Wright (vo, gtr) acc. pno; sax; dms	Sav 870		BB
303	C 1344	Wet Clothes Blues	Bumble Bee Slim (vo) acc. possibly Amos Easton (pno)	Vo 03267	2/4/36 Chicago	JRD
304	C 1231	I Done Caught My Death of Cold	Bumble Bee Slim (vo) acc. pno; gtr; bs	Vo 03767	6/2/36	JRD
305	15689	Pneumonia Blues	Blind Lemon Jefferson (vo, gtr)	Pm 12880 Lon AL 3564	-/10/29 Chicago	PHO
306	C 93846A	Bring Me Flowers While I'm Living	Peetie Wheatstraw (vo) acc. Lil Armstrong (pno); Chu Berry (sax)	De 7886	25/11/41 Chicago	JDe
307	22064	Hooting Owl Blues	Dolly Ross (vo) acc. Porter Grainger (pno); sax; dms	Br 7005B	-/-/27 N.Y.C.	PHO
308		Death Bells	Lightnin' Hopkins (vo, gtr)	GS 646	-/-/46	JDe

ITEM	MATRIX	TITLE	ARTIST AND ACCOMPANIMENT	CAT. NO.	DATE LOCATION	COLL.
309	WC 3141	Lost Lover Blues	Blind Boy Fuller (vo, gtr) acc. George Washington (wbd)	OK 05756	19/6/40 Chicago	PHO
310	2293	Coffin Blues	Ida Cox (vo) acc. Tommy Ladnier (cnt); Jesse Crump (pno)	Pm 12318 Lon AL 3517	–/–/25 Chicago	PHO
311	85516	Six Cold Feet In the Ground	Leroy Carr (vo, pno)	Bb 5963	25/2/35 Chicago	PHO
312	20374-1	See That My Grave Is Kept Clean	Blind Lemon Jefferson (vo, gtr)	Pm 12608	–/2/28	PHO
313		Death Valley Blues	Arthur 'Big Boy' Crudup (vo, gtr) acc. dms	Bb 8858	c./–/41 Chicago	DSB
314	DAL 398-1	Me and the Devil Blues	Robert Johnson (vo, gtr)	Vo 0418	20/6/37 Dallas	MV
315	90597	Crying Mother Blues	Red Nelson (vo) acc. Cripple Clarence Lofton (pno)	BrE 03508-A	–/–/35	PHO
316	147324	Down in the Cemetery	Billy Bird (vo, gtr)	Co 14381-D	27/10/28 Atlanta	JJ
317	C 3740	Shine On, Shine On	Big Bill Broonzy (vo, gtr) acc. Jazz Gillum (hca)	OK 06303	2/5/41 Chicago	DSB
318	90033	Death of Leroy Carr	Bumble Bee Slim (vo) acc. pno; gtr	De 7098	–/6/35 Chicago	JRD
319		Relief Blues	Red Nelson (vo) acc. pno; gtr; traps	Bb B-7265-A	c./–/38 Chicago	PHO
320		F.D.R. Blues	Champion Jack Dupree (vo, pno)	J.Dvs 5102	–/–/46	JDe
321	BS-049199	Decoration Day Blues	Sonny Boy Williamson (vo, hca) acc. Joshua Altheimer (pno); Fred Williams (dms)	Bb 34-0713	17/5/40 Chicago	JDe

ITEM	MATRIX	TITLE	ARTIST AND ACCOMPANIMENT	CAT. NO.	DATE LOCATION	COLL.
322	WC 2978	*Strange Place*	Bukka White (vo, gtr) acc. wbd	OK 05526	–/6/40	DSB
323	90922	*World's a Hard Place*	Georgia Pine Boy (vo, gtr) acc. vln	De 7828B	–/9/35 Chicago	PHO
324	91523A	*Between Midnight and Dawn*	Johnny Temple (vo) acc. Odell Rand (clt); Horace Malcolm (pno)?; bs	De 7547	17/10/38 Chicago	VS
325	65423A	*Shepard Blues (Pig Latin Blues)*	Ollie Shepard (vo) acc. and his Kentucky Boys: pno; sax; traps	De 7602	18/4/39 N.Y.C.	PHO
326		*Mother Fuyer*	Dirty Red (vo, pno) acc. gtr; dms	Ald 194A	–/–/46	PHO
327	WC 3204	*The Jive Blues*	Peter Chatman (vo, pno) acc. hca; bs; wbd	OK 05908	–/8/40 Chicago	JRD
328	C 91773	*Hard Way to Go*	Leroy's Buddy (vo) acc. Rob Cooper (pno)	De 7846	14/9/39 Chicago	PHO
329	64194	*Champ Joe Louis (King of the Gloves)*	Leroy's Buddy (vo) acc. Honey Hill (pno); gtr; sax	De 7476	23/6/38 N.Y.C.	PHO
330	146149	*Lonesome Blues*	Henry Williams (vo, gtr) and Eddie Anthony (vo, vln)	Co 14328-D	20/4/28 Atlanta	PHO
331	63529	*The Train Is Coming (No More Baby Talk)*	The Honey Dripper (vo, pno) acc. dms	De 7483	1/4/38 N.Y.C.	PHO
332	15671	*That Crawling Baby Blues*	Blind Lemon Jefferson (vo, gtr)	Pm 12880 Lon AL 3564	–/10/29	PHO
333	93849	*Mister Livingood*	Peetie Wheatstraw (vo) acc. pno, Lil Armstrong; bs	De 7879	25/11/41 Chicago	DJP

ITEM	MATRIX	TITLE	ARTIST AND ACCOMPANIMENT	CAT. NO.	DATE LOCATION	COLL.
334	BS 030828	I Like the Way You Spread Your Wings	Walter Davis (vo, pno)	Bb 7978	19/12/38 Chicago	DJP
335	C 3790	Key to My Door	Brownie McGhee (vo, gtr) acc. George Washington (wbd)	OK 06437	23/5/41 Chicago	PHO
336	B 11499	Midnight Hour Blues	Leroy Carr (vo, pno) acc. Scrapper Blackwell (gtr)	Vo 1703	16/3/32	PHO
337	C 1939	Blues Everywhere	Yas Yas Girl (vo) acc. Blind John Davis (pno); gtr; dms	OK 03638	22/6/37 Chicago	ET
338	W147608	Waking Blues	Otis Harris (vo, gtr)	Co 14428-D	8/12/28 Dallas	PHO
339	20193	Mr. Blues	Lucius Hardy (vo) acc. pno	Pm 12598	–/12/27	BD
340	BS 074101	Blues Trip Me This Morning	Tommy McClennan (vo, gtr) acc. str; bs	Bb B-9037-A	20/2/42 Chicago	PHO
341	4449-2:630	Jinx Blues	Ora Brown (vo) acc. Tiny Parham (pno)	Pm 12481	c.,/3/27 Chicago	MV
342	DAL 394-2	Hell Hound on My Tail	Robert Johnson (vo, gtr)	Vo 03623	20/6/37 Dallas	MV
343		Every Day of the Week	Pink Anderson (vo, gtr) acc. Jumbo Lewis (wbd)	Riv RLP 12-611	29/5/50 Charlottesville, Va.	PHO
344	BVE-37945	Rock Away Blues	Sadie McKinney (vo) acc. Charlie Williamson (cnt)	Vic 20565	24/2/27	BR

ITEM	MATRIX	TITLE	ARTIST AND ACCOMPANIMENT	CAT. NO.	DATE LOCATION	COLL.
345	151596	*Blues Blues*	Bessie Smith (vo) acc. Charlie Green (tmb); Clarence Williams (pno); Ed Allen (cnt)?; Floyd Casey (dms)?	Co 14611-D	11/6/31 N.Y.C.	PHO
346	C 3907	*Conversation With the Blues*	Big Bill Broonzy (vo, gtr) acc. Memphis Slim (pno); Washboard Sam (wbd)	Co 9932	17/7/41 Chicago	JRD
347	2294	*Rambling Blues*	Ida Cox (vo) acc. Tommy Ladnier (cnt); Jesse Crump (pno)	Pm 12318 (Lon AL 3517)	–/–/25 Chicago	PHO
348	146191	*Sunrise Blues*	Will Day (vo) acc. gtr, clt	Co 14318	25/4/28 New Orleans	BD
349	02644	*Tantalizing Blues*	Little Brother Montgomery (vo, pno)	Bb 6766	16/10/36	ET
350		*Worried Man Blues*	Walter Davis (vo, pno)	Bb 5129	–/–/31-2	BD

Acknowledgments in Discography

371

Index of Quoted Blues Singers

Blues singers who are quoted in the text are indexed in alphabetical order and the Item numbers allocated in the Discography follow the names. Where a singer uses a pseudonym the items are listed hereunder if the pseudonym is more generally known than the correct name of the singer. Correst names, where known, are also listed and cross-reference made. All listed names are of vocalists but instruments played are indicated where applicable.

Selected Bibliography

A listing of principal works of reference consulted:

ALLEN, Frederick Lewis, *The Big Change: America Transforms Itself.* Hamish Hamilton. 1952.

ALLEN, W. F., *Slave Songs of the United States.* New York. 1867.

ARCHER, William, *Through Afro-America: An English Reading of the Race Problem.* Chapman and Hall. 1910.

ARMITAGE, Merle, *The Railroads of America.* Duell, Sloan, & Pearce, Little, Brown. 1952. Illus.

ASBURY, Herbert, *The Underworld of Chicago: An Informal History of the Chicago Underworld.* Robert Hale. 1941. Illus.

BACKUS, E. M., *Negro Songs From Georgia. Journal of American Folk Lore.* Vol. 10. No. 11.

BAYTON, James A., *The Psychology of Race Morale. Journal of Negro Education.* Vol. 9. April 1942.

BLESH, Rudi, *Shining Trumpets: A History of Jazz.* Cassell. 1949. Illus.

BONTEMPS, Arna W., *The Story of the Negro.* Knopf. 1948.

BORNEMAN, Ernest, *A Critic Looks at Jazz.* Jazz Music Books. 1946.

BOTKIN, B. A. (Editor), *Lay My Burden Down: A Folk History of Slavery.* University of Chicago Press. 1945. Illus.

BROONZY, William 'Big Bill,' and BRUYNOGHE, Yannick, *Big Bill Blues: William Broonzy's Story.* Cassell. 1955. Illus.

BROWN, Earl, and LEIGHTON, George, *The Negro and The War. Public Affairs Pamphlets.* No. 71. 1942.

BROWN, Sterling; DAVIS, Arthur, and LEE, Ulysses (Editors), *The Negro Caravan.* Dryden. 1941.

BUCKMASTER, Henrietta, *Out of the House of Bondage: The Story of the Famous Underground Railroad of Negro Slaves.* Victor Gollancz. 1943.

BURLIN, Natalie Curtis, *Negro Folk Songs.* G. Schirmer. N.Y. 1918–19.

CALVERTON, V. F. (Editor), *Anthology of American Negro Literature.* Modern Library. 1929. Illus.

CARMER, Carl, *Stars Fell On Alabama.* Loval Dickson & Thompson. 1935. Illus.

CUNARD, Nancy, *Negro: Compiled and Edited by Nancy Cunard.* Nancy Cunard. 1934.

DAVIE, M. R., *Negroes in American Society,* Whittlesley House. 1949.

DAVIS, A., and DOLLARD, J., *Children of Bondage.* American Council of Education. 1940.

DE KRUIF, Paul, *The Fight For Life.* Jonathan Cape. 1938.

DRAKE, St. C., and CAYTON, H., *Black Metropolis.* Harcourt, Brace. 1945.

DuBOIS, W. E. B., *Black Reconstruction.* Harcourt, Brace. 1935.

EMBREE, E. R., *Brown Americans: The Story of a Tenth of a Nation.* Viking. 1944.

FAUSET, Arthur Huff, *Black Gods of the Metropolis: Negro Religious Cults of the Urban North.* University of Pennsylvania Press. 1944. Illus.

FEDERAL WRITERS' PROJECT, *Florida: A Guide to the Southernmost State.* Oxford University Press. (Ohio) 1939. Illus.

FEDERAL WRITERS' PROJECT, *Mississippi: A Guide to the Magnolia State.* Hastings House. 1949. Illus.

FEDERAL WRITERS' PROJECT, *Tennessee: A Guide to the State.* Hastings House. 1949. Illus.

FRANKLIN, John Hope, *From Slavery To Freedom.* Knopf. 1956.

FRAZIER, E. Franklin, *The Negro Family in the United States.* Dryden. 1939.

FRAZIER, E. Franklin, *The Negro in the United States.* Macmillan. 1949.

GELLERT, Lawrence, and SEIGMEISTER, Elie, *Negro Songs of Protest.* American Music League.

GOODWIN, R. B., *It's Good To Be Black.* Doubleday. 1954.

GREENAWAY, John, *American Folk Songs of Protest.* University of Pennsylvania Press. 1953. Illus.

GUNTHER, John, *Inside U.S.A.* Hamish Hamilton. 1948?

HAMILTON, Charles (Editor), *Men of the Underworld: The Professional Criminals' Own Story.* Victor Gollancz. 1953.

HANDY, W. C., *Father of the Blues: An Autobiography of W. C. Handy.* Edited by Arna Bontemps. Foreword by Abbe Niles. Macmillan. N.Y. 1955.

HARRIS, Sara, *The Incredible Father Divine.* W. H. Allen. 1954. Illus.

HERSKOVITS, Melville J., *The Myth of the Negro Past.* Harper. July 1941.

HURSTON, Zora Neale, *Mules and Men.* Introduction by Franz Boas, Ph.D. Kegan Paul; French, Taubner & Co. 1936.

JOHNSON, Charles S., *Growing Up In The Black Belt.* American Council on Education. 1941.

JOHNSON, Charles S., *Patterns of Negro Segregation.* Victor Gollancz. 1944.

JOHNSON, Charles S.; EMBREE, E., and ALEXANDER, W. W., *The Collapse of the Cotton Tenancy.* University of North Carolina Press. 1935.

JONES, Max, *On Blues.* Essay in *P.L. Yearbook of Jazz* 1946. Editor Albert McCarthy, q.v.

KENNEDY, R. Emmett, *Mellows, Work Songs, Street Cries and Spirituals from New Orleans.* A. & C. Boni. N.Y. 1925.

KLINEBERG, O., *Characteristics of the American Negro.* Harper. c. 1944.

KREHBIEL, H. E., *Afro-American Folk Songs.* G. Schirmer. 1924.

LAING, Iain, *Jazz In Perspective: The Background of the Blues.* Hutchinson. 1947.

LOMAX, John A., and LOMAX, Alan, *Our Singing Country.* Ruth Crawford Seeger, Music Editor. Macmillan. N.Y. 1949.

LOMAX, John A., and LOMAX, Alan, *Negro Folk Songs As Sung By Leadbelly.* Macmillan. N.Y. 1936.

LOMAX, John A., *The Adventures of a Ballad-hunter.* Macmillan. 1946.

LOMAX, Alan, *Mister Jelly Roll: The Fortunes of Jelly Roll Morton, New Orleans Creole and 'Inventor of Jazz.'* Cassell. 1952.

MARTIN, John Bartlow, *Break Down The Walls.* Victor Gollancz. 1955.

MATSCHAT, Cecile H., *Swanee River: Strange Green Land.* William Hodge. 1951. Illus.

McCARTHY, Albert (Editor), *P.L. Yearbook of Jazz.* Poetry London, 1946. Illus.

McILWAIN, Shields, *Memphis Down In Dixie.* J.P. Dutton. N.Y. 1948.

MYRDAL, Gunnar, *An American Dilemma.* Vols. I and II. Harper. 1942.

ODUM, Howard W., and JOHNSON, Guy B., *The Negro and His Songs: A Study of Typical Negro Songs in the South.* Chapel Hill. University of North Carolina Press. 1925.

ODUM, Howard W., and JOHNSON, Guy B., *Negro Workaday Songs.* Chapel Hill. University of North Carolina Press. 1926.

OTTLEY, Roi, *Black Odyssey: The Story of the Negro in America.* John Murray. 1949.

OTTLEY, Roi, *Inside Black America.* Eyre and Spottiswoode. 1948.

PATTERSON, Alexander, *The Prison Problem In America.* The Prison Commission. c. 1934.

PATTERSON, Heywood, and CONRAD, Earl, *Scottsboro Boy.* Victor Gollancz. 1950.

PEABODY, Charles, *Notes On Negro Music. Journal of American Folk-Lore.* Vol. 16.

PERROW, E. C., *Songs and Rhymes From The South. Journal of American Folk-Lore.* Vols. 25, 26, 28.

PETERKIN, Julia, and ULMANN, Doris, *Roll, Jordan, Roll.* Robert O. Ballou. N.Y. 1933. Illus.

POWELL, Adam Clayton, Jnr., *Marching Blacks: An Interpretive History of the Rise of the Black Common Man.* Dial Press. 1945.

PUCKETT, Newbell Niles, Ph.D., *Folk Beliefs of the Southern Negro.* Chapel Hill. University of North Carolina Press. 1926. Illus.

REID, Ed, *The Shame of New York.* Victor Gollancz. 1954.

SAXON, Lyle; DRYER, Ed, and TALLANT, Robert, *Gumbo Ya-Ya.* Houghton Mifflin. 1945. Illus.

SCARBOROUGH, Dorothy, assisted by GUTLEDGE, Ola Lee, *On the Trail of Negro Folk Songs.* Howard University Press. 1925.

SHAPIRO, Nat, and HENTOFF, Nat, *Hear Me Talkin' To Ya.* Peter Davies. 1955.

SIEGFRIED, André, *America Comes of Age.* Harcourt, Brace. 1927.

SMITH, Charles Edward; RAMSEY, Frederick, Jnr.; ROGERS, C. P., and RUSSELL, William, *The Jazz Record Book.* Smith and Durrell. N.Y. 1946.

SPERO, Sterling D., and HARRIS, Abraham L., *The Black Worker.* Columbia University Press. 1931.

SPRIGLE, Ray, *In the Land of Jim Crow.* Simon and Schuster. 1949.

STEARNS, Marshall W., *The Story of Jazz.* Sidgwick and Jackson. 1957. Illus.

STEGNER, Wallace, and Editors of *Look, One Nation.* Houghton Mifflin. 1945. Illus.

STERNER, R. M., and others, *The Negro's Share.* Harper. 1943.

SUTHERLAND, R. L., *Colour, Class and Personality.* American Council on Education. 1942.

TALLANT, Robert, *Voodoo In New Orleans*. Macmillan. N.Y. 1946.
TALLEY, Thomas W., *Negro Folk Rhymes*. Macmillan. N.Y. 1922.
THOMAS, Norman, *Human Exploitation in the United States*. Frederick A. Stokes. 1934.
UNITED STATES BUREAU OF LABOUR STATISTICS, *Negroes in the United States: Their Employment and Economic Status*. U.S. Government Publicity Office. 1952.
UNITED STATES INFORMATION SERVICE, *The Negro In American Life*. 1954. Illus.
UNITED STATES INFORMATION SERVICE, *The American Negro Today: Facts and Views of British and American Writers*. Illus.
UNITED STATES INFORMATION SERVICE, *The Negro In The United States*. (Bibliography.) c. 1953.
VAN DERSAL, William R., *The American Land: Its History and Its Uses*. Oxford University Press. 1943.
WARREN, R. Penn, *Segregation*. Random House. 1956.
WATERS, Ethel, and SAMUELS, Clark, *His Eye Is On The Sparrow*. Doubleday. 1951. Illus.
WHITE, Walter, *Rope and Faggot: A Biography of Judge Lynch*. Knopf. 1929.
WHITE, Walter, *A Man Called White*. Victor Gollancz. 1949.
WORK, John Wesley, *Folk Songs of the American Negro*. Fisk University. 1915.
WRIGHT, Richard, *Black Boy*. Victor Gollancz. 1945.
WRIGHT, Richard, *Twelve Million Black Voices*. Lindsay Drummond. 1947. Illus.
WRIGHT, Richard, *Native Son*. Victor Gollancz. 1940.
WRITERS' PROGRAM, *Alabama*. Smith. 1941. Illus.
WRITERS' PROGRAM, *Arkansas*. Hastings House. 1941. Illus.
WRITERS' PROGRAM, *Louisiana*. Hastings House. 1941. Illus.
WRITERS' PROGRAM, *South Carolina*. Oxford University Press. 1941.

Principal magazines and periodicals consulted:

Discophile. Editor: Derek Coller. Published by Derek Coller. Issues 1–60. 'Race Record Department.' Contributions by Anthony Rotante *et al.*
Jazz Hot. Editor: Charles Delaunay. Contributions of Jacques Demetre: 'Blues' (Series); 'La Mythologie Noire'; 'Histoire du Blues,' etc. Kurt Mohr *et al.*
Jazz Journal. Editor: Sinclair Traill. Contributions by Derrick Stewart-Baxter. 'Preaching the Blues' (Series); Hugues Panassié *et al.*
Jazz Monthly. Editor: Albert J. McCarthy. Published by Francis Anthony. Contributions by Frederick Ramsey, Jnr., Paul Oliver and others.
Melody Maker. Editor: Pat Brand. Published by Odhams Press. Contributions by Hugues Panassié. 'The Blues Singers' (Series); Max Jones *et al.*
Music Mirror. Editor: Tom Cundall. Contributions by Paul Oliver. 'Sources of Afro-American Folk Song' (Series); 'Blues and Views' (Series).
Record Changer. Editors: Gordon Gullickson, Bill Grauer. Contributions by Ernest Borneman, Kenneth Goldstein, Charles Edward Smith *et al.*
Record Research. Editors: Len Kunstadt and Bob Colton. Contributions by Len Kunstadt, Harrison Smith, Anthony Rotante. 'Rhythm and Blues' (Series).
St. Louis Jazz Report. Edited by Robert Koester. Blue Note Record Shop, St. Louis, Mo. Contributions by Robert Koester.

DISCOGRAPHY

Jazz Directory. Compiled by Albert McCarthy and Dave Carey. Now published by Cassell. London. Volumes I–VI.

Index